SCIENCE TEACHING IN SECONDARY SCHOOLS

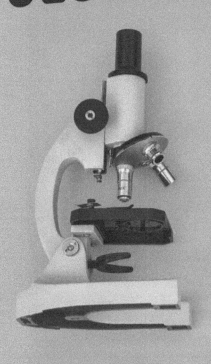
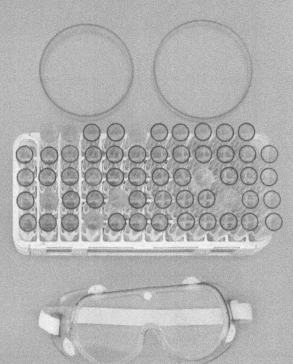

Sara Miller McCune founded SAGE Publishing in 1965 to support the dissemination of usable knowledge and educate a global community. SAGE publishes more than 1000 journals and over 800 new books each year, spanning a wide range of subject areas. Our growing selection of library products includes archives, data, case studies and video. SAGE remains majority owned by our founder and after her lifetime will become owned by a charitable trust that secures the company's continued independence.

Los Angeles | London | New Delhi | Singapore | Washington DC | Melbourne

SCIENCE TEACHING IN SECONDARY SCHOOLS

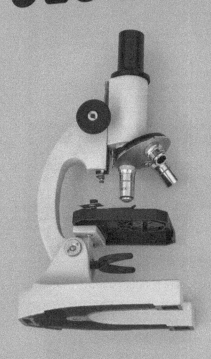
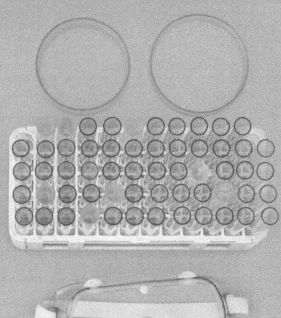

EDITED BY
LEIGH HOATH • MATTHEW LIVESEY

$SAGE

Los Angeles | London | New Delhi
Singapore | Washington DC | Melbourne

Los Angeles | London | New Delhi
Singapore | Washington DC | Melbourne

SAGE Publications Ltd
1 Oliver's Yard
55 City Road
London EC1Y 1SP

SAGE Publications Inc.
2455 Teller Road
Thousand Oaks, California 91320

SAGE Publications India Pvt Ltd
B 1/I 1 Mohan Cooperative Industrial Area
Mathura Road
New Delhi 110 044

SAGE Publications Asia-Pacific Pte Ltd
3 Church Street
#10-04 Samsung Hub
Singapore 049483

Editor: James Clark
Assistant editor: Diana Alves
Production editor: Sushant Nailwal
Copyeditor: Jill Birch
Proofreader: Sunrise Setting
Indexer: Cathryn Pritchard
Marketing manager: Lorna Patkai
Cover design: Naomi Robinson
Typeset by C&M Digitals (P) Ltd, Chennai, India
Printed in the UK

Editorial arrangement © Leigh Hoath and
Matthew Livesey 2022

Chapter 1 © Leigh Hoath and Matthew Livesey 2022
Chapter 2 © Matthew Livesey and Paul Smith 2022
Chapter 3 © Caroline Neuberg and Devinder Gill 2022
Chapter 4 © Alex Sinclair and Rebecca Riley 2022
Chapter 5 © Ed Podesta and Louise Cass 2022
Chapter 6 © Andy Chandler-Grevatt and Claire Davies 2022
Chapter 7 © Allison Cranmer and Andy Chandler-Grevatt 2022
Chapter 8 © Mark Langley and Jessie Mytum-Smithson 2022
Chapter 9 © Rania Maklad and Mick Dunne 2022
Chapter 10 © Rob Butler and Adam Higgins 2022
Chapter 11 © Jessie Mytum-Smithson and
    Matthew Livesey 2022
Chapter 12 © Stuart Bevins and Gareth Price 2022
Chapter 13 © Leigh Hoath and Matthew Livesey 2022

Library of Congress Control Number: 2021945671

British Library Cataloguing in Publication data

A catalogue record for this book is available from
the British Library

ISBN 978-1-5297-6259-4
ISBN 978-1-5297-6258-7 (pbk)
eISBN 978-1-5297-8796-2

At SAGE we take sustainability seriously. Most of our products are printed in the UK using responsibly sourced
papers and boards. When we print overseas we ensure sustainable papers are used as measured by the PREPS
grading system. We undertake an annual audit to monitor our sustainability.

CONTENTS

ABOUT THE EDITORS

Leigh Hoath is a Senior Professional Practice Fellow at Leeds Trinity University. She has worked in higher education since 2006 following a successful teaching career and leads science education at the University across the primary and secondary age phases as well as holding a wider role developing Continuous Professional Development (CPD) and Knowledge Exchange. Leigh's own studies focused on teaching in the outdoor setting which stemmed from her interests in enhancement activities such as the Duke of Edinburgh's Award and longer expeditions around the world with pupils. Leigh is the education consultant to the world's largest chemical business (BASF), where she develops their outreach provision, as well as for the BBC on their Blue Planet Live BBCTeach resources and their latest 'green curriculum' and sustainability campaigns – The Regenerators. She is an active member of the Association for Science Education on a regional and national level and, as well as being a trustee, sits on their Education Group and was awarded Chartered Science Teacher Status (CSciTeach) in 2009. Leigh is a regular author of science education articles and book chapters, and a national and international conference presenter.

Matthew Livesey is a teacher of biology at Bradford Grammar School. Alongside his main teaching role, Matthew is part of the teaching and learning team, leading CPD and pedagogy development within the department and more widely across the school. Matthew has mentored several student teachers on both their first and second placement of training. He is a former medical doctor and a keen outdoor enthusiast and regularly draws upon his experiences to contextualise learning. Matthew sits on the 11–19 Committee for the Association for Science Education, their Publications Group and the Yorkshire Regional Committee and is a frequent presenter at their conferences, focusing on supporting student teachers and early career teachers in their first years of teaching.

ABOUT THE CONTRIBUTORS

Allison Cranmer is a Senior Lecturer in Initial Teacher Education (PGCE Secondary Science) at the University of Huddersfield. She taught science at KS3–KS4 and physics to KS5 in secondary schools in southern England for over two decades. She is a qualified Occupational Health and Safety practitioner and a member of the Association for Science Education Health and Safety Specialist Group.

Stuart Bevins is a Principal Research Fellow at the Sheffield Institute of Education. He has designed and led both large and small-scale research and knowledge exchange projects including collaborative European projects. He is interested in social learning theories and science teacher professional development. Stuart is a member of the STEM Learning Research Advisory Group and has published widely in the field of science education and is editor for *Cogent Science Education*.

Rob Butler was a special school science teacher for 20 years, spending the last six as a deputy head. Before that he supported mainstream and special schools across his local authority as an advanced skills teacher (AST). After 25 years in the classroom, Rob stepped down from teaching to reduce his hours. He's now a Field Officer with the Association for Science Education (ASE) working with teachers across the North and East Midlands, keeping his finger on the pulse of science education. Rob holds Chartered Science Teacher Status (CSciTeach) and is a CPD facilitator for the STEM learning network. He has created resources for lower attaining students for a major publisher and blogs at his own website, fiendishlyclever.com.

Louise Cass is a Head of Science at Havelock Academy, Grimsby. Louise worked as a Forensic Scientist as a gunshot residue expert before training as a secondary Science teacher specialising in Chemistry. Louise is Chair of Governors for Phoenix Park and Sevenhills Academy, the local Alternative Provision, and works alongside them developing their science curriculum. Her main interests are ensuring that science, as a subject, is accessible for all. Louise is a mentor for student and Early Career teachers.

Louise is also the co-founder of BrewEdCleethorpes where she has worked to ensure that high-quality CPD, and research can be shared within North East Lincolnshire.

Andy Chandler-Grevatt taught secondary science for over a decade before becoming a science teacher educator. He is now a Senior Lecturer in science education at the University of Brighton training teachers in the South of England. Andy is the author of a large number of teaching and learning resources, international consultant for assessment, and the assessment and curriculum editor for Oxford University Press. Andy is a Chartered Science Teacher and long-standing member of the Association for Science Education.

Claire Davies is an Assistant Headteacher at Downlands Community School and has been a science teacher for the past 26 years. She has a keen interest in quality-first classroom teaching and stretch and challenge of all pupils. Claire is also the Lead of the Sussex and Surrey SLP (Science Learning Partnership) where she works with many science teachers providing high-quality CPD. Her particular focus is on the recruitment and retention of good classroom teachers.

Mick Dunne moved from being Head of Initial Teacher Education at the University Centre, Bradford College to a senior lectureship at Manchester Metropolitan University. He is now semi-retired and working as an education consultant, supporting Science Learning Partnerships, and is Visiting Lecturer for Leeds Trinity University, Leeds University, and Manchester Metropolitan University, primarily supporting science Initial Teacher Education (ITE) courses. Working in secondary and middle schools for ten years, he took on a range of roles including subject responsibility for science, ICT, and mathematics before moving into teacher education. He has published widely, has been a member of several editorial boards both in the UK and abroad, has actively supported the Association for Science Education (a member since 1980) and undertaken a wide range of international work. His doctorate studies focused on primary-aged children's perceptions on learning outside the classroom.

Devinder Gill has over 20 years of experience teaching in secondary schools in England. He is currently a Development Coach for the Institute of Physics, delivering CPD for teachers of physics at all stages of their career. He is also the Yorkshire Regional Representative for the Ogden Trust, developing school partnerships in both the primary and secondary sector.

Adam Higgins has been a science teacher at an all-boys school in Gidea Park since 2016. He has a keen interest in methods to raise the attainment of students of all abilities by allowing them all to experience success in the classroom. Adam is a strong believer in the collaboration of teachers, freely sharing both ideas and resources through a number of platforms.

Mark Langley is the Science CPD Lead at the National STEM Learning Centre, York. With a chemistry and physics background, Mark taught in a number of secondary schools and was head of department as well as an examiner and a health and safety officer, before moving to work within STEM learning in 2008. Mark's current role is to lead the primary and secondary science teams, developing and delivering effective immersive CPD to teachers, technicians and others involved in delivering STEM within UK schools. He also regularly designs and develops STEM projects overseas to help countries develop effective STEM teaching, through face-to-face training, as well as remote support. He specialises in practical STEM activities, linking different subject areas to develop students' understanding and application of their subject knowledge, with real life contexts and challenges. He sits on a number of UK organisations as an adviser for effective education and is regularly asked to present at national and international events.

Rania Maklad joined Manchester Metropolitan University in 2011 and has been in different leading roles since then. She was the Primary Science Subject Lead in 2015–2018 and contributed to the undergraduate and postgraduate teaching programmes in primary science. Rania is currently a member of the development team of the new teacher education undergraduate programme and is leading the changes starting at BA1 level. Her research interests include primary science, multilingualism, and Initial Teacher Education. Prior to joining the university, she taught primary aged children in Scotland and Egypt for 15 years.

Jessie Mytum-Smithson has worked as a teacher of science since 2013. Between September 2016 and July 2017 she took a secondment to the National STEM Learning Centre to support teachers in the classroom to develop a Science Capital approach to their teaching as part of the Enterprising Science project, a five-year research and development partnership between King's College London, University College London, Science Museum Group and funded by BP. Jessie Mytum-Smithson is the Action Research Lead in Science at St Bede's and St Joseph's Catholic College in Bradford.

Caroline Neuberg completed a PhD on physical volcanology in France and went into teaching via a School-Centred Initial Teacher Training (SCITT) route. She has been teaching mainly Physics for the past decade and also experienced New Zealand's education system for a year. She engaged with the Ogden Trust, coordinating a partnership and completing a teacher fellowship, and has worked for Scientix, a European network of science educators, as an ambassador for four years. She was awarded the 2020 Patrick Moore Medal for Education by the Royal Astronomical Society due to her engagement in promoting Geophysics and Astronomy.

Ed Podesta is a teacher educator who works at Leeds Trinity University. He trained as a history teacher and worked in state and private schools in that role for more than a decade. His experience and research interest is in teacher autonomy and agency, an area of education that Ed is published in and exploring further through his PhD.

Dr Gareth Price held his first job as a Records Clerk at the Royal Gwent Hospital in Newport but is now a Senior Research Fellow at Sheffield Institute of Education (SIOE). Between these roles he worked at Countesthorpe College in Leicestershire teaching science and humanities to 14–19 year olds, managed the science publishing at Collins Education and wrote science learning materials for traditional and online media. His interests centre around curriculum development with an emphasis on inquiry-led pedagogies which grant the learner greater power in the *what*, *how* and *why* of their learning. He has worked on projects that support this learner-empowered model in Thailand, Malaysia, the Philippines, Borneo and, most recently, India and Brussels. His current research is looking at creativity in the science classroom and the development of a novel approach to science education called 3D-Science.

Rebecca Riley is a practising primary teacher and Science Lead at Horbury Bridge Academy. She has been awarded Fellowship by the Primary Science Teaching Trust to their College in recognition of her outstanding practice. She is an active member of ASE.

Dr Alex Sinclair is a Senior Lecturer in Science Education at St Mary's University, Twickenham and has taught science in primary and secondary schools. He is an active member of the ASE and is Chair of the Futures Committee and Editor of Science Teacher Education. He is a regular conference presenter.

Paul Smith is an Early Career teacher following undertaking a PGCE in Secondary Science with a biology specialism at Leeds Trinity University. He is a science teacher at Woodkirk Academy in Wakefield. Before retraining as a teacher, Paul was an Ecommerce Marketing Manager and had graduated with a degree in genetics.

TABLE OF ABBREVIATIONS

AfL	Assessment for Learning
AO	Assessment Objective
[ASD/ASC]	Autism Spectrum Disorder/Autistic Spectrum Condition
ASE	Association for Science Education
AST	Advanced Skills Teacher
AT	Attainment Targets
BERA	British Educational Research Association
BEST	Best Evidence Science Teaching
CCF	Core Content Framework
CCT	Chartered College of Teaching
CK	Content Knowledge
CLEAPSS	Consortium of Local Education Authorities for the Provision of Science Services
CLP	Classification, Labelling and Packaging
CLT	Cognitive Load Theory
CPD	Continuous Professional Development
CSciTeach	Chartered Science Teacher
CTeach	Chartered Teacher
DfE	Department for Education
EAL	English as an Additional Language
ECF	Early Career Framework
ECT	Early Career Teacher
EEF	Education Endowment Foundation
EHCP	Education, Health and Care Plan
ELSE	Enquiry-Led Science Education

ESERO-UK	European Space Education Resource Office for the UK
GCE	General Certificate of Education
GCSE	General Certificate of Secondary Education
GHS	Globally Harmonised System
HASAWA	Health & Safety at Work, etc. Act 1974
HSE	Health & Safety Executive
IEP	Individual Education Plan
IoP	Institute of Physics
ICT	Information and Communication Technology
IT	Information Technology
ITE	Initial Teacher Education
ITT	Initial Teacher Training
KS	Key Stage
MFL	Modern Foreign Languages
MHSWR	Management of Health & Safety at Work Regulations 1999
MLD	Moderate Learning Difficulties
NAS	National Autistic Society
NGSS	Next Generation Science Standards
NHS	National Health Service
OEAP	Outdoor Education Advisers' Panel
Ofqual	Office of Qualifications and Examinations Regulation
Ofsted	Office for Standards in Education, Children's Services and Skills
PAT	Portable Appliance Testing
PBL	Problem-Based Learning
PCK	Pedagogical Content Knowledge
PGCE	Postgraduate Certificate in Education
PLAN	Pan-London Assessment Network
PoS	Programme of Study
PP	Pupil Premium
PPE	Personal Protective Equipment
PSTT	Primary Science Teaching Trust
QTS	Qualified Teacher Status
RSB	Royal Society of Biology
RSC	Royal Society of Chemistry

SATs	Standard Assessment Tests
SCITT	School Centred Initial Teacher Training
SEERIH	Science and Engineering Education Research and Innovation Hub
SEMH	Social, Emotional and Mental Health
SENCo	Special Educational Needs Coordinator
SEND	Special Educational Needs and Disability
SLP	Science Learning Partnership
SpLD	Specific Learning Difficulties
SSERC	Scottish Schools Education Research Centre
STEAM	Science, Technology, Engineering, Art and Maths
STEM	Science, Technology, Engineering and Maths
TA	Teaching/Learning Assistant
TAPS	Teacher Assessment in Primary Science
VLE	Virtual Learning Environment
ZPD	Zone of Proximal Development

FOREWORD

Back in 1982–83 when I did my year of initial teacher education (a PGCE, which was almost the only route in England back then), it all seemed a lot more straightforward than it does now. The excellent course I attended had a full range of sessions covering important aspects of education such as disadvantage, gender and race and there was enough time on the course to do options, each with 15 hours of contact time: I chose one on philosophy of education – which led to a life-long interest in the subject – and one on assessment. But the core content of the course dealt with two issues: how to manage a classroom and how to teach one's subject, in my case science, with biology as my specialism.

I loved my PGCE and got a huge amount from it – but I wish I had had this book to read too! Its chapters are valuably each co-authored by a school teacher and some-one working in Initial Teacher Education and cover a tremendous amount, with lots of guidance, suggestions for practice and pointers to think about. There are also great vignettes that highlight issues – so I'll end by telling what is really an anecdote, but which I could claim is a vignette.

My teaching practice (as we called it then) was conducted in a split-site 11–18 school. Staff were supposed to maintain student discipline while walking the several hundred yards between the two sites. However, almost all the 'real' teachers had cars and drove between the two sites, leaving those of us without cars (most of us doing our teaching practice) to try to stop several hundred students (or so it seemed at the time) from smoking, swearing, fighting and generally misbehaving. One 15 year-old, let's call him Reggie after the older of the Kray twins, ran rings round me. I was very relieved when the term came to an end, presuming I would never see him again. However, come September he turned up at the school at which I was starting my teaching career to redo his Biology 'O' level, which he had failed.

Reggie engaged little in my lessons and took no interest in the subject until one day, to my surprise, he asked me what the formula for salt was. It was the first sign he had ever shown in my presence of being interested in science. I told him that the formula for the most common salt was NaCl and somewhat sheepishly he pointed to a bottle of NaOH pellets which the lab technician, without me noticing, had left out in the lab and told me that he had swallowed some of them. Much to the class' amusement, I got him to wash his mouth out repeatedly and phoned for the lab technician (who had a car) to take him to the local A&E in case he needed his stomach pumped. Reggie was a lot better behaved for the remainder of the year.

Michael J. Reiss
UCL Institute of Education

1
INTRODUCTION
LEIGH HOATH AND MATTHEW LIVESEY

CHAPTER OVERVIEW

This chapter will introduce the content of this book and explore how to get the most from it. We will give you some ideas as to how this book can best support you through your training and early stages of your career as a science teacher. This chapter will set a scene for what is to come and also give you some insight into how the book was co-constructed with a view to sharing the views and expertise of a range of academics and classroom practitioners.

INTRODUCTION

Before outlining what this book is, it is important to let you know what it is *not*. This is not going to tell you what the authors think is the one 'right' way to approach an aspect of teaching. It is not a tick list of competencies that will enable you to pass your training or Early Career teaching. It is not just a handbook. This book offers the bringing together of minds, particularly those who are current teachers, often working with student teachers undertaking their training, and academics who support the teaching on Initial Teacher Training (ITT). This is often referred to as Initial Teacher

Education (ITE) but for the purpose of this book and to remain consistent with the Core Content Framework (CCF), we will use ITT.

The content of each chapter is shaped by the experiences of these teachers and academics. It is there to encourage you to think about developing as a teacher, highlight some of the related theory and principles behind the teaching and also offer some practical tips for how you can address gaps where you need to know more. This chapter will suggest some ideas around how you can use this book to support your development and hopefully will be something that you return to through the early stages of your career as a means of supporting your academic work and practice.

THE CONTENT OF THE BOOK

As mentioned, this book draws upon theory and practice and brings these elements together in a practical and accessible way to support you as a student teacher. We believe that as science teachers you have one of the greatest challenges of all the subject areas – perhaps on a par with other practical subjects or those such as modern foreign languages (MFL) where there are different disciplines within the one subject area.

As you read this book the chances are you will have a very different background to the student teacher who is next to you on your course or at the desk close by in the workroom. Not only are you likely to be training with individuals from different scientific specialisms (biology, chemistry or physics), but the routes taken to achieve these specialisms vary greatly. The challenge for you as a science student teacher, is that you are often expected to teach outside of your specialism from a very early point in your career. Not only are you expected to learn the craft of teaching but also develop subject knowledge on a level that is rather substantial, which may often be outside your comfort zone. It is rare to have student teachers start the course with pre-university qualifications in all the science disciplines. Often at the interview stage we find applicants have a strong first discipline, a secure and supporting second subject and what we affectionately refer to as a 'dodgy third' science. It is expected that on your training year your subject knowledge will be where it needs to be – and quite rightly so. There is no excuse for being underprepared in relation to this. At the same time, we know that many student teachers particularly have a 'needs must' approach to subject knowledge which means for those early stages of their teaching career they are one or two steps ahead of the pupils in some of their lessons.

The content of this book simply cannot tell you all the science you need to know and how to teach it. What we envisage this book doing is highlighting many of the key areas you have to engage with and demonstrate progression in during your training and early career. Hopefully, you will then be able to equip yourself with strategies and understanding around these key areas as a means of moving you forward to being an excellent science teacher.

The structure for each chapter is broadly the same – you will see an overview to the chapter at the start. The authors will share the chapter content, giving you some indication of what you can expect to get out of reading it. We are then going to show you where these are related to the Core Content Framework (CCF) and Early Career Framework (ECF) standards (see Table 1.1 for an overview of where the standards are addressed).

The main section will explore theory, practice and pedagogy in relation to the topic, which is something that can support you in your teacher training and potentially with academic assignments you may need to complete as part of your training. Most chapters draw upon the narrative of a student teacher or experienced science teacher, which are followed with reflective activities designed to give you an opportunity to relate their experience to your own.

Within the chapters there are links, where appropriate, with technology – although we recognise this is an ever-changing field and so these serve as a starting point for you to go and research further what works for you and your pupils. We have included indications of what to look for when you are observing others' teaching in your school-based experiences and a key part of the chapters is the reflective questions which you will find near the end. We encourage you to think about these as a means of working out what your own principles of practice are and how unpicking of ideas and concepts can enable you to develop further. Further reading accompanies the chapters, which will provide further information related to the specific content covered.

THE CHAPTERS

The following chapter and the final two are designed to 'top and tail' the book, outlining more generalised aspects of your training. The remaining chapters are in a suggested order, but that doesn't mean there is a requirement to have read the preceding one in order to make sense of whichever you have chosen. You will find that there are some themes discussed in more than one chapter – cognitive load theory (CLT) and pedagogical content knowledge (PCK) are two examples. In each chapter the context in which these are applied is different and so it is not merely repetition but rather what that particular aspect begins to 'look like' in action.

In Chapter 2 we have drawn upon the views of a range of people in respect to the journey of the student teacher. Within the chapter you will read of the experience of a very recently qualified student teacher with the purpose that his story, captured in multiple vignettes, will help manage your own expectations around this time. It will outline ways in which workload can be managed, approaches that will enable you to best succeed and importantly consider the training and early teaching years from the perspective of the school-based mentor.

As we have touched upon, subject knowledge is an important aspect of your role as a developing science teacher. Chapter 3 brings together experiences from a classroom teacher and former teacher who now works within one of the subject bodies – the Institute of Physics (IoP). They describe why secure subject knowledge goes beyond just knowing the facts and links this with pedagogy. The chapter is full of examples from across the science disciplines to support your thinking and direction of where to get additional support with this facet of your teaching. It is not about teaching you the subject knowledge you need to know, it is rather focused on ensuring you know where the challenging aspects come from and how they can be addressed.

As secondary science teachers we often think of the first year of secondary school as being when learners start 'proper' science. Chapter 4 encourages you to think differently about this and outlines the importance of being cognisant of not only what is taught in primary schools but how it is taught. At some point you should take the time to look in detail about what is covered within the National Curriculum for primary schools and be prepared to recognise that there is a significant volume of science content that enables you to teach what you need to in secondary schools.

Up to this point in the book you will have considered many of the ideas that underpin and support teaching and the next section moves on to thinking about more of the applications of this within the classroom. Planning is essential in order to ensure you have a clear direction of travel in relation to progress with your learners and Chapter 5 will encourage you to think about the nature of planning, what makes planning lessons for progress effective, and the strategies you can adopt throughout this process.

We often find that assessment is a challenge for student teachers and early career teachers (ECTs) and is a target that is carried through from training to being an ECT. Chapter 6 touches upon different approaches to assessment and offers a rationale around its importance, again supported by vignettes from one of the author's teaching experiences. There are various demands placed upon you as a science teacher in terms of assessment and this chapter will begin to unpick those and create a supportive framework for you to hang your own experiences on.

Teaching safely is one of the more unique points of being a science teacher and this is achieved through very active management of your classroom as well as working closely with others, including technician staff. In Chapter 7 there are the key contexts around the health and safety demands of the classroom from a policy perspective including strategies for how to approach achieving these and creating a safe working space within your classroom or laboratory setting. Following on from this is a chapter where the nuances around effective practical work are explored. Chapter 8 will enable you to see what makes practical work most effective, consider how substantive and disciplinary knowledge can be developed through it and how to 'do' purposeful practical work.

As new and developing teachers it is important that, through the practice of the approaches and strategies covered in the opening chapters of this book, you are able to apply these to ensure that all learners are able to access content as far as possible. Chapter 9 takes some examples of commonly thought of 'tricky topics' and considers ways in which these can be taught. It encourages you to consider the purpose of approaches and evaluate strategies such as modelling and use of analogies. It is key that you think about how you are meeting the needs of the range of learners you will teach and how to respond to them.

Adaptive teaching is addressed within Chapter 10 and what form this takes within the secondary science classroom. This chapter will also introduce you to a range of terms in relation to SEND and how you can begin to meet individual pupils' needs. An approach that is often encouraged within science teaching is bringing science to the learner in a context that they can make sense of on a personal level. Chapter 11 draws upon the principles from the Science Capital Teaching Approach to outline how science can be brought to the learner in a way that encourages them to see it as relevant to their own lives.

The final chapters are constructed so they bridge the transition from a student teacher to an ECT and beyond. They encourage you to think about what the curriculum is and how this can be best used by you to make it work for you. Although it is a framework of what must be taught to most learners, it can be challenged in a number of ways. Chapter 12 pushes you to think about the key debates in science education, how you are teaching the curriculum and working with what you have to do in order to make it more about how you do it and how this can increase and improve your pedagogical repertoire within the classroom. The concluding chapter will draw together support available from a range of subject association bodies and suggest ways in which you can continue to grow and develop as a teacher once your training period is over. It is there to support you moving into a space where you have greater ownership of your classroom, to develop autonomy and agency, and to highlight that the learning and developing as a teacher is never 'done'.

Although presented sequentially, it is worth noting that there are many links between the different chapters of this book. At the time of writing, authors shared content with each other to ensure that these links were meaningful. It would be remiss of us to suggest, for example, that planning and assessment are not linked, or that subject knowledge and adaptive teaching are dichotomous. With so many authors contributing to the book, each chapter has its own 'voice'. As Editors, we made a positive decision to ensure that these voices are heard within the words and there is no generic tone as you read. This co-construction is an important element within the book.

Having summarised the content, let us suggest how we envisage you use it.

WAYS TO USE THE BOOK

As stated at the start of this chapter, this book is not about telling you how to do something in one way. You may find a journey through this book that we do not mention in this section – and that is absolutely fine. The key point is that you are reading about your chosen profession with an interest in developing it.

We will start with the obvious approach. You could start at the beginning of the book and read it through from cover to cover. Our experience tells us that not many trainees have the time to commit in this way to their reading, so we anticipate it is used in a much more agile manner.

The chapters, although interrelated, are discrete in their design and you can dip in and out of the book to allow you to access what you need at that moment in time. It is a 'go to' resource which will give you enough of what you need to know to be able to make progress but also to establish what the next steps are for you.

The content has a dual purpose. As well as being a practical 'how to' guide, there are suggestions within each chapter around educational theory and relevant literature. This book will also not just allow you to develop what you do but also an understanding of why you do it. We therefore see this as a real starting point to support academic assignments as you move through your training or as you want to know more about a part of your teaching as an ECT.

The key point is that however you use it, you are developing, learning more and engaging with moving forward your own practice. We hope you will use the opportunities to reflect and link what you have read with your own experiences and enjoy what you read as you think about yourself as a teacher.

Table 1.1   Summary of the book content and CCF and ECF standards

	Chapter Title	CCF and ECF Standard							
		1	2	3	4	5	6	7	8
1	Introduction	x	x	x	x	x	x	x	x
2	Expectations for your training year	x		x	x				x
3	The importance of subject knowledge	x	x	x					
4	What we can learn from primary school science		x	x		x			
5	Planning for teaching science	x	x	x	x				
6	Effective assessment in science	x	x			x	x		
7	Health and Safety in Science	x		x				x	x
8	Practical work in science			x	x	x		x	
9	Teaching tricky topics and abstract concepts		x		x	x	x		
10	Teaching pupils with SEND		x		x	x			x
11	Putting science into context for pupils			x	x			x	x
12	Challenging the curriculum	x	x						x
13	From student teacher to ECT	x	x	x					x

SUMMARY

Now you have read this chapter you should have:

- An understanding of the content of the book chapters and their organisation.
- Identified ways in which you can make the content work for you in supporting your teaching and development.
- Been introduced to the principles that underpin the co-construction of the chapters.

REFLECTIVE QUESTIONS

- What difference will it make to your teaching, decision making and ability to reflect if you have more of an understanding of why you are doing something in the classroom as well as knowing what you are doing?
- What is the best way to use this book to make it work for you - are you going to dip in and out, target sections in a systematic manner or other?

2

EXPECTATIONS FOR YOUR TRAINING YEAR

MATTHEW LIVESEY AND PAUL SMITH

CHAPTER OVERVIEW

Having started to read this book, it may be the case that you are about to or have recently embarked on the journey to train as a secondary science teacher. You might be coming into your teacher training straight from your university degree course or contemplating a complete change in career later in life. The thoughts and feelings of the student teacher are often very similar no matter what your starting point. Come September, it is a level playing field and everyone is working towards the same goal. In this chapter, we will highlight some of the expectations for your training year, as well as some practical solutions to overcome these whilst on placement. Paul's experiences are shared through a series of vignettes outlining his recent training year.

> **LINKS TO ITT CORE CONTENT FRAMEWORK AND EARLY CAREER FRAMEWORK**
>
> This chapter supports development of:
>
> - Standard 1 - set high expectations
> - Standard 3 - demonstrate subject and curriculum knowledge
> - Standard 4 - plan and teach well-structured lessons
> - Standard 8 - fulfil wider professional responsibilities

INTRODUCTION

Embarking on your teacher training is an exciting prospect. Many student teachers come with preconceptions of what it is like to be a teacher having spent countless hours as a pupil themselves. Some even have visions of emulating one of their favourite teachers at school or ensuring that they are not like some they remember. However, most student teachers come with a degree of trepidation, commonly thinking 'how am I going to control a class of 30 teenagers when they all have Bunsen burners out?' It is natural to have some sort of nerves before starting a new career, but these early-stage jitters get washed away once the teaching starts and you begin to build confidence in your practice.

There is plenty of support available to you as a student teacher throughout your training which you can always seek out when you need it – and importantly, do not be afraid to do so. This chapter tries to alleviate some of the common worries and situations that you may experience from your course and encourages you not to suffer in silence. Shout out and seek help from the wide support network that is available to you.

VIGNETTE 2.1   BEFORE THE TRAINING STARTED

Before starting his training, Paul expected the course to be hard. Every piece of advice he had received from current teachers and people doing the PGCE was that it was difficult and tiring. Strangely, they never really went into much more detail or explained exactly in what way it would be hard. He found it odd that it was commonly known to be difficult but that nobody said specifically what was so hard about it.

Paul wasn't too sure about the format of the course beforehand, and how the university part and mentoring ties into the actual teaching. He didn't know what he would actually be spending his time doing over the course of a day or week or month, other than teaching, of course. Before starting the programme, Paul was told by university tutors that as student teachers they will be told what they would need to do at each point and he was happy to trust this process and felt he was right to do so.

As a fairly reserved person, Paul was under the impression that he would have to undergo a personality change in order to become a good teacher. He believed that he could become a great teacher but that his current self was not capable of being like all the teachers that he remembered from his own time in school. He had managed staff before but nothing like a class of 30 teenagers.

Paul prepared by buying some new shirts, shoes, trousers and ties. He stocked up on all the stationery that he thought a teacher would need - pens, exercise books, rulers, Tipp-Ex and he even treated himself to a new laptop to cope with all the work he would be doing. He also bought a printer just in case he ever forgot to print off worksheets at school (which he did).

The most important item Paul bought was an academic year diary. This was essential for keeping track of lessons, meetings and deadlines during the PGCE year. He quickly discovered that the option of not being organised didn't exist and a clear diary made life much easier. He also soon realised that the only way to remember all the different things he had to do was by having a well maintained 'to do' list.

As well as getting hold of the equipment he needed to teach, Paul spent the two weeks before the course relaxing and getting himself into a positive frame of mind and talking to himself positively. He knew it was going to be tough but also knew it would be a lot of fun. He'd often say 'enjoy yourself' before he taught a lesson that he was feeling worried about and that really helped, because he did enjoy himself.

Activity: Think carefully about how you will create a space and time for you to think calmly and positively about your work. How will you create relaxation time and space for yourself during the year(s) to come. Make a plan for how you will ring fence your time to achieve this.

WORRIES ABOUT YOUR SUBJECT KNOWLEDGE

Science teaching is unique. A student teacher will typically enter teacher training with a background in one science discipline but will ultimately be asked to teach two other science subjects often to GCSE level. This may well be out of their comfort zone and it is therefore not surprising that people embarking on a science teacher training course are often worried that their subject knowledge is not up to scratch.

Spending some time before you start the course refreshing some knowledge is often a good idea. Use textbooks, websites and videos to bring knowledge back to the forefront of your mind in preparation for the pupils asking questions. Using the science National Curriculum documentation for Key Stage 3 and 4 as a check list to perform a pre-course subject knowledge audit is often a good way of highlighting your areas of strength and weakness before the course starts, and may be a pre-course requirement. It is often the case that regardless of studying a science discipline to degree level, a lot of the content you will be delivering to pupils will not have been covered since you sat that exam yourself.

Chapter 3 looks at the development of your subject knowledge in more detail and gives you ways you can develop this approach effectively.

VIGNETTE 2.2   PAUL'S SUBJECT KNOWLEDGE DEVELOPMENT

Before starting the PGCE it had been nine years since Paul finished his first degree, and he hadn't worked in a scientific role since. This meant that his main concern before the course was his subject knowledge. Whatever your starting point, you'll need to constantly work on your subject knowledge.

Paul tried sitting down and revising from a textbook regularly, as if he were revising for his exams, but he found it difficult to focus. He learned that the very best way to improve his subject knowledge was by thinking about how he could explain this topic to another person by planning a mini-teaching activity. That way, he reviewed the content that needed to be included, made sure he was comfortable with it, and kept a track of any questions any of the content raised for him as he went along. Once he'd found the answers to those questions, he thought of ways he could explain them to a secondary school pupil. He found that he could guarantee that if an explanation didn't make sense to him, it wouldn't to a pupil either.

Activity: Think carefully about how you will refresh some of your knowledge you may not have studied in some years. Can you look at the GCSE past papers for common exam boards and test yourself by doing a few questions? Can you articulate multiple ways of explaining one concept?

ORGANISATION AND MANAGING WORKLOAD

Teaching is a challenging but extremely rewarding career. You will discover this as you go through your training year and beyond. There can be times when the workload – planning lessons, marking, responding to emails, meetings, assignments amongst others – can become overwhelming. It is therefore key to be organised with your work, to help prioritise your wellbeing.

In the early stages of training and your career, particularly, it can take quite a long time to plan a lesson or activity – often disproportionate for the duration of the teaching. This is incredibly common and is due to inexperience and lack of practise, but as time passes it will become slicker and much quicker to do. The key skill to learn quickly during your training years is the point at which you need to down tools and stop working for the day. Everyone is different and it is a hard point to identify. Teachers naturally set high expectations of their pupils and themselves, but it is imperative to learn that 'being good is good enough' and that you don't have to be outstanding all of the time (Ovenden-Hope and Brimacombe, 2020). If you feel you are spending long periods on certain tasks, or finding it tricky to balance your time, speak to your mentors and host teachers who will be able to support you (also see Chapter 5 which has a focus on planning).

To help with organisation and time management, set aside some time before you start the week, look ahead at your timetable and allocate time periods to certain tasks. If you have non-contact time between classes, ask yourself 'what can I do that adds value in this time period?' and assign a task. It might be observing a more experienced colleague, writing a lesson plan or simply having a cup of tea to take stock after a busy morning of teaching – time to reflect on what you have done and how you have done it. Allocating time slots is a good way to help map out your time to make it as efficient as possible. This technique can also be done at the start of the academic year, aiming to identify pinch points when time may be stretched, such as essay deadlines, parents' evenings, school trips and increasing teaching allocation.

The Department for Education (DfE) have set out plans to help Early Career Teachers and their mentors identify ways in which workload can be reduced to allow more time for tasks which add value to their training (Department for Education, 2019c). There is also an expectation as part of the ITT Core Content Framework and ECF that you should consider the impact of your workload on your wellbeing and take steps to manage these appropriately in discussion with your mentors, schools and training providers (Department for Education, 2019a, 2019b). There is plenty of support available from your training provider and mentors in school. In addition, the Association for Science Education (ASE) have published the Science Teacher SOS Guide with plenty of advice on managing workload and promoting wellbeing in schools (Association for Science Education, 2018).

VIGNETTE 2.3   PAUL'S EXPERIENCES OF MANAGING WORKLOAD

For Paul, the hardest part of the course was around April. He was now on the full timetable for a student teacher, meaning that he was teaching quite a few lessons per week, but he felt that he hadn't really got any quicker with his lesson planning. Paul also needed to complete a university assignment and apply for jobs at the same time. He could feel his free time being eaten away and still everything wasn't getting completed. He spoke to his mentor about how he could speed up his lesson planning and, as always, his mentor had so many practical tips for him. The workload did become manageable quite quickly and Paul was able to find time to send some job applications off and have time for his hobbies.

Paul found that planning good lessons was the most difficult part of the course, but delivering the lesson was the reward for that hard work. His favourite moment of the year came in the very first minute of the very first lesson he taught. Paul displayed an electron micrograph of a fly's eye on the board and asked a Year 7 class what they thought it was. Every hand in the class immediately shot up. He could not believe the level of enthusiasm the pupils had for an image he had seen so many times. He had a preconceived notion that secondary school pupils could be quite apathetic, but this year taught him the polar opposite and as long as a task was not too hard or too easy, every pupil wanted to give it their best. When a class was enjoying and engaging with a task that he had planned and given thought to, Paul found there wasn't a better feeling.

Activity: Think carefully about how you are going to manage your time and remember that you should include protected time during the week for doing the things you enjoy outside work. Reflect on the lessons you teach that engage the pupils and run smoothly. What strategies did you employ to plan these lessons that you can use again to reduce your planning time?

LESSON OBSERVATIONS

Lesson observations offer two layers of support as a developing teacher. The first is by watching experienced teachers to learn how to teach, and secondly through being observed and being assessed in your abilities to teach effectively. Over the course of your training year, you will undoubtedly observe experienced teachers deliver lessons, with the aim of picking up tips and strategies that you can incorporate into your own lessons at a later stage. It sounds straightforward; however, like most things, observing lessons effectively is a difficult task and one which a student teacher must begin to master from the early stages of their training year.

VIGNETTE 2.4 PAUL'S EXPERIENCE OF DOING OBSERVATIONS AND BEING OBSERVED

Paul found it very difficult to know what he should be looking at during lesson observations, particularly during the first few weeks of the teacher training course – which was when there was the most time to observe lessons. The most important things he took from those early observations were becoming comfortable just being in a classroom, getting a feel for the pace of a lesson and some of the more obvious elements of behaviour management. Once he had taught more lessons himself and set his weekly targets with his mentor, Paul was then given the chance to observe teachers who were particularly strong in the areas he was trying to most improve. At this point, it became much easier to take specific techniques away from an observed lesson and use them in his own practice.

Paul found being observed himself a far more supportive experience than a stressful one. He had a strong sense that his mentor, host teachers and link tutors were there to help him and he found himself not focusing on them at all. There was enough to think about with the lesson and the pupils, so he didn't have the headspace to worry about his observing teacher too. Link tutor visits (where your university-based tutor visits you in school) felt higher stakes, but they were there for support in exactly the same way that host teachers were, so he didn't change anything at all about his planning or delivery based on who was observing the lesson. Paul took every piece of advice he was given into consideration, especially if it was in an area which he hadn't realised he needed to develop and tried to show his host teacher in the next lesson that he had been listening and had acted upon it. This attitude stood him in good stead throughout the course and it really helped build good relationships with his host teachers.

Activity: Think about Paul's early experience of observing other teachers compared with later in his placement. Establish a clear idea of where you can gain most benefit from watching others teach their lesson. Consider what you can also get from observing teachers from other subject areas.

It is important to understand the difficulties in observing. Student teachers often think that after observing a lesson with an experienced teacher, teaching is an easy task to undertake. What can't be seen from direct observation is the dynamic and constant thought process going through the teacher's mind when delivering the lesson. The masking of this thought process and decision making can often lead the student teacher to only see what they know and understand from their preconceptions of teaching. These preconceptions stem from many years of being a pupil themselves when at school. The mindset needs to change from one of receiving the lesson, to one of delivering it as the teacher.

Whilst starting out and learning the skills of observation, it is a good idea to make notes and observe what is happening in the classroom at each stage of the lesson in general. Table 2.1 gives you some generic questions to think about as you are watching a lesson. These notes and observations can then be looked on with a critical eye later in the placement to identify the intricacies that were involved.

Later on in your placement, it is more useful to go into lesson observation with a focus or particular question you would like to answer, and that may link to your weekly development targets set in discussion with your mentor. Having a narrow focus will allow you to home in on those specific skills and techniques the experienced teacher is using. This may be looking at how the teacher starts a lesson, how

Table 2.1   Questions to think about when observing a lesson for the first time

Stage of Lesson	Prompt Questions
First 5 minutes	• How did the teacher get the pupils into the room? How were they settled? • Was there a task displayed on the board or on their desks? • How were high expectations established? • How was the register taken?
Start of the lesson	• How did the teacher start the lesson? • How did the teacher hook or engage the pupils into the content being taught? • How did the teacher assess any knowledge that was taught in the previous lessons?
Main teaching section	• How are the lesson intentions shared with the pupils? • What resources were used? (IT, worksheets, etc.) • How did the teacher hand out any resources? • What was the pace of the lesson like? • How long did the teacher give each activity before moving on? • How did the teacher deliver the lesson content to the pupils?
Plenary	• What did the teacher do to assess how much progress had been made in the lesson? • How did the teacher set any homework? • How were pupils dismissed?
General Questions	• How often did the teacher ask questions? Who to? • How did the teacher deal with any behaviour problems that arose? • How did the teacher set out any practical work/equipment? • How did the teacher group the pupils when working together? • Did the teacher make any considerations for any pupils who have SEND?

a teacher assess pupil progress or how effective support for pupils with SEND can be implemented. To help you along with this, each chapter in this book contains a list of questions which you can ask yourself when observing a lesson.

WORKING WITH YOUR MENTOR

Mentors play a critical role in the development of student teachers. Mentoring by experienced colleagues is at the heart of the ITT Core Content Framework (CCF) published in 2019, that stipulates the 'minimum entitlement of all trainee teachers' (Department for Education, 2019b: 3). Mentoring is also an integral component of the Early Career Framework (ECF), which together with the CCF, form the multi-year entitlement of a student teacher to support and professional development well into their Early Career Teacher (ECT) years. A student teacher should receive from their mentor 'structured feedback … on a particular approach – using the best available evidence – to provide a structured process for improving the trainee's practice' (Department for Education, 2019b: 5).

VIGNETTE 2.5   WORKING WITH MENTORS IN PAUL'S SCHOOLS

The role of the school mentor is crucial to the training year and beyond. Before starting the course, Paul expected his mentors and host teachers to observe his lessons and give him pointers afterwards. Beyond that, he hadn't appreciated the huge role that they played in his confidence and professional development. These are the people who are teaching him how to be a teacher, both in the classroom and out. Paul hoped they would make him feel comfortable and welcome and he found that they really did. Every teacher he has come across has been nothing but friendly, approachable and happy to help.

The most important thing Paul found was that he should not try to hide anything from his mentor or host teacher in terms of worries or lack of confidence at times. He was tempted to want to appear as a finished article straight away but realised quickly it wouldn't help at all to try to hide any concerns he might have. Being honest about any misgivings he had or where he didn't understand parts of the feedback received allowed a productive discussion which enabled him to make more progress than had he kept quiet. Paul definitely felt he wasted time by not asking more questions of his mentor.

Activity: Think about how you will ask for clarification around feedback. You may face some that you disagree with; however, you must approach these conversations respectfully and professionally. Write some sentence starters that will enable you to manage these conversations in this way should they arise.

MENTOR MEETINGS AND TARGET SETTING

As part of the support your mentor will give you, it is important to set aside a regular time on a weekly basis for a mentor meeting. Here, you will discuss what has occurred the week prior and then set development targets for the week ahead. To get the most out of these meetings, it is important for you to prepare for them in advance – think about the lessons that went particularly well or badly and why they may have done so. Have you done anything particularly interesting this week or tried something new? The more things you bring to discuss, the better the meeting will be.

Each week needs to be seen as a cycle. During your placement, you will be observed and be given formal, and informal, feedback for you to reflect upon which you will need to bring to discuss with your mentor. Together, you will evaluate your teaching as well as the progress made by the pupils. This evaluation will form the basis of your targets for the week to come.

Good targets are subject specific and focused to a particular development goal. To give a generalised target is near useless. For example, a general target could be:

• Focus on behaviour management techniques when pupils are doing group work.

Although this target has a focus of behaviour management and is an element of the ITT Core Content Framework and Early Career Framework, it doesn't provide any substance for evaluation and discussion at a mentor meeting later. A more specific target could be:

• Focus on using different behaviour management techniques and organisation strategies when class 10X are performing the effect of temperature on amylase practical on Friday afternoon.

This is both subject specific by focusing on organisation of practical equipment and managing the pupils in a laboratory environment, whilst also being class and time specific which will help when you come to write lesson plans.

These targets, set in conjunction with your mentor, will then form the basis of your planning for the week ahead. As you go to plan 10X's practical lesson, you can use the chapters in this book as a starting point to look at health and safety of a practical (Chapter 7) and managing the practical environment (Chapter 8) to look for ideas and techniques for you to research further and implement in your teaching practice. You would also be able to use this target as a focus for your lesson observations of other teachers in the department, identifying how they set up their lab environment whilst dealing with the practical management.

Once you have researched, planned and then delivered your lesson, you will be able to reflect and evaluate on the techniques you used and the impact they had on pupil progress.

VIGNETTE 2.6   TARGET SETTING ON PLACEMENT

Target setting is an integral part of the PGCE course and Paul found the process was well supported by the university. Together with his school mentor, he chose three targets per week which were always based on the 'areas for improvement' from his lesson observations that week. The targets needed to include specific actions that were subject specific and, by speaking through these with his mentor, and then with host teachers afterwards, it kept him accountable. Paul found it beneficial not to worry about setting the same or similar targets more than once, as sometimes it would take a couple of different techniques to see improvement and something which works with one class, might not work with another.

Activity: Create a check list to ensure that your targets are subject specific, class specific and will allow you to identify steps to achieving them.

WORKING WITH TECHNOLOGY

Pupils and teachers alike are more accustomed with technology than ever before. With all education stakeholders now reflecting on the steep learning curve that was remote learning due to the Coronavirus pandemic of 2020/21, technology in the classroom has never been more important. There are a plethora of fantastic resources available on the internet which need to be used as part of your armoury when it comes to delivering high-quality lessons. These range from tools to help pupils undertake independent learning to online quizzes and retrieval practice activities. Throughout some of the following chapters, the authors will highlight various tried and tested resources which you can use to boost your use of technology in the classroom.

VIGNETTE 2.7   TRAINING TO TEACH DURING A PANDEMIC

Under normal circumstances, the use of technology in the classroom is not much more complicated than preparing or adapting a simple presentation to help structure your lesson. During remote learning however, teachers had to be a little bit more creative. Because of the Covid19 national lockdown, Paul was delivering lessons via online platforms for about 10 weeks. The most challenging aspect of online teaching is that you have very little idea what

(Continued)

the pupils are doing. He found that by using virtual whiteboard sharing sites he was able to see pupils' work in real time and comment on the quality or correct any mistakes.

Paul described teaching online as challenging because it is so difficult to gauge engagement and understanding. He avoided lecture-style lessons, so it was a case of being as creative as possible to get the pupils involved. He found that getting pupils to do some work that he could see right at the beginning of the lesson worked well to get them invested in the lesson.

Activity: Consider what you have learned during the pandemic that might support your teaching - this might be about your own IT skills or communication skills, for example. Also think about how you will make the best use of technology in the classroom that adds value to the pupils' progress.

THE PROFESSIONAL TEACHER

Maintaining professional behaviours is an integral component of the CCF and ECF Standard 8 (Department for Education, 2019a) and encompasses the notion of professionalism. Professionalism is defined by the Oxford English Dictionary as the 'quality, character or conduct [and] the competence or skill expected of a professional' (Oxford English Dictionary, 2021). The general public have an impression of what a teacher is and how they should present themselves, which ultimately led to the profession being ranked the fourth most trusted occupation in the UK in 2020 (Ipsos MORI, 2020). Student teachers entering the career need to uphold this image and maintain professional standards.

Maintaining professionalism starts with simple measures such as treating colleagues with respect, turning up on time, handing lesson plans and resources to your mentors on time, handing essays in by the deadline or wearing professional attire. This then builds to develop yourself further by reflecting on your own teaching practice to become expert practitioner by engaging with CPD or contributing to whole school development plans.

Continual professional development (CPD) is something which you will become very familiar with once you finish your ITT course and embark on the early career years. As a professional, there is an expectation that you continually finesse and refine your skills to become an expert practitioner in the classroom. There is a wide variety of sources for this, some of which can be obtained through the school, but subject-specific CPD is at the heart of being an excellent science specialist. The Association for Science Education (ASE) and subject societies (Royal Society of Biology, Royal Society of Chemistry and the Institute of Physics) provide networking opportunities and CPD at national and regional conferences which can help you develop further. More generally, the Chartered College of Teaching (CCT) offers an abundance of support for ECTs. The opportunities these organisations and others provide can be found in Chapter 13.

Networking is a great way to find other science specialists to share ideas and resources for you to trial in the classroom, to continue to develop professionally. This may be within your training cohort, your host school or engaging with the science community on social media, such as Twitter. Social media can be an invaluable resource to connect with experienced and renowned colleagues worldwide, to share best practice and discover emerging ideas. A gentle reminder, however, that you need to follow the professional standards expected of you as a teacher when posting or commenting in the public domain on social media – you never know who might be reading what you post.

Overall, remember that there is a huge support network waiting for you to tap into. Everyone on your journey will support you to become the best teacher you possibly can be.

VIGNETTE 2.8   REFLECTIONS ON A CHALLENGING, BUT ENJOYABLE, YEAR

The reason that Paul had chosen to become a teacher was that he felt, in his previous job, that he was no longer progressing as a person or learning new skills. This training year has been easily the most enjoyable of his career and the fact that it is difficult is largely what makes it so enjoyable. He had previously had a range of jobs in terms of difficulty, and in terms of enjoyment and satisfaction he opted for more challenging every time. Paul was able to learn and talk about something he found hugely interesting every day - science. The enthusiasm and energy of his pupils gave him the energy and motivation needed to teach, and more. The reason, it seems, that nobody was able to describe for him exactly what he would find difficult about the PGCE before he started was that everyone finds it difficult in different ways and everyone finds it difficult at different points in the year.

Paul thought that to become a teacher, he would require a personality change. Before the course, he couldn't imagine himself standing in front of a class full of pupils. This couldn't be further from the truth. He found that when a class became his responsibility, he acted up to it, and teaching didn't feel unnatural at all. Behaviour management made more sense when he became responsible for the learning of the whole class. The more time he spent in a classroom, the more comfortable he started to feel and the easier it was to

(Continued)

enjoy himself when teaching. Paul couldn't imagine himself teaching like the teachers he had seen and been taught by, and that was because no one can teach with someone else's personality; his own would do just fine. Paul is exactly the same person he was before he started, he just has some new skills and confidence.

Activity: Think about your teacher identity and how this might change with time. As Paul says, you are still you, but how does the teacher 'you' draw upon your best communication and interpersonal skills?

PAUL'S TOP 3 TIPS FOR STUDENT TEACHERS

Get organised – you do not have the option of not being organised. You need to know exactly what you're doing every hour of every day so that you can teach the right lessons and get the resources ready in good time. There is a huge difference between having a lesson planned two weeks in advance and rushing around the night before. Look after your wellbeing by planning early.

Embrace being a beginner – this is something that your pupils will be brilliant at, but it comes less easily to a student teacher whose goal for the year is to show that they are a competent teacher. Take every piece of advice on board; thank host teachers for their feedback and aim to improve for next time they observe you. By embracing this beginner's mentality, you become free from the fear of looking inexperienced in front of an experienced teacher. You *are* inexperienced, they know that and are there to help.

Enjoy yourself – there is no point in any of this if you don't enjoy yourself. It can become easy to get bogged down in lesson planning and assignments, but we have all chosen to be a teacher because it is fun. This year is a hard one and that is what makes it so worthwhile; there is nothing more empowering that doing exactly what you have chosen to do and enjoying yourself while you do it.

SUMMARY

Now you have read this chapter you should have:

- Thought about common challenges faced by students as you embark on your individual journey to become a teacher.
- Read the experiences of a recent student teacher.
- Found support when you need to as you refer back to some of their advice and experiences.

REFLECTIVE QUESTIONS

- What can I do to ensure that I am organised for the start of the teacher training course?
- Have I got a plan I can use on a weekly basis, setting time aside for hobbies, interests and time to spend with loved ones to help me relax and unwind?
- What does professionalism mean to me? How can I ensure that I uphold public trust in the teaching profession?

FURTHER READING

The ASE's guides to teaching biology, chemistry or physics give a good background understanding to some of the topics you may encounter on placement. They help improve your subject knowledge and give tips on how to develop your explanation of these topics.

BIBLIOGRAPHY

Association for Science Education (2018). Science Teacher SOS. Available at: www.ase.org.uk/sos (accessed July 2021).

Department for Education (2019a). Early career framework – GOV.UK. Available at: www.gov.uk/government/publications/early-career-framework (accessed July 2021).

Department for Education (2019b). Initial teacher training (ITT) core content framework – GOV.UK. Available at: www.gov.uk/government/publications/initial-teacher-training-itt-core-content-framework (accessed July 2021).

Department for Education (2019c). Supporting early career teachers: reducing teacher workload – GOV.UK. Available at: www.gov.uk/government/publications/supporting-early-career-teachers-reducing-teacher-workload (accessed July 2021).

Ipsos MORI (2020) Ipsos MORI Veracity Index 2020. Available at: www.ipsos.com/ipsos-mori/en-uk/ipsos-mori-veracity-index-2020-trust-in-professions (accessed July 2021).

Ovenden-Hope, T. and Brimacombe, K. (2020). Teacher wellbeing and workload: Why a work–life balance is essential for the teaching profession – The Early Career Hub. Available at: https://earlycareer.chartered.college/teacher-wellbeing-and-workload-why-a-work-life-balance-is-essential-for-the-teaching-profession/ (accessed July 2021).

Oxford English Dictionary (2021). Available at: www.oed.com/ (accessed July 2021).

3

THE IMPORTANCE OF SUBJECT KNOWLEDGE

CAROLINE NEUBERG AND DEVINDER GILL

CHAPTER OVERVIEW

In this chapter, we will focus on one of the most, if not *the* most, exciting parts of being a science teacher, which is sharing subject knowledge with your pupils. We will focus on the importance of secure subject knowledge in teaching as well as exploring the pedagogical knowledge associated with the topics taught. We will also give you actionable recommendations to help you further develop your knowledge and emphasise the importance of Continuous Professional Development (CPD).

LINKS TO ITT CORE CONTENT FRAMEWORK AND EARLY CAREER FRAMEWORK

This chapter supports development of:

- Standard 1 – set high expectations
- Standard 2 – promote good progress
- Standard 3 – demonstrate good subject and curriculum knowledge

INTRODUCTION

Wherever you are on your journey to a teaching career, you will have selected this career path for different reasons such as wanting to share the love of your subject, feeling empowered when helping someone learn something new, being influenced by a previous teacher, enjoying the company of young learners or a combination of all the reasons above. However, at first, the classroom teaching can feel like an exercise in spinning plates; you will be welcoming and registering pupils, whilst having a range of activities ready for them to be engaged. You will be managing the more active pupils and identifying their strengths and weaknesses, whilst at the same time engaging the quiet pupils and encouraging them to actively contribute, teaching to the syllabus content, and having your practical equipment ready for a great lesson. During this lesson, as a teacher, you will not have the time to seek and learn for yourself the theoretical knowledge that underpins the pupils' learning. This theoretical subject knowledge is the most fundamental pillar at the heart of being a great teacher.

THEORETICAL KNOWLEDGE

In an ideal world, your first lesson with a class will involve the pupils settling quickly, with brand new stationery and a fresh-looking planner placed neatly on the desk in front of them, before they turn their attention to you and wait expectantly. They are ready to trust you and learn some exciting new science. However, you have been asked to start with a topic which is not within your area of specialism.

In preparation, it is likely that you have spent the previous evenings reading up on the topic from a generic textbook and are now ready to impart your freshly acquired knowledge to your class. Suddenly, invaded by doubts, you wonder if you have used the most appropriate source to learn the content and therefore are about to teach it in the 'wrong' style for their examination specification. You worry that your pupils may start asking probing questions that would expose your lack of deep knowledge of the subject. What if some of them become disillusioned by your answers and start to disengage?

Firstly, if you do have these doubts, you are not alone. Many science teachers, when they first embark on a career in teaching, encounter these thoughts, and it is likely that even as you gain experience in years to come there will be something you have to 'learn' before teaching. This is fully understandable given that you may well have dropped a particular science at A-Level or GCSE (or O-Level) and not looked at it since. It is a feature relatively exclusive to science that teachers are expected to teach subjects that are outside their specialism.

Whilst writing this chapter we carried out a small survey of PGCE science student teachers at Leeds Trinity University and unsurprisingly discovered that subject knowledge cropped up as a major concern for many of the trainees when having to teach outside their specialism. When asked about these concerns, one trainee responded with: 'being unable to answer the questions pupils may come up with, outside of the restrictions of the content of the lesson for which I have learnt/revised'. Another trainee said: 'Physics was not the best subject for me so obviously this would need more time to prepare lessons and sometimes feel less confident while teaching them.' Of the three sciences, the survey revealed that physics was the subject where the trainees lacked most confidence, with two-thirds of the trainees highlighting it as the subject they are most worried about.

It is crucial to stress that no teacher (science or any other subject) can teaching effectively, and with confidence, without depth and breadth of knowledge of the topic taught. Indeed, as a teacher, the fundamental aim in the classroom is to share knowledge and this goal is better achieved if the teacher has a secure command of the subject knowledge. Coe et al. (2014) stated that the most effective teachers have deep knowledge of the subjects they teach and also warned that it is a significant impediment to pupils' learning when teachers' knowledge falls below a certain level. 'Teachers cannot help children learn things they themselves do not understand' (Ball, 1991: 5).

As a teacher, you are placed in a position of trust: the cooperative pupils in the classroom come prepared with a belief that the person in front of them will be able to take them from ignorance to wisdom. Pupils often have an uncanny ability to identify lack of confidence, inexperience and uncertainty in a teacher's subject knowledge, which they could possibly exploit. Olasehinde-Williams et al. (2018) established that subject content knowledge of teachers was found to be a significant predictor of pupils' academic achievement. Abell (2007) and Wallace and Loughran (2012) restate the inextricable connection between teachers' knowledge and pupils' learning. Vignette 3.1 outlines how one trainee approached her need to address gaps in subject knowledge.

VIGNETTE 3.1 HUMAIRA'S APPROACH TO SUBJECT KNOWLEDGE DEVELOPMENT

Humaira was a mature student teacher who studied A-Level biology and chemistry before going on to study biology at university. By the time she had graduated she decided she wanted to be a teacher, having had experience of working with younger students in university and helping with youth clubs when she was at school. She embarked upon a PGCE Secondary Science with biology and realised this would also mean also teaching out of her specialism. To say that she was nervous about this is a massive understatement! She felt that her biology subject knowledge was secure, chemistry was strong enough for her to be confident, however her physics felt really quite distant. The other

(Continued)

realisation when she started her training was that there was actually a signifi-cant difference between the biology she had been studying in her degree and the science on the curriculum.

She decided to take a two-fold approach to addressing this. The first was to look at the subject knowledge in her strongest subjects and compare this closely with the National Curriculum - this allowed her to work out what she had simply forgotten compared with what she didn't know. The gaps here were the smallest so she felt that she could at least deal with these with some ease. Then she had to deal with the physics. Again, she tried to remember that much of what she was going to teach she had already done at school - although some years ago. She used revision guides and online resources to support her development. She wasn't able to relearn everything she had done but as soon as she knew what she had to teach on her school placement she focused on those areas. She felt really concerned going to speak to the other teachers about it and was worried about looking like she just shouldn't be there ... but it turned out that the major-ity of the teachers had been in the same position as her and were happy to help. She realised that asking for the support was far better than being in the position of not getting it right in class.

Activity: You are most likely to be asked to track your subject knowledge development throughout the year. How will you do this and how will you make this strategic rather than always being a 'needs must' response to what you have to teach?

Hopefully we have convinced you of the crucial demand for secure knowledge in the topics you will teach. As this chapter develops, we will provide you with practical approaches and steps you can take to further your knowledge. This knowledge can be gained from many sources, as long as you are prepared to identify your areas of development and work carefully at addressing them.

Key reference textbooks may form the backbone of this knowledge development – looking at GCSE or A-Level textbooks may be a mandatory and necessary step needed before facing a class. Reliable websites help provide the basic information that needs to be communicated to pupils and it is important that, as a science teacher, you look through several sources to develop your understanding in order to add layers of depth which will allow you to better contextualise the content. Experienced teachers have placed a huge wealth of resources on the internet, including videos on YouTube, that are readily accessible. In addition, there is a good chance that your school has a sys-tem in place for you to access shared resources from your colleagues. Speaking to colleagues prior to the lesson about how best to use these is essential and it is always a good idea to adapt them to your own approach and class. They will also be able to help you quality assure the plentiful material freely available online to ensure that it is correct scientifically and also pitched at the right level for the pupils you will be using it with.

However, learning science is not merely acquiring a collection of facts and information. It is important for the pupils to develop a scientific frame of mind that will help them apply concepts to contexts and independently investigate the reasons and scientific thinking behind the facts they will learn. As a teacher, you will need to be secure in your understanding of the material you are teaching to ensure these links can be established effectively, allowing your pupils to make good progress.

This also means you need to think about how to encourage pupils to have an inquisitive mindset, grounded in scientific content, to promote the development of effective enquiry (Dewey, 1910; Green, 2020). Acquiring knowledge to teach the next class does not only mean being ready to share facts but also to teach the scientific thinking behind the fact, as well as the stepping stones needed for the pupils to understand the concepts through the most appropriate methods and approaches.

PRACTICAL KNOWLEDGE AND RELATED SKILLS

As a science teacher, you are placed in a privileged and exciting situation of being able to carry out practical work. This should help your pupils secure their theoretical knowledge and provide them with a wide range of skills. Benchmark 3 from the Gatsby *Good Practical Science* (Holman, 2017) assumes that teachers should have had subject specialist training (both initial and continuing) in the subject (biology, chemistry, physics, etc.) and age range they teach, so they can carry out practical science with confidence and knowledge of the underlying principles.

The 21st-century skills educational movement advocates for the integrations of critical thinking and problem-solving skills in teaching young minds (Bellanca and Brandt, 2010). Society has dramatically changed since education became compulsory, leaving behind an industrial economy and moving towards a service economy that requires from its workforce – i.e. your pupils, in several years – many other competencies than the simple ability to recall facts. Science should be the subject at the forefront of these changes due to its exceptional character of being taught by problem-solving, critical thinking, team working, analytical processing and communication skills. All of these skills can be developed during practical work.

It can be quite daunting to perform a demonstration in front of a whole class for the first time and this is exacerbated further when covering a topic outside of your specialism. Therefore, it is imperative that you practise any demonstration or class practical before you plan to teach the lesson (see Box 3.1 for commonly used examples), working closely with the technicians in the department (this is elaborated upon in Chapter 7). As a student and relatively new teacher, ensure you make the most of the expertise on offer from your mentor, experienced teachers and the technicians within your school so that you develop a solid understanding of the underlying science. Further details on developing these skills can be found in Chapter 8.

BOX 3.1   COMMONLY TAUGHT DEMONSTRATION EXAMPLES

In biology, the opportunity to dissect tissue specimens can be a unique and memorable way to introduce organ systems to your pupils. Dissection specimens provided for schools often do not necessarily look like the diagrams you or your pupils will find in textbooks, which you may not realise until too late. This, coupled with managing the behaviour of an excited class, has the potential to cause problems. This indicates the value of liaison with more experienced colleagues and technicians to practise before undertaking your lesson live.

Group 1 metals in water is always an exciting and engaging demonstration in chemistry. It is essential that you practise this in order to learn how to facilitate discussion whilst doing, work out sizes of metal to cut, and how to manage the situation if there is a larger (or smaller) reaction than expected. The pupils always want a bigger piece of metal in the water - you must be very clear about when big enough is big enough.

Consider a simple circuit with a cell connected to a resistor in physics. According to the theory at key stage 3, when you place a voltmeter across the cell and then the resistor, you might expect the potential difference across the cell and resistor to be identical. This might not always be the case if there is a small potential difference across the connecting wires. Only by practising the demonstration and asking questions would you, as a non-specialist physics teacher, be aware of this and be ready to discuss it with your pupils.

In order to further prepare you to undertake practical work and demonstrations, there are some supportive websites from associations and subject bodies such as:

- Practical Physics by the Institute of Physics
- Nuffield practical collection by the Royal Society of Chemistry
- Practical Biology by the Royal Society of Biology
- Science and Plants for Schools (SAPS)
- CLEAPSS - see Chapter 7

They list an extensive number of practicals and demonstrations, each with a detailed procedure, health and safety guidance and most importantly, teaching notes provided for each practical. There is further information about support offered through such bodies and associations in Chapter 13.

VOCABULARY

The language of science is an area that can lead to much confusion due to the discrepancy between the everyday experience of the word and the scientific one. Teaching science also needs to include the disciplinary literacy, such is the unique lexicon used in each of the three sciences (Hendrick and Macpherson, 2017). As teachers, we need to encourage pupils towards more accurate expression in the verbal form, to articulate sound verbal reasoning, and accurately use technical vocabulary. Hirsch (2003) argues that such skills are essential for developing subject knowledge – and in turn are built by subject knowledge. So, it is important to use the appropriate and rigorous terminology of scientific jargon to develop the pupils' needs.

As a new teacher, do not expect to get the use of precise scientific vocabulary correct from the very beginning. Experience in the classroom with plenty of practise teaching a particular topic will enable you to develop this skill. Observe your colleagues in lessons, paying particular attention to the language they use. In the same way, you want your pupils to hear the key language so that they gain fluency in reading examination questions and develop comprehension of the questions – a common stumbling block that often impedes progress.

Words in science often have a different contextual meaning than their everyday definitional use (see Box 3.2 which gives some common examples). This is why, as a science teacher, it is so important to pause and think very carefully before you offer scientific descriptions and explanations and be meticulous to avoid the casual use of scientific language that would only reinforce some of these difficulties.

BOX 3.2   EXAMPLES OF THE USE OF WORDS IN EVERYDAY LANGUAGE AND IN A SCIENTIFIC CONTEXT

IN CHEMISTRY

In everyday language, the term gas tends to be used to describe a range of combustible fuels such as camping gas, BBQ gas bottles, car fuel, or natural gas used in homes for cooking or heating. Primary pupils will experience the use of the word gas as a combustible fuel that is burnt to release heat. Hence pupils often do not define air as a gas because a gas is seen as something that is flammable and air is not. This may lead to initial difficulties and typical misconceptions when teaching the three states of matter.

(Continued)

IN BIOLOGY

The ordinary usage of the word 'plant' commonly refers to small, leafy shrubs. When the scientific term 'Plant Kingdom' is presented to pupils they often have difficulty with the classification encompassing mosses or very large trees and therefore believe trees and plants to be different.

IN PHYSICS

The word 'moment' is used as a turning effect of a force in physics rather than a very brief period of time in everyday language. More importantly, the difficulties in assimilating the difference between mass and weight is exacerbated by an improper use of the word weight in everyday language. This misuse of the term 'weight' is so ingrained it is even used in official documentation such as the weight of allowed baggage on flights expressed in kg, the unit of mass.

MATHEMATICAL SKILLS

Fear of maths can be a factor that prevents pupils from embarking on a rewarding science-based career: it will be part of your job to alleviate this often-unfounded fear. You will need to display confidence in the mathematical skills needed. One of the pitfalls to avoid is the potential discrepancy between the language and methods you use in science compared with those used by the mathematics teachers in your school.

To combat the compartmentalisation of subjects, it is useful to have some consistency between mathematics and science. According to the report *The Language of Mathematics in Science* (Boohan and Needham, 2016: 2) 'it is unhelpful to have arbitrary differences in approaches and terminology between the subjects'. If your mathematics department uses the term 'make x the subject' with algebraic functions, but the science department within the same school use the term 'rearrange the formula', is it little wonder that pupils are left puzzled. It is important within any school for there to be a close collaboration between mathematics and science departments to develop such consistency. As a student teacher, it is worth sitting down and having a chat with your colleagues in the mathematics department to establish when they teach fundamental skills such as plotting graphs, calculating a gradient and converting units that are commonly used across the three science disciplines. Student teachers need to be confident in these basic mathematics skills themselves before introducing often tricky contextual problems to the pupils.

Subject knowledge of an equation we might use in science must go beyond being able to simply recall a formula. Consider the following:

$$density = \frac{mass}{volume}$$

The robotic use of this formula by inserting values, rearranging and obtaining a suitable answer without a genuine understanding will leave gaps in the learning that should occur. For example, water has a density of 1000 kg/m³. But what does this *actually* mean? For an understanding of this value, our pupils would need to know what we mean by a volume of 1m³. They would then need to have some grasp on how 'heavy' a mass of 1000kg is (whilst ensuring not to add confusion by introducing the term weight). Only then would they have an understanding of what 1000 kg/m³ means and be able to compare effectively with other materials.

A commonly used formula in both biology and physics relates to the calculation of magnification:

$$magnification = \frac{image\ size}{actual\ size}$$

Pupils are expected to manipulate this formula whilst simultaneously dealing with the conversion of, often complex, units of measurement. When teaching this equation, it is vital to ensure that pupils are comfortable with rearranging formulae to ensure this fundamental mathematical skill is achieved before moving on to converting units of measurement. It is worth emphasising to pupils the use of applying common sense to the answer obtained with sizes of objects – ensuring the answer seems relatable to real life and sensible.

ESSENTIAL MATHEMATICAL SKILLS FOR SCIENCE TEACHERS

At GCSE level, mathematical skills are a requirement that account for up to 10% in biology, 20% in chemistry and 30% in physics. The mathematical skills can be divided into five broad areas: arithmetic and numerical computation (as outlined in Table 3.1), algebra, handling data, graphs, and geometry and trigonometry. The aim of Table 3.1 is to provide a brief overview of the most used prefixes in the science curriculum for pupils aged 11 to 16.

PEDAGOGICAL CONTENT KNOWLEDGE

We have seen that teachers must have secure subject knowledge to teach effectively and assess progress of pupils adequately. This simply cannot be done without a good understanding of the subject material. However, this is only half the story. You must also consider *how* you impart this knowledge and ensure that the content is accessible to all your pupils. In other words, teachers need an understanding and appreciation of Pedagogical Content Knowledge (PCK). Teachers need to look at subject content and be able to transform it so that it can be readily digested by pupils with different abilities and backgrounds. The concept of PCK is also developed in Chapter 9 discussing tricky topics.

Table 3.1 Prefixes frequently used within the science curriculum

Prefix Name	Giga	Mega	Kilo	Hecto	Deca	Deci	Centi	Milli	Micro	Nano
Symbol	G	M	k	h	da	dc	c	m	·	n
Magnitude	10^9	10^6	10^3	10^2	10^1	10^{-1}	10^{-2}	10^{-3}	10^{-6}	10^{-9}
Multiply by	1,000,000,000	1,000,000	1,000	100	10	0.1	0.01	0.001	0.000,001	0.000,000,001
Relation to every day scale	Sun, Earth's orbit	Moon, Earth	Suez Canal, Kilimanjaro	Fields, Eiffel Tower	Houses, sperm whales	Human	Ping Pong ball, mouse	Head of pin or Mosquitoes	Red blood cells size or bacteria	Atoms spacing or carbon nanotubes

Shulman distinguished between content as it is studied and learned in disciplinary settings and the 'special amalgam of content and pedagogy' (Shulman, 1987: 8) needed for teaching the subject. These ideas had a major impact on the research community, immediately focusing attention on the foundational importance of content knowledge in teaching and on PCK in particular. PCK allows teachers to ask and answer some important questions (Saeli et al., 2011) such as:

- What is the best way for me to teach...?
- How do I explore what my pupils already know about...?
- What misconceptions are pupils likely to have about...?
- Which is the best model to teach pupils about...?
- What do pupils find difficult about...?

It is important to stress that you will develop your PCK over many years 'by engaging with research, reading books, working with colleagues, training and through reflecting on classroom practice' (Green, 2020: 83).

We will now explore in further detail some of the PCK that should be considered in science lessons: knowledge of cognitive load theory, retrieval practice and knowledge of preconceptions. These topics are also discussed in Chapter 5 in the context of planning, Chapter 9 in relation to tricky topics and in Chapter 10 focused on teaching pupils with SEND.

IMPORTANCE OF MANAGING COGNITIVE LOAD

There has been a good deal of research over the last few years on understanding how our brains are able to process and store information. Cognitive load theory was developed by a psychologist, John Sweller (1988), who explained that information will be stored in the long-term memory, provided it has been processed sufficiently in the working memory. If too much information is presented at once, the working memory can become overloaded and much of the information is lost. Hence, the aim of a lesson is to ensure that we can load the long-term memory of our pupils as effectively as possible by not burdening the working memory with too much information at any one time.

As a teacher this means you need to think carefully about the sequencing of a topic and practical work so that you do not provide too much detail at the beginning which would lead to the working memory being overloaded. An example might be a sequence of lessons in chemistry on the particle model of matter. Launching into all the definitions along with descriptions for the three states of matter within a short space of time would saturate the working memory and some of the information would therefore not filter across into the long-term memory. As mentioned earlier in this chapter when we looked at vocabulary, we want our pupils to be scientifically literate, but we cannot expect them to be efficient learners if we bombard them with many terms in a short space of time. Any comprehensive description of the states of matter would contain terms such as molecules, atoms, ions, density, volume, compressible, incompressible, melting point, boiling point, vibrations and forces. You need to navigate through a topic such that pupils do not suffer from cognitive overload when confronted with too many terms too quickly.

Even within a single lesson, you need to consider carefully how you might reduce cognitive load. When you ask your pupils to complete a practical task, you significantly increase their cognitive load. Pupils are often so preoccupied with following written tasks, gathering, setting up and using scientific apparatus, that they often lose sight of the reasons why they are completing the practicals, let alone the underlying science. Breaking a practical into sections with systems in place that pupils are familiar with, such as collecting and returning equipment, can reduce their cognitive load (see Chapter 5 for use of integrated instructions to support practical work). A model set-up of the experiment can also be displayed so that your pupils have a clear picture of how to set up the equipment. Although tabulating data and plotting suitable graphs are important skills, consider providing frames or tables if this is not the focus of the lesson, in order that the pupils can focus on the science.

Rogers (2018) highlights several techniques to reduce cognitive load in lessons such as worked examples. This makes transparent what might be considered the hidden process of problem solving or structuring questions in such a way to provide the support pupils might need whilst removing the extraneous information. However, it should be stressed that reducing the cognitive load should not be at the expense of limiting the appropriate level of challenge, which you should keep in mind at all times.

IMPORTANCE IN CONTINUITY OF LEARNING THROUGH RETRIEVAL

Have you ever been in a position where you think you understand a particular piece of information, but when asked to explain it, you suddenly struggle to recall some of the finer details? Retrieval practice in one way is looking at how we can extract the information we have learnt from our memory. As a teacher, you need to consider the strategies you can employ to develop and improve the ability of your pupils to retrieve information that has been stored for days, weeks, months and even years. This is not solely for the pupils to apply this knowledge in assessments, but rather to develop their learning and identify any gaps in their knowledge and understanding.

Student teachers need to have a clear progression map that details what subject knowledge has been taught in previous lessons. It is easy as a student teacher to plan lesson by lesson and not see the links. You need to ensure that opportunities are available in lessons for pupils to recall some of the information that has been covered earlier, which means there is an impact on how you need to think about and plan subject content.

Let's consider what this might look like in a lesson. Starting a lesson with a five-minute, low threat, whole class questioning on the content of the previous lesson will help your pupils cement the new concepts in their long-term memory. It is important that this is not just a hands-up exercise, but that all pupils are able to access information from their memories. This could be done by providing mini-whiteboards for pupils to respond to true/false questions or perhaps to recall word equations or sketch graphs to show patterns. Another idea could be to have pupils produce their own flashcards with key words and definitions. Pupils could then work in pairs to quiz each other using the cards as prompts.

Retrieval practice techniques would be vital across all year groups but are especially so with any A-Level classes you may be teaching. Pupils are bombarded with a huge amount of information and, with the nature of science, these ideas are often inter-linked. Well-spaced interventions to look at retrieving some of the earlier material covered will enable your pupils to see the inherent links and connections.

IMPORTANCE OF KNOWING PRECONCEPTIONS AND PRE-KNOWLEDGE

Pupils will come to your class with preconceived ideas about science gained from their everyday experiences, previous teaching, their environment and surroundings. As a teacher, preconceived ideas need to be identified, challenged and then finally replaced if incorrect or inaccurate. Student teachers often find identifying preconceptions challenging. This is fully understandable as a genuine concern for teachers would be if they further perpetuate these alternative conceptions. Some of these preconceived ideas are based on our everyday experiences. Consider a shopping trip and pushing a supermarket trolley. Without the pushing force, the trolley quickly comes to a stop. Therefore, it is no wonder pupils arrive at lessons convinced that anything moving *must* need a force pushing it in the direction of movement. Even when these ideas are refuted according to Newton's Laws of Motion, it is so easy for pupils to fall back to their preconceived ideas. This is especially true when the concepts are non-intuitive and do not align with everyday observations. As student teachers, we must ensure that our own subject knowledge is secure enough to be able to identify the errors pupils hold and also the ability to address these.

Care must be taken, as misconceptions may sometimes surface during a lesson when diagrams are drawn or models are applied to explain scientific phenomena such as the example in Box 3.3. This is especially the case when trying to link the microscopic with macroscopic observations and explanations.

BOX 3.3   EXAMPLES OF HOW PUPILS' WORK CAN BE USED TO ELICIT THEIR PRIOR KNOWLEDGE

A pupil drew this diagram (Figure 3.1) as part of their homework. This highlights the importance of you having secure subject knowledge, why identification of preconceived knowledge is key and how you might go about tackling inaccuracies.

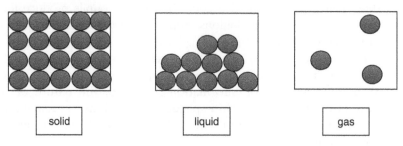

solid	liquid	gas

Figure 3.1   The particle model for the three states of matter as drawn by a pupil during homework

Questions to consider about this pupil's understanding:

1. Where do you think the misconceptions may arise here?
2. How do you assess preconceived ideas?
3. How could you address these misconceptions?
4. Which alternative conceptual model(s) do pupils hold?
5. How do you move pupils from current thinking towards accepted ideas?

Typically, we find that pupils believe that a container of gas only contains a handful of particles. They may also assume that the gaps between the gas particles are filled with air and their preconceived ideas on forces suggest that there must be forces acting on gas particles as they move in a container. Teachers need to be watchful for these misconceptions and set tasks to address these issues. The Best Evidence Science Teaching (BEST) resources produced by the Education Group at the University of York have used the evidence available from educational research to produce a comprehensive list of diagnostic questions to reveal preconceptions and common misunderstandings (see annotated reading). In addition, the use of 'Concept Cartoons in Science Education' (Naylor and Keogh, 2000) or 'Next time questions' (see further reading) are able to highlight some of the conceptual difficulties pupils may have.

Once you have revealed the misconceptions of your pupils, you will need to consider carefully how you might challenge these ideas. Rogers (2018: 13–14) suggests a very explicit approach using refutation texts where the learner does three things:

1. States the misconception.
2. Explicitly says that this is not correct.
3. States the accepted scientific viewpoint.

An example might be:

1. Many people believe there is air between gas particles.
2. However, this is not correct.
3. There is only empty space between the gas particles.

Finally, it is important that you aim to address and assess misconceptions in a variety of contexts. For example, you could ask pupils to think about the particles that would be present in bubbles when water boils. You could ensure that the particle model is not taught in isolation but integrated into other areas such as changes of state, gas pressure and convection currents in air.

SUPPORTING YOUR SUBJECT KNOWLEDGE

As we have established so far in this chapter, it is your responsibility as a teacher to make sure that you have the adequate and fundamental knowledge to deliver an appropriate lesson. In this next section we give you a list of tried and tested, reliable resources that have formed the backbone of knowledge improvement for many other science teachers.

TEXTBOOKS AND WEBSITES

There are numerous textbooks that are available to support subject knowledge development. A starting point might be to select a textbook that matches the course content that is in line with the specific examination body you are teaching. The book needs to contain the appropriate material at the correct level you are planning to teach, with accurate information. You could explore within your new school the books they use and many will lend you these for the duration of your time with them. Subject associations such as the Association for Science Education have a range of supportive publications, and books such as *Powerful Ideas of Science and How To Teach Them* (Green, 2021) begin to draw together what to teach in science and how to approach this.

Websites associated with teaching and learning of science are plentiful – with time and experience you will favour some over others. Any list will become quickly outdated and we recommend speaking with colleagues and peers for recommendations. As with anything, they are not all good, so do not always trust everything in front of you.

Practising past papers related to your exam board is the best tool you can use to identify potential gaps in your knowledge. This is a really practical strategy which might enable you to tailor your actions for developing subject knowledge more efficiently in the beginning of your career.

THE IMPORTANCE OF CONTINUOUS PROFESSIONAL DEVELOPMENT (CPD)

It has been claimed that teachers typically stop improving after three to five years of teaching (Coe et al., 2014). As a professional in your field you should constantly strive to process and evaluate education research and evidence that may emerge to improve your practice. Reading articles in newspapers and scientific journals to keep abreast of current discoveries in science is a simple approach that you can take … remember, you as a science teacher might be the *only* person to share this information with your pupils. Your job is not solely to impart knowledge and develop understanding through effective use of lesson time but to share that passion for your subject in the hope that this enthusiasm rubs off on to your pupils. Only then will subject knowledge play its part in promoting a love of learning (see also Chapter 11 which considers the science capital teaching approach).

Continuous Professional Development (CPD) ensures that you are keeping pace with the standards of teaching. This can take the form of an informal in-school meeting with a more established teacher or an external provider, and it is important to move away from thinking of CPD as only going on a course. Online or face-to-face events are great ways to feel reinvigorated as they can provide you with a deeper understanding, new teaching ideas and demos as well as progression steps to teach a topic, along with developing a supportive network of colleagues. CPD can also enable you to appreciate and be more aware of the impacts and implications of your work. Thus, it is important that you engage with support networks. Many trusts and organisations can form a support network from which to gain new or more in-depth knowledge. You will find numerous sources of CPD. However, we would encourage you, in Physics, to register with the Institute of Physics, in Chemistry, with the Royal Society of Chemistry and in Biology, with the Royal Society of Biology. The overarching Association for Science Education (ASE), STEM Learning, Royal Society and Professional Teaching Institute are highly recognised and recommended sources of CPD (see Chapter 13 for more information). More locally you will also find that some universities provide ad hoc CPD for teachers.

Finally, we encourage you to engage with CPD events provided by your examination board. These events may focus more on the application of knowledge and curriculum knowledge rather than pure subject knowledge, but they will still inform your teaching and help make you a better teacher.

As a new science teacher, we hope that a bright and enjoyable future in teaching awaits, but also that you experience the fun and satisfaction in developing your own subject knowledge and learning some amazing new science. Teaching allows you to share that love and enthusiasm you probably had for science when you were at school. You will even question some of the science that you regard as your specialist subject when the pupils ask questions that you had not even considered. This is the beauty of science. You will constantly be learning the subject – subject knowledge should not be seen as a static body of knowledge.

WHAT TO LOOK FOR WHEN OBSERVING LESSONS

- How do experienced teachers approach the identification of preconceptions in science lessons?
- What ways do teachers introduce new subject knowledge to pupils and how do they develop this through a lesson?
- How do teachers deal with tangential questions in relation to the subject being taught?

SUMMARY

Now you have read this chapter you should have:

- A better understanding of the importance of having secure subject knowledge when teaching.
- Realised the importance of correct use of vocabulary and mathematical approaches to support teaching and learning.
- Greater knowledge of the theories associated with developing subject knowledge.

REFLECTIVE QUESTIONS

- What strategies will you use to identify gaps in your own subject knowledge and how will you address these systematically as an ECT of Science?
- How will you find the best way to teach subject content as well as learning what to teach, i.e. how do you develop your pedagogical repertoire?
- Reflect on lessons to consider those where you felt more secure or less secure in terms of subject knowledge - how did this impact on the lesson?

FURTHER READING

Best Evidence Science Teaching (BEST) addresses all three sciences and was developed by the University of York and supported by Salter's Institute. It reinforces subject knowledge development and assessment of your pupils. Available: www.york.ac.uk/education/research/uyseg/research-projects/bestevidencescienceteaching/

Next Time Questions focus on physics subject knowledge and enable teachers to challenge some preconceptions that pupils may have. Available: www.arborsci.com/pages/next-time-questions

Dr Jasper Green, known on social media as 'The science teacher' and Ofsted Subject Lead for Science offers science thinking resources and support with pedagogy. Available: https://thescienceteacher.co.uk/

BIBLIOGRAPHY

Abell, S.K. (2007). Research on science teacher knowledge. In S.K. Abell and N.G. Lederman (Eds), *Handbook of research on science education*. Mahwah, NJ: Lawrence Erlbaum Associates, Inc.

Ball, D.L. (1991). Teaching mathematics for understanding: What do teachers need to know about subject matter? In M. Kennedy (Ed.), *Teaching academic subjects to diverse learners* (pp. 63–83). New York: Teachers College Press.

Bellanca, J. and Brandt, R. (Eds) (2010). *21st century skills: Rethinking how students learn*. Bloomington, IN: Solution Tree Press. Available: DOI: 10.1007/s11858-012-0429-7

Boohan, R. and Needham, R. (2016). *The language of mathematics in science: a guide for teachers of 11–16 science*. Hatfield: Association for Science Education.

Coe, R., Aloisi, S., Higgins, S. and Major, L.E. (2014). *What makes great teaching? Review of the underpinning research*. London: The Sutton Trust.

Department for Education (2018). Initial teacher training: trainee number census 2018 to 2019 (Report on Official Statistics). Retrieved from: www.gov.uk/government/statistics/initial-teacher-training-trainee-number-census-2018-to-2019

Dewey, J. (1910). Science as subject-matter and as a method. *Science*, 31(787): 121–127.

Green, J. (2021). *Powerful ideas of science and how to teach them*. Abingdon: Routledge.

Hendrick, C. and Macpherson, R. (2017). *What does this look like in the classroom?: Bridging the gap between research and practice* Woodbridge: John Catt Educational.

Hirsch, Jr., E.D. (2003). Reading comprehension requires knowledge – of words and the world: scientific insights into the fourth-grade slump and the nation's stagnant comprehension scores, *American Educator*, Spring, pp 10–29. Available: www.aft.org/sites/default/files/periodicals/AE_SPRNG.pdf

Holman, J. (2017). *Good practical science*. London: Gatsby Charitable Foundation.

Naylor, S. and Keogh, B. (2000). *Concept cartoons in science education*. Stafford: Millgate House Publishing.

Olasehinde-Williams, F., Yahaya, L. and Owolabi H. (2018). Teachers' knowledge indices as predictors of secondary school students' academic achievement in Kwara State, Nigeria. *IAFOR Journal of Education*, 6(1): 73–90.

Rogers, B. (2018). *The big ideas in physics and how to teach them*. Abingdon: Routledge.

Saeli, M., Perrenet, J., Jochems, W. and Zwaneveld, B. (2011). Teaching programming in secondary school: A pedagogical content knowledge perspective. *Informatics in Education*, 10(1): 73–88.

Shulman, L.S. (1987). Knowledge and teaching: Foundations of the new reform. *Harvard Educational Review*, 57(1): 1–23.

Sweller, J. (1988). Cognitive load during problem solving: Effects on learning. *Cognitive Science*, 12(2): 257–285.

Wallace J. and Loughran J. (2012). Science teacher learning. In B. Fraser, K. Tobin and C. McRobbie (Eds), *Second International Handbook of Science Education. Springer International Handbooks of Education*, 24. Dordrecht: Springer.

4

WHAT WE CAN LEARN FROM PRIMARY SCHOOL SCIENCE

ALEX SINCLAIR AND REBECCA RILEY

CHAPTER OVERVIEW

This chapter will outline the common experiences pupils starting secondary school will have gained from their primary science education. We will provide you with guidance and preparation when first teaching a Year 7 class by outlining some of the issues related to transition and detailing an overview of primary science education. We will also make suggestions for working with your Year 7 class that build upon and value their primary school science learning.

LINKS TO ITT CORE CONTENT FRAMEWORK AND EARLY CAREER FRAMEWORK

This chapter supports development of:

- Standard 2 – promote good progress
- Standard 3 – demonstrate good subject and curriculum knowledge
- Standard 5 – adapt teaching

INTRODUCTION

As a student teacher you may start reading this feeling that many of the points raised in the chapter are beyond your remit and control. You will be in the difficult position of being placed in a science department and school where you may have very little agency over the structure and ethos of the department you are teaching in. You are unlikely to have the status, or experience, to make recommendations about how best to aid the transition process from primary to secondary school. However, there is much that you can do on a personal and professional level to ensure that your pupils have the best learning experiences. This chapter will aid you in doing this by helping you to appreciate some of the historical contexts around transition; give you a flavour of what a Year 7 child will have covered in their primary years; and suggest strategies for integrating into your practice which demonstrate that you value the pupils' previous learning experiences.

ISSUES AROUND TRANSITION

We will first address the often-perennial debate about transition which, at its heart, is related to ideological and pedagogical positions about the purpose of primary and secondary science education. Usually drawn from a lack of knowledge and experience, both primary and secondary teachers can hold strongly held stereotyped images about each other's practices. This unhelpful situation has led Sutherland et al. (2010) to describe there being a 'two tribes', them and us, mentality between teachers of the two age phases. This is further compounded by reporting of 'dips' in attainment progress between primary and secondary. The purpose of this chapter is not to offer solutions to transition-related problems but to provide a brief topography of the situation in which you may be placed as a student teacher. It is written with the caveat that, while there are often clear differences between primary and secondary science, it has been necessary to make some generalisations about the teaching and learning at these age phases so that you have a starting point for your classes.

SCIENCE PROFILE

It is important to remember that pupils who arrive at secondary school may have had differing experiences of science in primary school. Although recognised as a core subject in the National Curriculum (DfE, 2013), science is not always acknowledged as a priority due to increased weighting on the progress being made in English and Mathematics. Science is no longer formally tested at the end of primary school in England and instead, the class teacher provides a statutory assessment as a part of the end of year data submission; this can cause schools to view the subject as less important. However, what this means is that pupils should have the necessary writing and mathematical skills which are so important for learning science. As a beginner teacher, it is beneficial to find out both the quality and quantity of written work that is expected from Year 6 pupils to guide what you can expect in your class.

At this stage it may be useful for you to interrogate your assumptions about the primary–secondary divide (see reflective questions section at the end of the chapter). Sutton (2000) offers a suggestion why so many applicants to PGCE courses acknowledge that it is only at secondary school that 'proper' science is taught. She generalises the approaches towards teaching pupils at the different age phases and proposes that primary teachers take a more holistic approach; this could be described as teaching the 'child', with secondary teachers focusing on teaching their 'subject'. This does not mean that there is no science in primary schools, and articles such as those which ask 'Should we teach chemistry at primary school?' (Stuart, 2020) show a misunderstanding of what happens in primary classrooms.

However, it is important to appreciate that evidence from reports across a number of years suggest that some pupils' attitude towards learning science decreases alongside their expected attainment in the early years of their secondary education (Galton et al., 1999; Ofsted, 2015) and that largely these are related to issues to do with transition. While some of this can be attributed to social factors (such as making new friends, moving to a new school and the anxiety this process can induce), this for many pupils, is temporary. The progression dip appears to be particularly pertinent to learning science as it is not experienced in the same way in subjects such as English and mathematics (Barmby et al., 2008). Braund (2016) provides reasons for lack of progress by those making the transition into the new school, and these can be broadly classified into two interrelated areas: curriculum content and pedagogical approach.

CURRICULUM CONTENT

Ofsted's (2015) research, entitled *Key Stage 3: The wasted years?*, identified that 9–17% of what was taught in Key Stage 3 science was repeated content. Braund (2016) recognised it was not just the same learning, but the very similar contexts and equipment which were being employed. Pleasingly, the amount of curriculum repetition is lower in science than in other subjects, such as English and Mathematics, which may be because of the introduction of new concepts such as cells, atomic structure and energy. While Braund and Driver's (2005) research showed that some secondary teachers lacked awareness of the primary curriculum, Ofsted (2015) highlighted that particularly successful transitions could occur when the primary leads reviewed the secondary curriculum for repetition.

PEDAGOGICAL APPROACH

There is much debate about the appropriate pedagogical approaches that should be adopted at different age phases and these are often related to one's view on the purpose of science education. Sutton (2000) acknowledges that many primary schools have values-based philosophies and that helping pupils to identify and practise these values is their key role. As a consequence of this, the pedagogy used in science lessons is likely to be more child-led and enquiry based. When making the transition to secondary schools, pupils are likely to experience lessons where the teaching style focuses far more on direct instruction.

Bridging projects/units which have been undertaken between secondary and feeder primary schools have been employed as a way of improving transition for many years. They have had varying success, with Symonds (2015) highlighting that there are no nationally agreed procedures for bridging projects and that recently far fewer schools are using them. The lack of consistent success is understandable. The nature of teachers' workloads often makes it impossible for the necessary subject-specific communication to take place. In addition to this, the disparate nature of primary feeder schools can mean that ensuring all transitioning pupils have engaged with these projects is challenging.

The bridging projects which worked well had a focus on the skills of working scientifically, which are taught both in Key Stage 2 and 3 (Braund, 2016). It is important to note that if this strategy is adopted there needs to be a shared understanding of the key stage appropriate language of working scientifically. This understanding about progression will be returned to later in this chapter.

Braund (2016: 23) stresses the importance of teachers at both age phases articulating to pupils the significance of their science learning. He suggests that:

> [Year 6 teachers talk] to the class about what they have done at key stage 2 and how this will be progressed and valued when they look at a similar topic again in key stage 3. Even more crucial is that the key stage 3 teacher talks with the class to show how what they have done at primary school is now being valued and built on in the secondary school. The whole point is to prevent pupils feeling that their primary science means nothing and that just because they see the title of a lesson or a topic at secondary school that they have already studied at primary school, this does not mean that the work will be just boring repetition.

We appreciate that it is unlikely that you will have the opportunity to communicate with primary school teachers and explore with them what they have covered in their science lessons. We will, therefore, provide a brief and very generalised outline of what a pupil starting in secondary school may have experienced in their primary school science lessons. This will hopefully ensure that you have the background context to talk with your Year 7s and 8s about what they achieved in their primary school years.

The next section is divided into the following areas:

a.   A generic science profile of a child leaving primary school;
b.   The substantive content knowledge that pupils develop in their primary years;
c.   The skills and ways of working scientifically which are developed at primary school;
d.   An overview of ways in which science capital is developed.

EXPERIENCES OF A YEAR 6 CHILD

The primary science curriculum differs from that in secondary in several ways and it is important that you are aware of the science journey the pupils have been on before arriving at secondary school. By being aware of what they already know, you can be prepared to establish a starting point to build upon and extend.

This section will outline the learning journey a child may have experienced from Reception (ages 4–5) through to the end of Key Stage 2 (age 11). It will first detail how science is learnt and taught in Reception. It will then provide an overview of the substantive content knowledge outlined in the National Curriculum in Key Stage 1 and 2 and then turn to the development of working scientifically across the age phases.

SCIENCE IN RECEPTION

Predominantly, primary school science is concrete and relatable, drawing inspiration from the world in which the child finds themselves. When pupils begin their primary school journey in Reception, they are still in the latter stages of infancy. At this point of their education, science is not taught discretely (much of it can be found in Understanding the World) but scientific skills are a focus and are often in context with the natural world. Learning at this point usually takes place through continuous provision. This is when the teacher provides pupils with resources and opportunities to explore, develop and consolidate their learning as independently as possible. Pupils in Reception are encouraged to make observations and draw comparisons based on their own experiences. They are exposed to, and begin to develop some understanding of, natural processes and changes which are facilitated by teachers based on the pupils' interests as well as using the local environment. For example, this can include pupils discussing why the outdoor water tray has frozen or noticing that there are conkers on the ground. This learning is often driven by the pupils, involving activities they enjoy and following their interests; these opportunities are facilitated by the teacher and are often linked to raising science capital (see below and Chapter 11).

KEY STAGE 1 AND 2 SUBSTANTIVE CONTENT KNOWLEDGE

In Key Stage 1 (age 5–7 years) and 2 (age 7–11), science is an umbrella term which includes biology, chemistry, physics and working scientifically. While there are distinct topics (such as animals, including humans, and electricity) within the programmes of study, these are not always directly referred to by their subject titles. Biology and chemistry topics are studied throughout, whereas physics appears primarily in Key Stage 2.

In Key Stage 1, curriculum science content remains relatable with meaningful links to the pupils' everyday experiences. Although the idea of science as a subject is introduced, the subject matter remains real and applicable to the outside world. Biology strands, such as living things (including plants and animals) and keeping healthy, are often taught as discrete learning topics at this stage (in contrast to the continuous provision provided in Reception), enabling pupils to build upon the foundation of knowledge already developed in Reception. Chemistry, in the form of materials science, also begins, giving pupils the opportunity to identify properties of different substances, their appropriate uses and how the application of a physical force can change them. At this stage there is a focus on identifying and classifying, and this is underpinned by vocabulary development and the necessary identification of an object's properties. While simple comparative tests are performed there is a greater emphasis on pupils gaining first-hand experiences of natural phenomenon through observations over time.

Opportunities for studying more abstract scientific concepts occur in lower Key Stage 2 (ages 7–9). This includes the appearance of the physics topics of light, electricity, and forces (in the form of magnets). This is still achieved by pupils manipulating concrete objects. For instance, they will be encouraged to feel the north poles of two magnet repel without understanding the role of magnetic fields or observe a bulb illuminate in a complete circuit without needing to appreciate that current is the flow of charge. States of matter and changes of state are an addition to the teaching of chemistry; however, this is only at the physical level and particles are not usually introduced.

In upper Key Stage 2 (ages 9–11), pupils will have learnt about the abstract concepts of space, forces and evolution. There is an increasing complexity in teaching and learning at this point, as pupils are often unable to experience these ideas first-hand. Although teachers will endeavour to relate these topics to everyday life, most of the learning will rely on the pupils' ability to access and understand pictorial and written representations. In electricity, pupils are only introduced to voltage in the form of changing the number of batteries and the effect it has on lamp brightness. In chemistry, they will have covered how physical changes differ from irreversible changes as well as how to separate simple mixtures using filtering and evaporation.

Many primary schools are using the PLAN (Pan-London Assessment Network) Examples of Work (see suggested reading at the end of the chapter) as guidance for their planning. The PLAN Team has provided examples of a pupil's work for each topic and year group. An annotated commentary is given which explains why a pupil has achieved (or not) age-related expectations in all the activities she or he has conducted throughout the topic.

In addition to consulting the primary National Curriculum for England, we highly recommend that you refer to the Year 5 and 6 PLAN documents. Reading these will highlight how primary teachers interpret the abstract statutory statements from the National Curriculum and turn them into learning experiences for their pupils. Not only will these provide examples of the types of activities that are carried out for each topic, thus showing you how you can relate to your pupils' prior experience, but it will also demonstrate the quality and quantity of work that primary pupils are capable of. Vignette 4.1 outlines a teacher's experience of working with different age phases.

There is no expectation in the National Curriculum that pupils should be introduced to cells, particles or the concept of energy during their primary science career, although it is relatively common to find that some may have been exposed to these learning areas – something which again highlights the need to find out what prior learning has taken place.

VIGNETTE 4.1   CHARLOTTE'S REFLECTION ON TEACHING DIFFERENT AGE PHASES

Charlotte made an unusual move in her teaching career. She was a secondary science teacher and had been for a number of years before taking a break to have her family. As the children grew older, she started to volunteer at their primary school – first of all reading with some Year 1 and Year 2 pupils but then doing more and more as the teachers realised she had once been a teacher herself. It came to the point where Charlotte decided she wanted to go back to work as a full-time teacher but that she would like to teach in primary school. It took a while for her to get the wider experience she needed around teaching phonics and the wider curriculum, for example, but after a year she managed to secure a job as a Key Stage 2 teacher and (the best bit!) she was going to teach all of the science across Years 3–6.

(Continued)

When she was a secondary teacher, Charlotte genuinely believed that the science in primary schools wasn't proper science. She dismissed it and considered it, in part, her role to start teaching these pupils what they needed to know. She didn't look at what they had done before - she had already made up her mind that it wasn't worth looking at. Having then taught in primary school, and even before getting that first primary job, she realised how very wrong she had been. The pupils in primary school had so much to offer in terms of how they engaged with their learning of science. The demands on language exceeded her expectations - they were using scientific vocabulary and doing so well. Charlotte wished she could go back to her time as a secondary teacher. She recognised that she may have missed a trick in terms of drawing out what primary pupils had done. Of course, they were not going to voluntarily offer that information - they were dealing with a significant transition to secondary school, which brings far more challenges distracting them from thinking about the science they learned at primary school. Charlotte considers herself very lucky to have taught in both age phases - and realises how important it is to value what has gone on before.

Activity: Before looking at the primary National Curriculum look at the Key Stage 3 science content and create a list of the prior learning you think the pupils need before teaching that. Compare your list to the curriculum content for Key Stage 1 and Key Stage 2. Challenge your own preconceived ideas about the content of this curriculum and how you can draw upon this to support your teaching in secondary school.

SKILLS, WORKING SCIENTIFICALLY AND SKILL DEVELOPMENT

Due to the aforementioned need to help pupils access concrete and relatable experiences there is often a large emphasis on practical work, and in many instances this is focused on the process of enquiry. At this point it would be useful if you reviewed the statements from the Year 5 and 6 section of 'Working scientifically' in the National Curriculum and compare it with what is expected from Key Stage 3 pupils. You will notice that much has been covered and there is a lot of prior experience to draw upon. This section will briefly 'unpick' how the upper Key Stage 2 'Working scientifically' statements translate in the classroom.

In primary science there has been a big push, since the current iteration of the National Curriculum, to move away from the premise that there is one scientific method and for teachers to help pupils to understand that scientific questions can be answered through five main enquiry types: identifying, classifying and grouping; comparative and fair testing; observation over time, pattern seeking and research using secondary sources. Pupils are encouraged to identify the way in which they are working scientifically and, often, symbols are used to help classify their approach. A copy of these symbols can be obtained from the Primary Science Teaching Trust (PSTT) and the Science and Engineering Education Research and Innovation Hub (SEERIH). (The PSTT enquiry approach symbols are available at https://pstt.org.uk/resources/curriculum-materials/enquiry-approaches and the SEERIH symbols from https://seerih-innovations.org/enquiringscience4all/downloads/). Both organisations summarise the enquiry types and provide examples of the age-related activities pupils could undertake when working scientifically. You should notice that much of the work in Key Stage 1 is premised upon identifying, classifying and grouping, which develops the necessary vocabulary required for future learning.

Pupils are encouraged to take measurements, beginning with the use of non-standard units in Key Stage 1. This could include using blocks or markers or they may just make simple direct comparisons such as which object travelled the furthest. In Key Stage 2, the use of standard units is introduced, and the accuracy of measurement is expected to improve as they get older. The equipment that pupils should have experienced are rulers, thermometers and weighing balances/scales. By Year 6 they should be measuring in mm, to 0.5°C, and to one decimal place when weighing. Many schools are now using dataloggers and a variety of apps to measure temperature, light and sound level and digital microscopes to make more detailed observations, usually of invertebrates and different fabrics (see the section below on technology). It is important to note however, that a child's proficiency in the use of scientific equipment can vary from school to school. This is generally because appropriate resources may not always be available. They will be in the habit of taking repeat measurements (3 is the magic number) and will be familiar with the term reliability (although many will confuse – as do secondary pupils – reliability with the ability to carry out a fair test).

As far as recording data is concerned, Year 6 pupils will have had experience of drawing their own dichotomous keys, a range of tables, scatter graphs and bar and line graphs. At this point it is worth reviewing the Teacher Assessment in Primary Science (TAPS) Focused Assessment examples of work (see suggested reading at the end of the chapter). These are the working scientifically equivalent of the PLAN Examples of work. Each assessment focuses on the development of one particular skill so will provide examples of age-related expectations across all of working scientifically. However, in this instance, reading these will show pupils' recording abilities.

In terms of recording learning, this can vary from one school to another. In some cases, pupils complete their work in exercise books; this could include written explanations, reports or diagrams, giving each child a clear portfolio of the learning that has taken place. In other cases, very little written work takes place during science lessons and there is a focus on the pupils' science learning and doing rather than their writing. Evidence can be collected on online platforms or in floor books which summarise learning from the whole class. Using these methods, understanding can be documented by filming or photographing pupils' explanations or work. Other, more creative methods of documenting pupils' progression include creative writing, crafts, artwork, drama and even dance. In addition to these methods, quotations can be scribed by the child, or an adult, to explain any creative work where the knowledge gained may not be clear upon first inspection. As you will note, most pupils are used to presenting their results and findings in front of the class in a variety of different ways and is something that could be considered still in a secondary classroom.

As part of working scientifically the pupils will be used to evaluating their own risks when carrying out practical work. However, a quick scan through the primary National Curriculum will show you that the equipment used is not beyond that readily accessible within most households. At its most extreme, pupils will have experimented with bicarbonate of soda and vinegar, heated various objects using a tealight, and made simple circuits with 1.5V batteries.

Most primary school pupils who move into Key Stage 3 will have little to no lab-based experience in terms of equipment or setting. In many cases, primary teachers work to avoid the lab-based scientist stereotype and focus on a variation of scientific settings and a diverse range of scientists. Primary school pupils usually carry out their science lessons in the same classroom in which they do the rest of their learning, and rarely have the opportunity to access a specific space allocated for science. This can make it difficult for some pupils to separate their science learning from the rest of the curriculum.

The use of outdoor settings is also popular in the teaching of primary science, and if schools are able to access a suitable outdoor learning environment pupils are able to experience some of their learning outside the classroom – a further step away from the secondary school science lab which has a more traditional approach to field work.

In addition to learning and practising these practical scientific methods, processes and skills, pupils will also have been introduced to specific aspects of the nature of science and will have been given an opportunity to learn about incidences when 'scientific evidence … has been used to support or refute ideas or arguments' (DfE, 2013: 25). There will have been two specific occasions when this will have occurred. In Year 5, during the topic of Earth and space, they will have come across Ptolemy, Ibn al-Haytham and Copernicus when learning how the geocentric model for the solar system gave way to the heliocentric model. Year 6's topic of evolution highlights how natural selection as an explanation for the evolution of species was adopted. Studying the work of Mary Anning, Charles Darwin and Alfred Wallace helps place this shift in thinking in context. You may notice that there is quite a feature of studying scientists and many schools have adopted an approach which links old, famous scientists to more contemporary and diverse scientists as a way of demonstrating how ideas have changed (Sinclair et al., 2019). Pupils should have been exposed to an array of diverse scientists, and those that use science in their work, as a way of developing science capital; more of which will be detailed below.

SCIENCE CAPITAL – EVERYDAY EXPERIENCES

Despite much of the research on science capital being based around secondary education, pupils' attitudes and ideas towards science are often formed before they progress from primary school. Archer and DeWitt (2017) identify that pupils, from the age of 10, state they enjoy doing science but do not necessarily want to be a scientist. In order to try to change this outcome, promoting and improving pupils' science capital has become an important part of primary science education as well. It is important to understand the science capital opportunities pupils experience in primary school so that you are able to nurture pupils' attitudes towards science once they transition to secondary. There is further detail in Chapter 11 for you to consider this in the secondary age context.

As previously mentioned, primary science is based around real life experiences and, especially in Reception, is driven by the interests of pupils and the surrounding environment. It is hoped that by 'personalising and localising' and 'eliciting, valuing and linking' pupils' interests and day-to-day experiences (Godec et al., 2017: 33) to their science learning that their perception of what counts as science is broadened. For example, if pupils are learning to classify living things, they may go into the school grounds or local area to find creatures in the locality rather than looking at images of animals in the classroom. Additionally, when learning about materials and their properties, they may observe their school coats and identify why specific fabrics have been used or they could focus on their trainers to figure out how they have been made to prevent them from slipping when playing at breaktime.

In primary, there is a large focus on moving away from the Einstein-like scientist stereotype: there is more to science than white men wearing goggles in laboratories. This is achieved by exposing pupils to a wide range of science careers through classroom experiences, school trips and visitors. During science lessons, pupils may be encouraged to be scientists. For example, when learning about plants, pupils could become botanists or arborists.

To further promote the idea that anyone can be a scientist, primary teachers aim to ensure that pupils are aware of a range of scientists (both historical and modern) within their science teaching. It is important to ensure a broad representation of historical scientists as well as elevating the scientists we have today so that a more diverse science culture can be celebrated within your classroom. By ensuring that pupils continue to have attainable and relatable role models, you will be able to promote the idea that science is for them – especially if these inspirational people look like, have similar backgrounds, or face the same challenges as they do.

Additionally, parents can be a valuable resource, and primary teachers should encourage parents with relevant careers to come into the classroom and share their experiences. In turn, this gives pupils more of an awareness of the breadth of science careers that are available and increases relatability, as the role models are adults that they are familiar with. This promotes the idea that everyone can be a scientist. In many cases, parents are more likely to offer to visit their child's primary school than secondary so it may be valuable to discuss parent careers with your pupils, which will give them the opportunity to share their own knowledge of careers in science.

You will know already that assessing and building upon young people's prior learning is the cornerstone of your teaching. As you will have gleaned from this chapter, pupils' primary science learning experiences are rich and extensive; you are not dealing with a 'tabula rasa'. For this reason, it is incumbent on you to know the relevant curricula areas they have studied and how what you are teaching them develops this. Reading the documents outlined previously (PLAN, TAPS and the National Curriculum) will provide you with this knowledge-base. You will, of course, need to consider how you will formatively assess your pupils' understanding and the future actions you will take. However, you should also remind yourself of Braund's (2016) advice to communicate your appreciation of the significance of their learning from primary school. As well as assessing 'what they know', you should consider the strategies you will adopt which will allow them to share these prior experiences, thus showing how you value them.

TECHNOLOGY

A range of technology can be used to support primary science, enabling pupils to develop skills that will support them when moving up to Year 7 and beyond. It is important to be aware of the elements of the primary computing curriculum that can act as a foundation and underpin elements of working scientifically and skill development in the primary classroom.

In Key Stage 1, the computing curriculum requires pupils to use technology purposefully in order to retrieve digital content – a skill that is developed and extended upon in Key Stage 2. When these skills are considered in a primary science context, they assist pupils in carrying out scientific enquiries that call for the use of simple secondary sources by enabling them to use the internet to locate specific information.

The Key Stage 2 computing curriculum calls for pupils to use and combine a variety of software to create content and accomplish given goals including collecting, analysing, evaluating and presenting data. To achieve the lower Key Stage 2 working scientifically strands, pupils are expected to present and report their findings in a variety of ways. By using skills gained when computing, they should therefore be able to use a range of publishing and data analysis software to create graphs and charts, labelled diagrams, tables, keys and presentations. When progressing to upper Key Stage 2, expectations include the above, but with increased accuracy, precision and complexity.

The use of algorithms and coding is prominent throughout the primary computing curriculum, and in many cases, parallels can be drawn that aid primary science teaching and learning. Pupils may be encouraged to use and write algorithms to carry out different scientific enquiries, and the process of evaluating the success of investigations require the same skills as debugging computer programs.

Working scientifically in Key Stage 2 introduces the use of dataloggers when taking accurate measurements of temperature, light and sound. Although all schools may not have access to these devices, there are a range of applications that enable the collection and exploration of data in a similar way. These devices promote problem-solving skills and allow pupils to analyse their findings. Using this equipment in the primary classroom helps to build confidence when using technology that is not readily available. This helps to prepare pupils for the Key Stage 3 classroom, when using appropriate techniques to collect data during field work, as well as analysing and evaluating the reliability of data collection, is an important element of working scientifically. Pupils may have also been exposed to digital microscopes to make more detailed observations, although these invariably are of invertebrates and different fabrics.

In addition, you should be aware that primary school pupils will be familiar with a range of other technological devices used within their science lessons. As well as a large number of apps that can be used to support learning (whether giving pupils the opportunity to investigate the human anatomy or explore space), different recording devices may also be used. Digital cameras give pupils an opportunity to record their learning in different ways, whether by taking photos and videos or creating vlogs and podcasts.

WHAT TO LOOK FOR WHEN OBSERVING LESSONS

- What strategies do teachers use to identify prior learning?
- To what extent do teachers of Year 7 refer back to primary school content?
- Can you observe any ways of teaching you would consider 'primary' approaches in Year 7 science teaching?

SUMMARY

Now you have read this chapter you should have:

- A better understanding of the issues related to transition.
- A clearer view of primary science education.
- Strategies to build upon your Year 7 class' previous science learning.

REFLECTIVE QUESTIONS

- Has this chapter changed or reinforced your point of view of teaching the 'child' or the subject of science?
- How will you gain an insight into your Year 7 class' experiences from their primary schools?
- When you revisit and retrieve topics and skills that your pupils will have addressed in their primary schools, how will you demonstrate that they are of significance and of value to you?

FURTHER READING

The PLAN Examples of Work show a child's work for each topic and year group. These are available at www.planassessment.com/copy-of-plan-knowledge-matrices-tea

The TAPS Focused Assessment Examples of work provide samples of how children work scientifically across all year groups and topics. These are available at https://pstt.org.uk/resources/curriculum-materials/assessment

This article in *Science Teacher Education* outlines how the teaching of science can act as a medium for supporting the transition between primary and secondary school: Hoath, L. (2021). Primary to secondary transition – it is more than it seems. *STE*, 90: 28–33.

BIBLIOGRAPHY

Archer, L. and DeWitt, J. (2017). *Understanding young people's science aspirations: How students form ideas about 'becoming a scientist'*. London: Routledge.

Barmby, P., Kind, P. and Jones, K. (2008). Examining changing attitudes in secondary school science. *International Journal of Science Education*, 30(5): 1075–1093.

Braund, M. (2016). 'Oh no, not this again!' Improving continuity and progression from primary to secondary science. *School Science Review*, September, 98(362): 19–26.

Braund, M. and Driver, M. (2005). Pupils' perceptions of practical science in primary and secondary school: Implications for improving progression and continuity of learning. *Educational Research*, 47(1): 79–93.

Department for Education (2013). The National Curriculum in England: Key Stages 1 and 2 framework document [online]. Available from: www.gov.uk/government/publications/national-curriculum-in-england-primarycurriculum (accessed 6 December 2020).

Galton, M., Gray, J. and Ruddock, J. (1996). *The impact of school transitions and transfers on pupil progress and attainment*. Norwich: Crown Copyright.

Godec, S., King, H.C. and Archer, L. (2017). *The science capital teaching approach: Engaging students with science, promoting social justice*. London: University College London.

Ofsted (2015). *Key Stage 3: The wasted years?* Manchester: Crown Copyright.

Sinclair, A., Strachan, A. and Trew, A. (2019). *Standing on the shoulders of giants*. Bristol: Primary Science Teaching Trust.

Stuart, I. (2020) Should we teach chemistry at primary school? [online]. Available from: https://edu.rsc.org/opinion/should-we-teach-chemistry-from-primary/4012529.article (accessed 6 February 2020).

Sutherland, R., Yee, W., MacNess, E. and Harris, R. (2010) Supporting learning in the transition from primary to secondary schools [online]. Available from: https://bristol.ac.uk/media-library/sites/cmpo/documents/transition.pdf (accessed 12 March 2020).

Sutton, R. (2000). *Primary to secondary – overcoming the muddle in the middle*. Salford: Trinity Press.

Symonds, J. (2015). *Understanding school transition: What happens to children and how to help them*. London: Routledge.

5
PLANNING FOR TEACHING SCIENCE

ED PODESTA AND LOUISE CASS

CHAPTER OVERVIEW

This chapter is focused on helping you learn more about how to develop your planning. We will consider how to support you in getting better at it, including ideas about activities that you can take part in with your mentor that will boost this learning. The content will enable you to divide planning lessons into steps, and see planning as a cyclical, developmental activity. We will also consider the implications of some important and influential cognitive theories of learning. A number of vignettes capture Mack's journey through learning to plan lessons as a student teacher.

LINKS TO ITT CORE CONTENT FRAMEWORK AND EARLY CAREER FRAMEWORK

This chapter supports development of:

- Standard 1 – set high expectations
- Standard 2 – promote good progress
- Standard 3 – demonstrate good subject and curriculum knowledge
- Standard 4 – plan and teach well-structured lessons

INTRODUCTION

You will sometimes hear teachers saying that they don't spend much time planning because they share resources, or use plans that their department has created. Often what is really happening is that these experienced teachers have already done their planning without being aware of that work. In preparing for hundreds of lessons and through thousands of interactions between their plans and pupils, experienced teachers build up a library of plans in their minds, related to topics and concepts they have taught before. It only seems to these teachers that they are not planning. We refer to this as a teacher's *tacit* knowledge, because it is knowledge that is sometimes hard to explain, or to articulate.

Sometimes these teachers might even say that you do not need to learn to plan lessons at all, because good science departments have centralised sequences, lesson plans and resources. However, our view is that these teachers can only use these centralised resources well, or quickly put lessons and resources together with them, because of this tacit knowledge, and the experiences of planning and teaching that it is based on. You are at the beginning of the same journey and will develop this ability to plan quickly and effectively.

VIGNETTE 5.1   MACK'S LESSON PLANNING

Mack had just started on his second school-based experience, following a successful first placement. Mack's specialism was biology, but as a first task he had been asked to teach some physics, specifically 'electricity generation', to a Year 10 group. Mack wanted this lesson to look good so that he could impress his mentor. He worked hard on a detailed presentation and resources about AC and DC generation, the National Grid, transformers, and even how to wire a plug. Two nights before the lesson was to be taught, he started to record his plan on the lesson plan proforma that he was supposed to use. It took him a long time, and in the early hours of the morning he was finally able to send it to his mentor.

The next morning Mack received an email on the bus on the way into school. His mentor was not happy with the plan, nor that she got it so late. She told him that there wasn't enough time to change the plan before the lesson, so she would have to teach the class. Mack was worried, confused and perhaps a bit angry - he felt his hard work on the lesson should have been recognised, and didn't see why he shouldn't be able teach it.

Activity: What do you think has gone wrong? What could Mack have done differently in terms of prioritising his focus for preparation? What could his mentor have changed? Jot down some ideas, and as you go through this chapter, see if you can add to or refine this list.

PLANNING IS A PROCESS OF DEVELOPMENT

To get to the same point as your more experienced teachers with planning you will need to give it conscious thought. You will also have to get your mentor to think consciously about planning, and this too has its challenges, as they often describe doing things 'intuitively' or habitually. In this sense, it is important that you think of planning as an ongoing process and one which you will continue to develop for a number of years after qualifying.

THINGS TO THINK ABOUT WHEN LEARNING ABOUT PLANNING

Box 5.1 outlines questions as prompts for the things that you need to think about when you are learning about planning lessons.

BOX 5.1   PROMPTS FOR LESSON PLANNING

- What am I teaching - knowledge, skills, outlooks and values? Do I know enough about this myself?
- Who am I teaching - what do they know already, what common sense ideas and preconceptions do they bring? What will they find difficult or confusing?
- How shall I source and arrange the content and activities of my lesson or sequence?
- How shall I consolidate the things I'm teaching?
- What assessment and feedback will aid learning and help me develop my teaching?

This is a cyclical process, as Figure 5.1 shows. You will set out knowledge objectives, then plan activities or read resources, and then after more planning realise you need to re-address your objectives, or seek further help, or other resources. So, sometimes it's best to go through the process in draft a couple of times before you firm up your ideas. At first this will take time. That is one of the reasons why, most training will only expose you to a few classes or give you plenty of time on your timetable in which to take these first steps.

For the rest of this chapter, we will go through these steps. Whilst we do this, it would be a good idea to plan one lesson as you read. This does not need to be a lesson you are teaching, just something to practise. We will illustrate these steps with some more examples from Mack's story. When we have done that, we will go

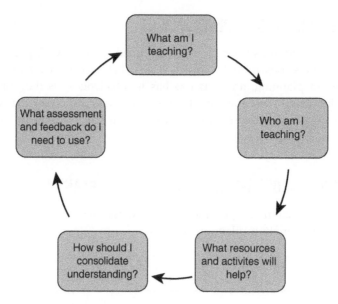

Figure 5.1   The cyclical nature of lesson planning

through some other ways in which you can learn about planning lessons. Remember – you are doing a course in teacher training because you are learning and no one should expect you to be an expert at this, even at the end of your course.

WHAT AM I TEACHING?

Finding out what you're teaching can be hard, and there are several people and kinds of resources that you will need to consult, question or investigate:

- Your mentor or the host teacher of the class might give you a topic.
- The school's sequences or schemes of work, or the specification from an exam board or the National Curriculum, might give you some further details.
- The textbooks you find in your department, or in the library of the ITT partnership provider will give you more idea about how this topic and content is covered.
- Professional Literature, which will tell you how other teachers have approached this topic, or similar classes or pupils to those that you are teaching.

You do not always need to take all these steps or read all you can find on each topic you teach. However, as our vignette suggested, one of the ways in which you can firmly ground your development, and how you plan for the progress of your pupils, is to be clear about the aims, in terms of knowledge and skills that you want to teach in each lesson or sequence of lessons.

Your mentor will usually refer you to documents that the school uses, such as their schemes of work, or examination specifications, but even these might not give you enough detail to know what to plan for. You might need to go back to clarify things further with a host teacher or mentor and the sooner you do this, the better.

All too often objectives in schemes of work or exam specifications (for example, 'explain the importance of photosynthesis'), do not provide the detail of the knowledge and skills that you want your pupils to have gained by the end of the lesson. It is likely that Mack's lesson objective (as outlined in Vignette 5.1) would have been 'to be able to explain electricity generation', but we can see now that this objective is too general, too vague for you to build a lesson around. For him to have successfully planned this lesson, he needed to take time to map out the intricate pieces of knowledge that would allow him to finally ensure that his pupils could explain how electricity is generated. He would have been able to see that to explain electricity generation was a long-term aim, achieved over several carefully sequenced lessons that built the necessary knowledge and skills.

A good objective for a lesson provides clarity of the knowledge and skills that need to be acquired by the pupils (see also Chapter 8 for writing lesson objectives for practical work). A way to ensure that this is achieved is to write objectives as a key question rather than an ambiguous learning objective (Green, 2020). If we want our pupils to be able to explain the importance of photosynthesis, we need to establish the key questions pupils must be able to answer, and what knowledge we need to teach, to ensure they can develop clear understanding. This will enable them to achieve such objectives. Examples of key questions include:

1.   What is the word and symbol equation for photosynthesis?
2.   Where do plants get the reactants for photosynthesis and how? (Water from the soil via the roots and the process of osmosis, carbon dioxide from the air via the stomata through the process of diffusion.)
3.   What are the products of photosynthesis and how are they used? (Glucose and oxygen, these are transported to where they are needed by the plant.)
4.   What is respiration? (Chemical reaction between glucose and oxygen which releases energy.)
5.   In a plant, what is the energy released from respiration used for? (Chemical reactions such as building glucose into starch for storage, building sugars into cellulose for cell walls, combining nitrate ions and other minerals to make amino acids for protein synthesis, building fats and oils for storage.)

By writing out the questions we want our pupils to be able to answer, we can see how all of the curriculum content links together, and can ensure that we help pupils strengthen and build those links. In the example above, we can see that photosynthesis is an important process because the products are used in respiration, which releases energy and in turn is used in metabolic reactions that keep the plant alive. How much of this you will cover in a lesson or sequence will depend on discussions with your mentor, and on the knowledge the pupils already have.

DO I KNOW ENOUGH?

You should not be afraid or ashamed to ask: 'Do I know enough about this topic for teaching it at this level?'. Chapter 3 outlined ways in which your subject knowledge can be increased to develop your own understanding, and by virtue ensure your explanations to the pupils are the best they can be. Whilst planning a lesson on a topic that is unfamiliar to you, it is a good idea to spend time reading around the subject, gathering material from different textbook sources and the internet to further your understanding and structure of the lesson.

As a student teacher you might wonder how your own development aims fit in with planning a lesson. Most teacher training programmes involve a regular meeting with a mentor at which targets are set (see Chapter 2). The important thing is to make sure that when these targets are being discussed, you and your mentor both have in mind the lessons that you are planning and teaching in the days ahead. This will allow you to tailor your lesson planning and your targets to each other.

WHAT DO THE PUPILS I AM TEACHING ALREADY KNOW?

One of the most important things that you are learning to do, in becoming a teacher, is to attempt to put yourself in the shoes of a pupil learning your subject. You need to be able to develop explanations (often even scripted explanations) that take into account what pupils know, or think they know, about a topic or concept. You will need to anticipate conceptual and practical difficulties that pupils will have in the specific topics you are teaching (Leach and Scott, 2008). It is worth bearing in mind that as well as planning content you need to take into account specific needs of learners and adapt your resources and teaching to meet these. Chapter 10 will offer some strategies that you can adopt to develop this.

Knowing the sequence of learning that a pupil has gone through prior to you teaching them is a good place to start. Review the learning journey that they have been on, the knowledge that they should have encountered. For example, in Year 5, children will learn about properties and changes of materials and should be able to use their knowledge of solids, liquids and gases to decide how to separate mixtures. This prior knowledge is built on in Key Stage 3, Key Stage 4 and Key Stage 5 chemistry

(Chapter 4 indicates how you can make best use of primary science learning as you teach Key Stage 3 pupils).

Even when you are clear about a topic, you will need to consider the depth and detail of the content that you will be teaching to. Pupils meet some science concepts on several occasions in the curriculum, each time working at a greater level of complexity or joining up their knowledge of one concept with another. As a teacher, you need to know where they are in this spiral. You will sometimes be teaching familiar material in ways that asks pupils to go beyond traditional science activities. You may be teaching about values or attitudes of enquiry, or you might have been asked to give space to enable pupils to debate an issue, in the context of this concept taught previously.

Science tends to have a hierarchical structure of knowledge where prior knowledge is a pre-requisite for later understanding (Howard and Hill, 2020). When planning a lesson, you will need to think about how the new knowledge that you are presenting will be integrated with the knowledge that pupils already have, ensuring it is meaningful (Ausubel, 1963). This new knowledge could be in a sequence of lessons planned over the medium term. For example, when teaching about electronic structure of an atom, you should make sure that the pupils know the structure of an atom and that there are protons and neutrons in the nucleus, with the electrons in a shell (or energy level), before moving on to the more complex theory. Another example might be learning and securing the knowledge of the ultrastructure of eukaryotic cells in Key Stage 3, before moving onto specific adaptations and roles of specialised cells and differentiation at Key Stage 4 and beyond. During the early stage of your training, you may not realise or fully appreciate these links, but dedicating time with your mentor or experienced host teachers to unpick the curriculum will help take your planning to another level. Being aware these links exist is a good first step, even though you might not put all the pieces together at first.

One way to organise this knowledge is with a concept map (Novak, 1990). Concept maps will allow you to see the relationships between the different ideas you are teaching and help you to identify the links between the areas. They can be organised in many ways, but giving yourself a basic structure can help. An example of a concept map in use to plan a curriculum can be found at: https://mcsbrent.co.uk/bunsen-blue-designing-a-science-curriculum/. Maps like these can also help you identify concepts that you need to update or refresh your own understanding of. There are science books such as *Powerful Ideas of Science and How to Teach Them* (Green, 2020) and *Cracking Key Concepts* in Secondary Science (Boxer et al., 2021) that you can use as a reference to check and improve your understanding of key concepts and relationships.

Look at the lesson you have planned: can you build a concept map which shows the prior knowledge needed to understand the new topic and how this will fit with the new knowledge that you are presenting? This will also give you a starting point for subsequent lessons so is not wasted time.

> ### VIGNETTE 5.2   MACK'S STORY
>
> Mack met with his mentor and looked at his lessons ahead. He appreciated that he had tried to put too much information into one lesson and that they should have been a sequence of several lessons. He started again, first by looking at the exam specification to see what he needed to plan for. Mack could see his pupils needed to know that 'electrical power is transferred from power stations to consumers' and that a 'step-up transformer increases potential difference from a power station to the transmission cables and then step-down decreases it' and that 'the National Grid system is an efficient way to transfer energy'. Mack set out a set of key questions that he wanted the pupils to be able to answer. He realised that he didn't know 'why the national grid is an efficient way to transfer energy', and so he decided to speak with a physics specialist in the department.
>
> **Activity:** As you develop your plans or learn more about the topic or concepts you are teaching, consider if you want (or need) to change the objectives of your lessons, or go back to an explanation that you have already scripted, or change a diagram. This is a good thing; it will help you construct a better lesson.

WHAT PRECONCEPTIONS DO THE PUPILS BRING?

This is an area where your peers, your host teachers, and mentor, and the professional community which you have joined can help. You can ask these people what issues they have faced in teaching a particular topic or tricky concepts. They may suggest solutions that you can adapt. Professional journals of subject associations, such as the Association for Science Education, will often have case studies which will outline these issues and potential solutions too. Chapter 9 also gives some suggestions to think about when dealing with tricky topics.

Sometimes, you can add to this collective wisdom by doing some thinking about, or by talking through, issues such as:

- What everyday understandings are there of this concept or these objects?
- What *things* will these pupils be meeting in this plan that are totally new to them?
- What are the overarching themes and underpinning elements in the concept you want to teach? How can you arrange the content and activities in your lesson to ensure that the pupils gain a deep understanding?
- What common misconceptions might arise in approaching these concepts and objects?

- What do you want them to do with this new knowledge that might also be mis-understood or difficult to achieve? What kinds of analogies might help clear up these issues? What dangers are there in these analogies?

One of the challenges in teaching science is that we teach it at a visible level, but many of the concepts and underlying processes cannot be directly observed by pupils in their everyday lives. Therefore, what the pupils *think* they understand can be different to what is true based on the scientific theory. Alex Johnstone (Johnstone, 1991) proposed that chemistry knowledge is understood (and misunderstood) at three fundamental 'levels' or 'representations': the macroscopic, the symbolic and the sub-microscopic. For example, when observing electrolysis of copper chloride, the pupils might experience the following levels of understanding:

- Macroscopic (or observations) – what can be seen or observed by pupils from their lives or in class: watching copper form on the cathode and smelling the bubbles of chlorine gas forming on the anode.
- Symbolic (or concepts) – concepts that are used to explain and understand underlying processes: a word and symbol equation to show what is happening at the electrodes.
- Sub-microscopic (or explanations) – explanatory model using fundamental concepts: in this case how the chlorine gains two electrons and forms a gas.

Thinking about the concepts and experiences in your lesson in this way can be a great way of considering the kinds of ideas and misconceptions that your pupils bring with them – and also the conceptual barriers and potential misunderstandings they might pick up whilst you teach them about it.

WHAT RESOURCES AND ACTIVITIES WILL HELP?

Keep in mind the steps you have already taken. Once you have worked out what is to be learned, what it is that the pupils already know, and what they already bring ideas or even misconceptions about, you can focus on the kinds of activities that will help achieve this new knowledge or understanding. This will enable you to keep checking each part of your plan to make sure that you are working towards your aims.

THE PROBLEM WITH 'PARTS'

Some teachers, some lesson proformas and some guidance on lesson planning advise teachers to split their lessons into several parts – such as a 'hook', starter, main activities and plenary.

Whilst some might find this a useful structure, it is also important to consider some of its limitations. Sometimes, it is not always possible to parcel learning up into discrete units of a lesson – you may want to teach complex issues, concepts or systems over several lessons to allow for consolidation and develop understanding. It can mean that your plan does not include good opportunities for assessment or evaluation of understanding in the parts of the lesson when it is needed most. Don't assume that checking understanding should wait until the end of the lesson because of a rigid lesson structure. In short, this common idea of a three- or five-part lesson is sometimes too much of a restriction on planning – even if it has some valid aims.

You might be training in a school which insists on standard formats or approaches. Don't worry, you can work and develop within most of these, as long as you do not lose sight of the science you are teaching.

THEORIES OF LEARNING AND PLANNING

Important theories about how children process, store and consolidate new knowledge can help you design the sequence of a lesson or lessons. Cognitive load theory (CLT), first described in 1988 by John Sweller and updated by Sweller et al. in 2019, is one such set of ideas and can provide a useful way of thinking about learning. However, it needs to be used carefully. 'CogSci' research seeks to understand the cognitive (to do with our thinking) functions and processes that underlie learning. Our understanding about how to apply CogSci and CLT in the classroom is developing, but there is still a lot of work to do. The Education Endowment Foundation report (Perry et al., 2021) suggests some promising results from some techniques, but also some dangers and negative effects from poorly implemented methods.

Cognitive load theory, for instance, suggests important ideas which need to be taken into account when planning sequences. The most important is that our working memory is limited – people can only process a small number of items of knowledge at one time. Asking people to switch between new items of knowledge in order to process them puts a burden on their thinking that can get in the way of learning.

According to CLT, using knowledge stored in long-term memory frees up the resources of the working memory. Complex combinations of information, such as those involved in completing a calculation, or working out the results of a reaction or a process, are much easier when using information, knowledge, or techniques stored in long-term memory.

The load on the learner's mind is therefore an important concept in cognitive load theory, which describes different kinds of load, of which we will focus on:

- **Intrinsic cognitive load** – the inherent difficulty of the content you are teaching.
- **Extrinsic cognitive load** – the cognitive load created by the way you are teaching, presenting or laying out information, or by other things in the environment that prevent learning.

In some publications, you will also see reference to Germane Load – this is load which might look like 'extraneous' load, but actually seems to help with the acquiring, construction and automation of schemas. Models of working memory have developed over time. More recent models suggest that Germane Load is no longer part of the overall 'load', but rather part of the processing that contributes to new mental models of a concept (Skulmowski and Xu, 2021).

A much simplified summary of the theory could be that teachers should manage intrinsic load and seek to reduce extrinsic load. There are lots of different pieces of advice that have emerged from CLT that relate to these aims, but the main ones are:

Worked example effect: This finding suggests that worked examples, which take pupils step by step through solutions to problems, are more effective at first than giving pupils all the information and techniques that they need to solve a problem, and then asking them to do so. A worked example can be done by modelling how to go through a technique or problem, or by setting our guidance on a worksheet that goes through a complete problem from start to finish. The evidence also suggests that this effect fades quite quickly, and that worked examples should be followed up with partially completed examples. An approach of using side-by-side examples for using equations can be found in Chapter 10.

Partially completed example effect: This finding suggests that pupils can also benefit, at the right time in a sequence, from being given problems that have been solved to an extent, or where the solutions contain errors that the pupils have to finish or correct. This is also an example of a technique which requires very careful use – presenting errors to pupils might even reinforce or consolidate those conceptual problems. Further examples of this in action can be found in Chapter 10.

Modality effect: This effect suggests that pupils can expand the extent of their working memory if teachers use two 'modes' of communication at the same time – so a presentation which involves audible explanation and diagrammatic explanation would in theory be more effective than just audible explanation or just diagrammatic explanation. This is quite a subtle effect and does not apply, for instance, when a teacher reads out words that are already shown on a screen or describes a picture. The Education Endowment Foundation (EEF) report (Perry et al., 2021) also suggests that this is a technique which is often misused through the production of complicated diagrams or confusing accompanying explanation.

Variability effect: After initially working through completed examples and then less and less example problems, this finding suggests that pupils will consolidate their understanding much more effectively if they encounter different problem-solving scenarios (Sweller et al., 2019).

The risk in over relying on thinking about cognitive load when planning lessons is that we can focus too much on *how* we're teaching at the expense of considering *what* we are teaching. It can also encourage us to continually treat pupils as if they are meeting information for the first time, every time. If we are not increasing the level of challenge, moving from worked examples to more complex problem solving, enabling the use of information already in long-term memory, as sequences and school years go on, we might not be planning as effectively as we should.

CHUNKING

We often find that student teachers when faced with a difficult topic will assert that all they need to do is 'chunk it' – that is, to make it easier for that information to pass through working memory by giving the information to the pupils in small, manageable and achievable sections. This is a useful technique to use when relaying such information; however, relying on chunking alone prevents us from considering what makes *this* topic difficult and about how best to explain or illustrate things with clarity. Our key message is therefore simple: keep in mind the science you are teaching.

PRACTICAL WORK

The Gatsby *Rapid Evidence Review of Good Practical Science* (Cukurova et al., 2017) recommends that the purpose of a science practical activity needs to be known and that it should be planned and executed so it is effective. This brings us to our next issue when planning a practical activity: should it be a teacher demonstration or whole class activity? Some practical activities must be done as teacher demonstration for health and safety reasons. However, just because a practical activity can be done as a whole class activity doesn't mean that it always should be. This is where it is important to refer back to your lesson objectives. What key questions do you want the pupils to be able to answer at the end of the lesson? Is this more achievable with a teacher demonstration or a whole class practical? Chapters 7 and 8 will also support you with such decisions.

THE POWER OF DIAGRAMS WHEN PLANNING PRACTICALS

Practical science is often challenging for pupils, so we need to ensure that a practical activity is purposeful and enables knowledge and skills to be developed. However, practical activities often cause cognitive burden with pupils' working memory being overloaded with all the information that they are required to pay attention to. Johnstone and Wham (1982) suggest that working memory during a practical activity has to deal with many different elements including:

- Names of apparatus and materials
- Skills to be recalled
- New written instructions

- Input from the actual experiment
- Theory to be recalled
- New skills
- New verbal instructions

How we present practical instructions to pupils will affect their extraneous load. If a pupil has to switch between two or more pieces of information, they are likely to experience split attention deficit (Chandler and Sweller, 1991). You will see in most textbooks and exam board schemes of learning that practical activities are given as a diagram of the apparatus and a separate step-by-step list of instructions. This format can increase extraneous load. A way to minimise this is to use 'integrated instructions', an example of which is shown in Figure 5.2.

This frees up the working memory and allows pupils to focus their attention on the concepts and skills they are developing. Pupils find completing practicals easier with this approach, cognitive load is reduced, and confidence and overall understanding of the practical is increased (Paterson, 2019).

HOW SHOULD I CONSOLIDATE WHAT HAS BEEN LEARNED?

We have already seen how sequencing increasingly independent and complex problems will help transfer information to long-term memory. A really useful and well-summarised resource is Zoe and Mark Enser's book *Generative Learning in Action* (Enser and Enser, 2020) which describes several processes that can help this transfer, and which also presents interesting ways of helping pupils manipulate the knowledge that they are working with. You can find similar ideas in *Making Every Science Lesson Count* (Allison, 2017). What will be crucial is thinking about what these techniques look like in science teaching:

- Drawing models and diagrams of processes
- Explaining issues, processes and problems
- Answering factual questions
- Completing exercises, which might also ask pupils to use this knowledge to analyse something, or complete a calculation, describe a process or predict its outcomes.

Some teachers have found using 'spaced recall', in which pupils are asked questions about topics and knowledge that they learned less recently, can help build a solid foundation of disciplinary knowledge on which to develop new learning. However, recall can happen in several ways beyond a formal test or even an informal quiz, though teachers have found both of these to be really useful (Perry et al., 2021).

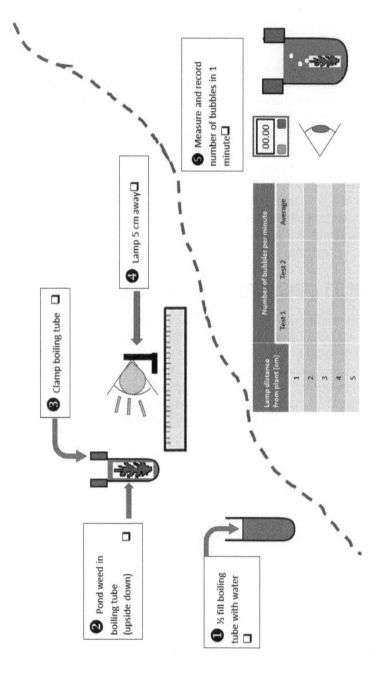

Figure 5.2 An example of use of integrated instructions for practical work (Louise Cass). The example shown can be easily constructed using software at http://chemix.org (Software credit: https://help.chemix.org/article/24-license)

WHAT ASSESSMENT AND FEEDBACK DO YOU NEED TO USE?

At this stage in the planning process, you will probably already be thinking – 'how will I know if they have understood?' and 'how will I know what they are thinking and learning?'. You can find more about assessment in Chapter 6, but for the purposes of this chapter our key message is that assessment is most effective when you have a clear purpose in mind, both in your teaching and in setting up any assessment.

A good place to start is to think about the different reasons and times that you might plan to assess during a lesson and some of these are outlined in Table 5.1. Being clear about these different purposes will then help you work out different ways of fulfilling these.

Table 5.1 The purpose of assessment and examples of strategies

Timing and Purposes of Assessment	Activities and Methods
At the very start: Do they know the things that you assume they already understand? Do they remember things previously taught that you will be building on?	Recalling key terms, quizzing, defining key terms.
As you explain things: Do they understand the key concepts or processes you have outlined? Do you need to explore things again, or explain them in a different way?	Q&A - choosing pupils to answer key questions about important concepts. Asking pupils to explain or describe processes. Matching definitions. Reviewing or completing knowledge trackers or organisers.
As they are working on things: Can you extend or challenge their learning?	Asking pupils to explain tasks, or recap discussions or experiments. Changing parameters or adding in elements to problems or scenarios.
When problems occur: What is causing a misunderstanding or error?	Asking pupils to revisit steps in processes, checking understanding of key terms, formulas or processes.
At the end of a lesson, or a unit of work: Have they reached a level of understanding that you planned? Are there any things you might need to re-teach in order to move on to the next unit of work?	Summative style questions or tasks that address a range of specific areas of knowledge and understanding that the unit has addressed.

HOW CAN YOU LEARN *ABOUT* PLANNING?

At the start of this chapter, we said that learning to plan was a developmental process – that you can learn more about it by reading, talking with others, and by doing other learning activities. What sort of activities should you take part in so that you learn more about planning and improve your practice?

USING A PROFORMA

A good lesson planning proforma will take you through the steps in thinking outlined in this chapter and can also act as a framework or key questions for discussion with your mentor or host teacher. However, even a good proforma only works well if used properly. Use it to help develop your thinking about that lesson or sequence by writing as much as you need, scripting bits of the lesson if helps your focus. Remember you might want to refer to it 'on the fly', so if you make it too long or too detailed, your plan might not help you in the classroom. An example of a proforma that you might like to use based on the ideas in this chapter can be found in Appendix 1.

TALKING TO AND THEN OBSERVING EXPERIENCED TEACHERS PLANNING AND TEACHING THEIR LESSONS

One of the best ways to get the most of your colleagues is by co-planning lessons with them, and then observing these lessons being taught. This helps you understand teachers' decision making during planning, and how these decisions have to be altered or adapted in the lesson itself. It is important to ask questions, but in the right way. For instance, 'I noticed you did X; can you help me understand the idea behind that?' or 'What makes Y such a good way of explaining [X]?' are great ways of starting a conversation about planning.

Even quite experienced teachers can be nervous about talking about their teaching or having people in to observe. Building up trust between you and a teacher or mentor is an important part of enabling this cooperation.

PLANNING LESSONS AND THEN WATCHING SOMEONE ELSE TEACH THE LESSON

Watching someone else teach your plan can help you see very clearly:

• What difference a particular approach to teaching has on your plan
• How your pupils might experience a lesson, resource or activity

- Why some things are taking more or less time, or are easier or harder than you expected
- How a diagram or explanation works (or doesn't).

Not only does this allow you to see your planning unfold in a lesson but also takes away the worries associated with other elements of teaching practice, such as having to deal with behaviour management. You will be able to critique your own resources and timings to develop your planning in future.

TEACHING THE SAME LESSON TWICE

Teaching the same topic to groups with different pupils can help you understand a different range of misconceptions and cater for different levels of understanding or confidence. Having two classes learning the same thing allows you to adapt and improve resources as well as change approaches to reflect these differences between classes. It will also emphasise the notion that there is no 'one size fits all' approach to teaching, as a plan you make for one class will have to be altered and modified for it to be a success in another.

ENGAGING WITH THE SCIENCE TEACHING COMMUNITY

Most obviously you can find articles and examples of how other science teachers have dealt with particular topics in specific circumstances (see Chapter 13 for how to develop networks and communities). You can also use the schemes of work, lesson plans, resources and textbooks you can find in your placement school. This will let you know how topics have been taught by other teachers, might give a clue about misconceptions and difficulties, help you understand what the vital aspects of a topic are, and give ideas for resources and activities.

WORKING YOUR PLANNING INTO YOUR OWN DEVELOPMENT AND REFLECTION

Student teachers who are focused on their own development tend to make sure they have taken their own targets into account when planning lessons. For instance, if you have a target of developing your explanations, or your use of diagrams, or more effectively using Q&A to assess your pupils' understanding, then you should be focusing on these things in your plans for teaching and, evaluating the extent to which your understanding of these things, and your practice, have improved.

VIGNETTE 5.3   MACK'S STORY – FEELING LIKE A TEACHER

Mack was preparing for a lesson with his mentor. He would be teaching electrolysis. Mack could see from the specification that pupils needed to know about the process, electrolysis of molten compounds, how it was used to extract metals and the electrolysis of aqueous solutions.

With his mentor, he then set about using sticky notes to figure out the prior knowledge that was needed, and the concepts that would be built as the sequence of lessons progressed. Soon, laid out in front of him, Mack could see the key questions his pupils needed to be able to answer to meet the lesson objectives. Mack planned his lesson and had included a practical (which he had decided to demonstrate) and he was feeling confident.

On the day of the lesson, Mack began with a knowledge retrieval exercise. He deliberately included questions that linked to the new learning. He then explained that electrolysis was the splitting of a compound using electricity and its purpose was to extract metals that were more reactive than carbon, followed by his demonstration of the electrolysis of copper chloride. He had chosen this so he could show how the copper collected at the cathode and, using litmus paper (which would bleach), that chlorine was collected at the anode.

He and his mentor thought carefully about his explanation of this. Mack used his visualiser to draw out the diagram of the electrolysis set-up; he talked through what was happening to the ions in the liquid and why they migrated to either the anode or the cathode. He asked the pupils to copy his diagram and then explained that there would be a set of questions related to the diagram and their observations of the demonstration. When he questioned the pupils, Mack felt he got more errors and questions back to him than answers.

Discussing this with his mentor after the lesson, and despite how confident he was at the start, Mack suggested that the pupils had not gained a clear understanding of the process, what was happening and why. They just couldn't grasp why one product went to the electrode that it did (and why chlorine suddenly became chloride). He and his mentor looked back at their mapping of the sequence of prior learning that pupils needed a clear understanding of to be able to explain electrolysis. Mack also reflected on some of the new terminology he'd introduced, e.g. anode and cathode.

Together they decided that Mack needed to revisit electron transfer and what an ion was. This wasn't the planned next lesson, but without this knowledge being revisited, continuing may have been a fruitless exercise. Mack and his mentor planned not only how to incorporate prior learning needed to move forward, but also how they would adapt his lesson the second time around. Mack suggested that introducing terms such as anode and cathode early on added to the confusion.

He made the decision that next time he would only introduce the basics and then bring in this terminology later.

Mack didn't have the perfect lesson but wasn't feeling frustrated by this any-more. As he worked with his mentor to plan their next steps Mack felt like he was now a teacher.

Activity: What kinds of problems, examples or activities can you use to help pupils remember the key ideas and issues you want them to learn? Are there dia-grams, models, animations that might help? Find out in discussion with your mentor.

Planning will feel like a never-ending process and be one of the most time-consuming and challenging elements of your training and early career teaching. By getting things right in the early stages and generating the habits of mind which will allow you to plan lessons which meet pupils' needs, expectations and progress their learning, you will develop that tacit knowledge which takes away some of the sense of burden. Giving it the consideration it needs at this point in your career will enable you to become more proficient, more quickly as you progress.

THINGS TO LOOK FOR IN AN OBSERVATION

- Thinking about the differences between practical and non-practical lessons – how do teachers structure their teaching?
- What kinds of activities do teachers in your department use throughout the lesson that you have not tried?
- What resources do teachers use from school in their lessons?

SUMMARY

Now you have read this chapter you should have:

- Learned that planning is a developmental process, and that you can accelerate this development by working in dialogue and collaboration with your mentor.
- Understood that there is a need when planning a lesson or sequence to start by thinking about objectives before activities, explanations, tasks and assessment, but that the process involves back and forth. Thinking about each aspect might cause you to readdress some of the others.
- Grasped the importance of planning lessons as a *science* teacher – generic tech-niques and theories can help, but the wisdom of your peers, mentor and the science teaching community will help you contextualise your approach.

> **REFLECTIVE QUESTIONS**
> - Looking at a lesson plan as a whole, consider where you need to ask questions. Where can you check that your explanations have been well understood?
> - What information will you need to be able to plan the next lesson or series of lessons?
> - When planning a practical activity, can you identify what key items of knowledge, key vocabulary and skills are involved? If it is for the whole class or a teacher demonstration, can you try to make a set of integrated instructions for it?

FURTHER READING

This book takes you through the process of planning in detail and helps think about how to teach your plan through to the end of the lesson: Allison, S. (2017). *Making every science lesson count*. London: Crown House Publishing

This is a good reference book to help you revisit things you have already learned, or approach topics that you are asked to teach that you are unfamiliar with: Boxer, A., Dave, H. and Jones, G. (2021). *Cracking key concepts in secondary science*. Thousand Oaks, CA: Corwin.

This is a review of the impact of popular cognitive science pedagogies. The report suggests which approaches have the most support, and also outlines some problems and common pitfalls. Written by Perry et al. (2021) and published by the EEF: *Cognitive science in the classroom*. Available at: https://educationendowmentfoundation.org.uk/public/files/Publications/Cognitive_science_approaches_in_the_classroom_-_A_review_of_the_evidence.pdf

BIBLIOGRAPHY

Allison, S. (2017). *Making every science lesson count*. London: Crown House Publishing.

Ausubel, D.P. (1963). *The psychology of meaningful verbal learning*. New York: Grune & Stratton.

Boxer, A., Dave, H. and Jones, G. (2021). *Cracking key concepts in secondary science*. Thousand Oaks, CA: Corwin.

Chandler, P. and Sweller, J. (1991). Cognitive load theory and the format of instruction. *Cognition and Instruction*, 8(4): 293–332.

Cukurova, M., Hanley, P. and Lewis, A. (2017). *Rapid evidence review of good practical science*. London: Gatsby Charitable Foundation.

Enser, M. and Enser, Z. (2020). *Fiorella & Mayer's Generative learning in action*. Woodbridge: John Catt Educational.

Green, J. (2020). *Powerful ideas of science and how to teach them*. Abingdon: Routledge.

Howard, K. and Hill, C. (2020). *Symbiosis: The curriculum and the classroom*. Woodbridge: John Catt Educational.

Johnstone, A.H. (1991), Why is science difficult to learn? Things are seldom what they seem. *Journal of Computer Assisted Learning*, 7(2), 75–83.

Johnstone, A. H. and Wham, A. J. B. (1982) The demands of practical work. *Education in Chemistry*, 19: 71–73.

Leach, J. and Scott, P. (2008). Designing and evaluating science teaching sequences: An approach drawing upon the concept of learning demand and a social constructivist perspective on learning. *Studies in Science Education*, 38(1): 115–142.

Novak, J.D. (1990). Concept mapping: A useful tool for science education. *Journal of Research in Science Teaching*, 27(10): 937–949.

Paterson, D.J. (2019). Design and evaluation of integrated instructions in secondary-level chemistry practical work. *Journal of Chemical Education*, 96(11): 2510–2517.

Perry, T., Lea, R., Jørgenson, C., Cordingley, P., Shapiro, K. and Youdell, D. (2021). *Cognitive science in the classroom*. London: Education Endowment Foundation.

Rogers, B. (2018). *The big ideas in physics and how to teach them*. Abingdon: Routledge.

Skulmowski, A. and Xu, K.M. (2021) Understanding cognitive load in digital and online learning: A new perspective on extraneous cognitive load. *Educational Psychology Review*. DOI: 10.1007/s10648-021-09624-7.

Sweller, J., van Merriënboer, J. and Paas, F. (2019). Cognitive architecture and instructional design: 20 years later. *Educational Psychological Review*, 31(2): 261–292.

6
EFFECTIVE ASSESSMENT IN SCIENCE

ANDY CHANDLER-GREVATT AND CLAIRE DAVIES

CHAPTER OVERVIEW

When we hear the word assessment, most people immediately think of 'examinations' or 'testing'. Although these are features of assessment, effective assessment practice takes place in every lesson where a science teacher is continually evaluating what each pupil knows, understands and can do before using this information to inform what they should do next. This chapter considers four themes that you should develop throughout your training, based on the ITT Core Content Framework and Early Career Framework: classroom assessment, monitoring progress, effective feedback and the role of examinations. It will introduce you to the basic ideas and raise questions to explore as you become more experienced. This chapter will encourage you to consider classroom assessment in terms of formative and summative assessments. You will develop a greater understanding of how to monitor and track progress effectively as well as how to plan and use feedback effectively, so pupils can respond to it. We will also outline strategies to improve success in formal examinations.

> **LINKS TO ITT CORE CONTENT FRAMEWORK AND EARLY CAREER FRAMEWORK**
>
> This chapter supports development of:
>
> - Standard 1 – set high expectations
> - Standard 2 – promote good progress
> - Standard 5 – adapt teaching
> - Standard 6 – make accurate and productive use of assessment

INTRODUCTION

There are many ways to assess pupils. We can observe them doing an experiment, ask them verbal questions about photosynthesis, ask them to write down a description and example of a neutralisation reaction, give them multiple choice questions about mass and weight, or ask them to research and write an essay about the environmental, economic and social impact of burning fossil fuels. Short of being a mind reader, we can only judge what a pupil knows, understands and can do by proxy of what they do, say, or write.

ASSESSMENT: TYPES, PURPOSE AND USE

One of the big debates in education is whether assessment is best done *to* the pupil or *with* the pupil (Harlen, 2007). The former is a traditional model of the pupil being taught, the pupil learning, before being tested and given a result. This outcome focused approach is also called summative assessment: it is what most examinations do. On the contrary, formative assessment is often done with the pupil, with the pupil knowing the purpose of the learning, how it will be assessed and what success looks like. Pupils are part of the learning and assessment process, receiving feedback regularly, and having opportunities to improve as well as developing skills in self-assessment and peer-assessment. However, some teachers and schools may have a stronger formative culture than others (Chandler-Grevatt, 2018). In terms of current policy, based on their research Ofsted (2021) offer a clear steer on their understanding of assessment in science.

You will hear the terms summative assessment, formative assessment, and diagnostic assessment used at different times within your career, however they are all related. For example, an end of topic test is used in a summative way to assess where the pupil is at that moment in their knowledge, understanding and skills. However, if the teacher or pupil analyses what they got wrong and takes action to improve, the end of topic test result is being used formatively, that is, it is informing the next steps in teaching and learning.

Formative assessment in schools is often called Assessment for Learning (AfL) and is based on a seminal paper by Black and Wiliam (1998a) who established that class-room assessment was too focused on summative values and proposed through extensive examples that formative assessment is the key to improved learning. This paper is summarised in the booklet *Inside the Black Box* (Black and Wiliam, 1998b). You will see some schools using 'AfL techniques', which you may want to try in your lessons, but with a critical approach. For example, you will need to consider the pur-pose of the task or activity: is it just a tokenistic part of the lesson or is it an embedded strategy to identify how the teacher establishes prior knowledge, sets age-related development targets, seeks to challenge misconceptions and provides effective feed-back. Assessment with purpose is key.

Diagnostic assessment is a particular approach to establish prior knowledge and decide on appropriate interventions or next steps in learning. This is a specialised approach to formative assessment. Diagnostic questions are often focused on particu-larly tricky areas of science – for example, looking at particle models of solids, liquids and gases, pupils can often incorrectly think that liquids are compressible under nor-mal conditions or that air exists between the particles of a gas. Well-written diagnostic questions can challenge these misconceptions. The BEST (Best Evidence Science Teaching, 2019) activities do this particularly successfully. Further detail on utilising these diagnostic questions and challenging the misconceptions can be found in Chapter 3.

Teachers use a combination of assessment techniques in their classroom. One use-ful mantra is 'Where are they now? Where do they need to be? How do we get them there?' If you consider these three questions during lesson planning, you will not go far wrong.

ASSESSMENT CAUTIONS: RELIABILITY AND VALIDITY

Before we move on, we need a bit of caution. When we assess, we need to understand some critical features of assessments and assessing. There are whole books written about this, so this is just a taster to get you thinking.

Reliability refers to the assessment having the same outcome for every pupil who takes that assessment. Formative assessment is less concerned about reliability; how-ever, it is important in high-stakes assessments such as examinations where pupils are being compared to one another. To what extent would an exam, if repeated, give the same result?

With respect to validity, an assessment, test or examination itself is neither valid nor invalid. It is how the assessment is interpreted and used to make inferences about learn-ing that determines validity. There are several types of validity that get quite complex.

Tests usually only sample knowledge, so how confident can you be from the assessment provided to the pupils that they know all the science well, or whether they just got lucky on those questions?

ASSESSMENT IN SCIENCE

The activities of teaching and learning are lost without assessment. Assessment allows the teacher to judge what their pupils have learnt, how well they have learnt it, and what to do next, as well as to make a judgement of a pupil's success, or otherwise, at a specific qualification. Good teachers tacitly know how to assess because they have gained experience in developing:

- Good subject knowledge that is linked into a coherent mental map
- Knowledge of common misconceptions, misunderstandings and mistakes
- The ability to notice, interpret and intervene to pupil responses
- Knowledge of statutory examinations and examination techniques
- A critical understanding of the purposes and uses of different assessment approaches.

This is known as teacher assessment literacy (Xu and Brown, 2016), an important aspect of teacher professional development. This is actually a very complex set of skills that may take several years to develop, and which evolve with experience.

Early in your training, observe some lessons where you focus on the assessment practices in the lesson. Box 6.1 gives some questions to ask the teacher beforehand and to discuss and deconstruct the assessment in the lesson with them afterwards.

BOX 6.1   QUESTIONS FOR DISCUSSION AROUND ASSESSMENT IN TEACHING

How does the teacher:

- Establish the prior knowledge of the class?
- Communicate learning intentions of the lesson?
- Share or model the expected outcomes of the lesson?
- Check how the class is progressing?
- Check how individual pupils are progressing?
- Feedback about learning on a class level?
- Feedback about learning on an individual level?
- Give opportunities for pupil self-assessment or peer-assessment?
- Deal with mistakes made by the pupils?
- Pre-empt any mistakes or misconceptions?
- Make reference to expectations in examinations (where applicable)?
- Use the end of the lesson to establish progress and/or next steps in learning?

USING ASSESSMENT TO SUPPORT PROGRESS

To ensure that each class you teach is making suitable progress and learning, you need to use both formative and summative assessment process. However, before you start teaching a group, it is useful to look at any data that will give you insights to prior attainment and anything that may inhibit progress in science. Some schools use baseline tests to establish a starting point when pupils join, and most schools have some type of monitoring or tracking system to establish progress. As a student teacher it is often tricky to work out where to begin with data, as you have not had a great deal of experience collating and presenting it. Box 6.2 offers some questions you can ask your mentors and host teachers about the data for your classes and how progress is tracked.

BOX 6.2   QUESTIONS FOR YOUR MENTOR ABOUT DATA AND PROGRESS

- Which Data Management System is being used?
- Which Progress Management System is being used?
- What Baseline Data is available (if any)?
- What Target Data is available? What type of target?
- What Individual Data is available? (SEND, PP, etc.)
- How is progress measured (if at all)?
- How is pupil progress tracked? What can you do with the data?

ASSESSING SCIENCE

Science is often divided into content (what you need to know) and skills (how you do science). These can be loosely equated with substantive knowledge and disciplinary knowledge, respectively. The National Curriculum (DfE, 2013) reflects this by splitting the science into content and 'Working Scientifically', but they are intended to be taught together. When it comes to assessing these, there are different challenges and strategies.

At GCSE, there are three areas that are assessed in combined or separate sciences. In any specification there will be a description of the Assessment Objectives (AOs) and usually the weighting of that AO in the examinations. Typical AOs are:

AO1: Demonstrate knowledge and understanding of scientific ideas, techniques and procedures.

AO2: Apply knowledge and understanding of scientific ideas, enquiry, techniques and procedures.

AO3: Analyse information and ideas to interpret and evaluate, make judgements and draw conclusions. This also includes developing and improving experimental procedures.

You can see that not only is knowledge and understanding important, but also the application of that knowledge and using that knowledge to analyse practical applications. A greater weighting is given to how pupils apply and use their knowledge in practical situations, than just recalling knowledge.

ASSESSING SCIENTIFIC KNOWLEDGE AND UNDERSTANDING

Science can seem to be a lot of facts, but it is more a series of concepts within the scientific way of looking at the world. Learning those concepts is composed of understanding the key words, having examples (and non-examples) of the concepts and being able to apply this to unfamiliar situations. Assessment forms an important part of the learning process, informal knowledge checks, quizzes and activities that support learning.

In the classroom, we can assess knowledge and understanding through verbal questioning and getting individual, paired, group or whole class responses. Commonly, retrieval questions are used to recall knowledge from previous learning with the aim to embed it in long-term memory. Low-stakes retrieval exercises can be used in the form of self-testing; when the act of assessment becomes the act of learning, that is the testing effect.

Science teachers use topic tests as summative assessments of knowledge and understanding at set points in the academic year. These are often higher stakes, as the results inform grades given in reports and inform predications. Prior to these tests, teachers often support revision or diagnostic activities and targeted interventions.

ASSESSING SCIENTIFIC SKILLS (WORKING SCIENTIFICALLY)

Working Scientifically is part of the National Curriculum and considers the way that scientific knowledge is applied. Practicals, experiments and investigations are all considered to be part of working scientifically. The actual doing of science is an important skill but less frequently assessed. For example, measuring accurately using a force meter, electronic balance or a measuring cylinder are often overlooked up to GCSE, as with the effective use of a microscope, burette or multimeter. However, there are now required practicals at GCSE, specified by the examination boards, which focus more on knowledge of the procedures and analysis, rather than the competency of doing the activity. Topic tests usually reflect external examinations in that only about 20% of the examination is based on knowledge and understanding (AO1) with the rest on the application of that knowledge (AO2) and the ability to analyse scientific data (AO3).

The Required Practicals at GCSE are a compulsory element of the course, supported by resources from the exam boards. These need to be carried out by all pupils within class time and the teacher needs to keep accurate records of when they are performed. In the GCSE written examination papers, these practicals are assessed using mostly AO2 and AO3, ensuring that all pupils have experience and understanding of key practical techniques and analysis.

England is unusual in its approach to practical work in science. Other countries have practical examinations, where skills are assessed or have a greater emphasis on assessing scientific inquiry skills. To find out more you could investigate the SAILS project (Harrison, 2014), which addresses how teachers can go about assessing and feeding back on scientific enquiry skills.

USING ASSESSMENT FOR LEARNING STRATEGIES

Assessment for learning strategies can be summarised as:

- setting meaningful learning objectives and outcomes
- planned, targeted questioning
- giving and responding to effective feedback.

LEARNING OBJECTIVES AND OUTCOMES

An important part of formative assessment is to have a shared understanding of what you are aiming for (learning objectives) and what success looks like (learning outcomes). Learning objectives can be used effectively if made part of the planning and lesson sequence. They can take various forms. For example:

A specific question:

What is aerobic respiration?

A big question:

How do animals and plants get energy from food?

A content statement:

Aerobic respiration and energy

A 'By the end of the lesson I will be able to…'

Describe the process of respiration

Explain how the reactants get to the cell and what happens to the products.

Learning outcomes are used to communicate what success might look like to pupils and have many iterations in lessons. You will find that many schools have recently adopted a three-tiered approach. For example:

- Working towards ... achieving ... working beyond.
- Developing ... secure ... extending.
- Learning ... mastered ... fluent.

The cautions with this approach are that both teachers and pupils should have a shared understanding of what these mean and should be used to support progress rather than a summative judgement of pupil learning. Finally, they should never be used to label the pupil, only their performance in a task or over a learning episode.

EFFECTIVE QUESTIONING

Effective questioning is a set of skills that take a while to hone through your early years of teaching. Questioning is a low resource way of assessing the knowledge gained by the pupils and is used by the majority of teachers in all disciplines. You can dynamically assess how your lesson is progressing and then alter the plan depending on the feedback obtained from the class.

Here are some useful ideas to develop a good set of questioning skills.

- Read about effective questions, establishing the reasons to ask questions and when to ask them. Key features are increasing wait time, strategies that maximise whole class participation, targeted questioning and knowing when to stretch a pupil's thinking with another question and when to move on. Always ask the question first, before targeting a particular pupil. This way, all the pupils are engaged in thinking about the question posed for the maximum length of time.
- Observe how your host teachers use questioning techniques and build a repertoire of techniques to try in your lessons. Think about targeting questions at specific pupils, scaffolding responses, and coaching pupils to make links between different pieces of information.
- Plan your questioning: write down the three questions you want every pupil to be able to answer by the end of the lesson and use them when you circulate while the class works. Link your questions to your learning objectives and outcomes and rehearse the types of answers you might get and the responses you could use.

FEEDBACK AND MARKING

One of the most effective approaches of supporting pupil progress and attainment is the receiving of good-quality feedback and allowing the pupil the opportunity to respond to the feedback.

MANAGING MARKING

The 'tick and flick' approach to marking is becoming a thing of a past. It is recognised as not being effective in learning and a waste of teacher time. Marking needs to be focused and manageable. It is impossible to mark everything a pupil writes in their book; instead, teachers now use various methods that have worthwhile outcomes and do not take too long. Each school and usually the science department has a marking or assessment policy you will need to adhere to. Pick this up early in your placement to follow as you go through your training.

Marking strategies you may see include:

- Focused marking: telling pupils which piece of work will be assessed and what will be assessed, e.g. writing a plan for an experiment with a focus on the use of the key words validity, reproducibility and accuracy.
- Whole class assessment and feedback: a sample of exercise books are looked at and then some general feedback of what is going well and what needs to be improved is given.
- Self- or peer-marking: pupils are encouraged to mark specific tasks themselves (or each other's) with the guidance of the teacher.

USING A MARK BOOK

If a parent of one of your pupils calls in and wants to know how their child is doing in science, what evidence do you have? You could look at the pupil's exercise book; however, most teachers have a mark book in which they record various aspects of a pupil's participation and performance in their lessons. You should avoid duplicating data, but having a mark book that has baseline data, useful information about learning support and general performance in your lessons will be key to analysing and recording the pupil's progress over the time they are in your class. The information in Box 6.3 can support you to find out how your mentor or other colleagues use mark books in your school setting to maximise their utility.

BOX 6.3   USING A TEACHERS' MARK BOOK

- What basic information is recorded?
- What baseline data is recorded?
- What SEND (other data) is recorded?
- What other information is recorded? Classwork, homework, attendance, punctuality, activities?
- In what form? Words/Letters/Numbers/Scores/Grades?
- Paper or electronic?
- Considerations of data protection in line with school policies?

VIGNETTE 6.1   CLAIRE'S MARK BOOK

Data collection is pointless unless that collection is being used effectively to monitor progress, highlight the need for intervention, or predict future outcomes. Claire's mark book helps her build a picture of pupil progress over time. She draws upon a range of information in forms such as homework, end of module assessments, and online learning platforms. This variety of tasks and data can then facilitate the scrutiny required to move to an overall picture of pupil progress. The mark book allows her to assess progress across AO1, AO2 and AO3, thus enabling intervention to be truly personalised and targeted based upon a diagnostic process as opposed to a collection of marks.

When Claire teaches her Year 10 class the structure and bonding topic, her mark book is invaluable for looking at historic data on atomic structure to see where the pupils' starting points are. She uses this historic data to plan diagnostic questions to establish retained knowledge before encouraging retrieval of this knowledge and moving on to more complex material.

In addition, Claire has data from online quizzing platforms – to which a school or department can purchase subscriptions – which can be a useful way for pupils to independently improve their progress. These platforms can highlight areas of strength and weakness in a pupils' understanding and give them opportunity to resolve areas of weakness.

Activity: Make a plan around the information you want and need to know about a class and how this can be gathered and stored (safely) to support your lessons. Ask other teachers what they do with this information and how it helps them better meet the needs of the pupil.

COMMUNICATING ATTAINMENT AND PROGRESS

As a teacher you will need to be able to communicate the attainment and progress of individual pupils and of whole classes with other people. You need to consider who you are communicating with, what information will be most useful and how best to present it. Regular communication with pupils about their performance is called feedback and is discussed in the next section. You will also have to communicate with parents or guardians, usually at parents' evenings. It would be a good idea to try shadowing your mentor or a classroom teacher for at least one of these before you qualify to gain an insight in the styles of conversation you might be having with parents or guardians. You also will need to communicate with other teachers, the head of department, colleagues that share your class, teachers from other subjects or colleagues who oversee the pupils' pastoral care. These conversations may take a different tone and require a greater use of data and knowledge of the pupil's progress.

FEEDBACK

Black and Wiliam (1998b) recognised that feedback was an essential component of assessment for learning to improve pupil outcomes. It was not until several years later that Hattie and Timperley (2007) wrote that effective feedback is one of the most powerful strategies to improve outcomes.

Hattie and Yates (2014) conceptualised feedback as 'types' and 'levels'. The three types are:

- Feed up – where am I going?
- Feed back – how am I going?
- Feed forward – where to next?

The levels of feedback are:

- **Task level:** How well tasks are understood or performed.
- **Process level:** The process needed to understand and perform tasks.
- **Self-regulation level:** Self-monitoring, directing and regulating of actions.
- **Self-level:** Personal evaluations and effect (usually positive) on the pupil.

When observing a teacher give feedback and as you develop this for yourself, analyse the types and levels of feedback that you are giving.

EFFECTIVE FEEDBACK

For feedback to be effective it has to be personal to the pupil, positive and specific. Saying, 'You are all doing really badly at calculating kinetic energy' (impersonal, negative and non-specific) is not nearly as effective as saying, 'Emma (personal), you have selected the correct equation (positive), now check the values for mass and velocity are in the SI units before putting them in the equation (specific)'.

There remains debate about how soon after the assessment activity that feedback should occur. Some argue that it should be immediate, others that there are benefits to delaying feedback. It depends on the task and purpose of the feedback. Observe what other teachers do and try out different approaches for yourself and find what works best for you and your specific pupils and classes. There is no one size fits all approach to feedback.

OPPORTUNITIES TO FEEDBACK

Lessons have lots of opportunity for informal, immediate feedback to individuals and the class. One approach that can be used is the rule of three, where if three individuals have required correction through making the same mistake, the teacher stops the class and addresses it with them all. It is useful to plan a formal immediate approach in the form of a plenary after an episode of learning. This is often during the last ten minutes of a lesson, but it can be midway through a lesson, or sometimes after a sequence of lessons. The purpose of these reviews is to:

- Refer back to learning outcomes/objectives
- Check knowledge, understanding and/or skills
- Check for competence, rather than confidence
- Inform pupils of next steps
- Inform teachers of next steps.

RESPONDING TO FEEDBACK

Feedback is often most effective if pupils have an opportunity to respond to that feedback. This can be achieved in a number of ways, often due to the type of feedback given. Just giving back the work to try again is not usually enough. It is essential to unpick where they have gone wrong, correct that and then give them some more examples or practice, often known as 'improve the child, not the work'.

Many schools recognise the importance of giving lesson time to improvement or intervention, but often this can be directed for homework and out of lesson learning, particular for the later key stages. After a period of learning and a form of assessment, the teacher can feedback what has gone well, but also what is needed to be improved. This can also be done at a whole class level, whereby the teacher notes down any errors, misconceptions or particularly well-answered pieces of work during the marking and assessment stage, before providing written feedback to the class during the lesson time.

In Vignette 6.2, Claire discusses how feedback is planned and organised in her school.

VIGNETTE 6.2   CLAIRE'S USE OF FEEDBACK

Claire tries to establish a culture whereby assessment is not regarded as a series of high-stakes events but as a shared process between pupils and teachers. For this to be effective, its ownership needs to be established across all stakeholders in all curriculum areas. This is articulated in a Whole School Policy, but that policy needs translation into widespread practice. Statements such as 'Pupils should be writing double the amount that the teacher has fed back' need to go beyond words into deeds.

For example, on marking the latest piece of work from a Year 10 class on moles, Claire picked out the three key areas for each individual pupil that she felt they hadn't grasped. This included finding the relative atomic mass, working out the number of moles of a substance, or balancing an equation. She got the pupil to write a user's guide on how to do this and give examples for them to try. Claire always tries to look back at this work to ensure they completed it and understood the work.

Dedicated time for feedback can give the process value and purpose. The response to feedback may be seen as a valuable lesson, which is given timely to establish a path forward that can be effectively used in the short term, not just in an exam term. Teaching the skill or content is integral, but so is the need for pupils to trial, practise, review and retrieve this knowledge accordingly. Effective feedback and the response to this feedback will be crucial in ensuring the success of this process.

Activity: Think about the types of feedback you give to pupils and what you want them to get from this. Write some sentence starters that will support you in offering productive feedback in written and verbal forms to your classes.

SELF-REGULATION AND METACOGNITION

A key aspect of formative assessment in the classroom is supporting the development of your pupils' self-regulation and metacognitive skills. We aim for pupils to be able to solve learning problems themselves, have a range of strategies to learn, and to monitor their own progress and success at learning. Self-regulation is closely associated with assessment for learning (Andrade and Heritage, 2017), and schools are being encouraged to embed self-regulation and metacognitive skills in teaching and learning across all subjects (e.g. Education Endowment Foundation, 2018; Mannion and McAllister, 2021). This could be an area to develop through your training assignments or as a focus in your early teaching.

SUPPORTING SUCCESS IN EXAMINATIONS

Of course, when it comes to it, the majority of pupils want to leave school with good qualifications, and most of those are assessed using externally set and marked examinations. Supporting their success in these can be considered in four parts.

- **Long-term planning:** Carefully planning how you will teach the material over the two years towards a qualification is important, as is how you will assess progress and intervene when necessary. This needs some flexibility to deal with the needs of individual pupils and cohorts. Generally, this is performed at the department level but will require you to tailor the scheme of work to your own class and their abilities.
- **Developing revision skills:** This is linked to the previously mentioned self-regulation skills. Pupils do have preferred ways of revising, and establishing those early in the course is useful to ensure success. These can be developed at each assessment point throughout the course. This is often a key skill which pupils need to be explicitly taught in the first instance, before becoming more independent as they progress through the school.
- **Exam technique:** Not only do pupils need to be taught the knowledge and skills from the specification, with effective revision strategies, but they also need to know how to tackle specific questions in the examinations. For example, reading the question carefully, understanding what specific command words you are looking for, knowing how to respond succinctly to short answer questions and how to tackle longer answer questions. The 'BUS' technique can be particularly useful in this regard – Boxing the command word, Underlining key information and Scribbling key knowledge and information.
- **Knowing your specification:** Different parts of the specification are covered in different papers. Ensuring that your pupils know what is covered in each paper and the types of questions to expect can aid their revision and confidence when sitting a paper.

PREPARING FOR EXAMINATIONS

Revision can often be a means of simply adding another coat of paint on to an already established body of knowledge and it simply replicates what they already know as well as the misconceptions and gaps within their knowledge. This does not allow them any means of progression. A check list for any examination is akin to a passport for revision. However, a check can be a cursory glance, but what is really required is more rigorous.

Getting pupils to RAG (Red-Amber-Green – also known as traffic lighting) allows a dialogue, a diagnosis and then a development strategy. Revision is multi-layered like an onion and a skill that pupils need to be explicitly taught.

- The first layer is learning the knowledge to impart. Pupils need to be confident in utilising flash cards, concept maps, revision notes and other active revision strategies for converting knowledge to different forms.
- The second layer is the practical application of that knowledge which must involve the regular and spaced self-testing of the material. The pupils may also use their revision flash cards and the online quizzing platforms previously mentioned.
- The third layer is contextualised practice. Revisiting past papers and their assessment questions, practising to a time limit, comparing your answer to mark schemes and

exemplar materials can all help. Their use is much more effective, however, if it is part of a planned, systematic approach, rather than sporadic events or cramming.

Using past examination material takes time to master. To develop exam technique, pupils need to be able to dissect questions to (a) identify the specific focus and content being assessed, (b) analyse key command words, and (c) anticipate the response that is expected. Once again this should be established as a developmental process not as a rite of passage to terminal assessment. Taking the fear out of the question through familiarity and understanding can be very reassuring to the pupil. Finally, as far as possible involving parents and guardians in the revision process helps pupils' success in their examinations, as they have support from both home and school.

LINKS WITH TECHNOLOGY

There are apps available to schools that can be used to support classroom assessment and feedback.

Classroom assessment apps: These are usually downloadable on a smartphone or tablet. They can use multiple choice questions to quickly assess knowledge and understanding of each pupil and the class overall. This is immediate feedback for the teacher, who can then intervene immediately or plan to do so in the next lesson. There are also many websites which are free for pupils to sign up to which provide large questions banks for pupils to undertake independent retrieval practice of the information.

Homework apps or platforms: Many schools now subscribe to online homework platforms. The best ones provide specific activities to specific pupils based on their performance, that is they provide an intervention. The teacher has access to what each pupil (and class) has done and how well they have done, which can allow for planning of classroom interventions.

Online summative tests databases: Having access to carefully developed, tried and tested summative exam questions is important when making judgements about attainment. Using these in topic tests improves the quality of the examinations. Often based on past papers, these databases can provide sample questions on specific concepts, whole test papers on topics, or mock examination papers.

WHAT TO LOOK FOR WHEN OBSERVING LESSONS

- What strategies does the teacher use to identify how the pupils are developing their knowledge at the start, throughout and at the end of the lesson?
- Does the teacher use a range of questions and how do they organise questioning throughout the lesson?
- Listen to the verbal feedback in class - can you discern the purpose of it and language that is used within it?

SUMMARY

Now you have read this chapter you should have:

- Knowledge of what formative assessment and summative assessment look like in the classroom.
- Information that supports what you need to know and to do to be able to track and support progress in your science lessons.
- An understanding of the features of effective feedback and some strategies that might be used in your science department.
- A grasp of how science is assessed using external examinations and how you can best support your pupils' success in these examinations.

REFLECTIVE QUESTIONS

- How can you create the right balance and range of formative and summative assessment in your lessons?
- How do you monitor your pupils' progress over time? What different strategies do you use? How effective are they? How could you improve?
- How do you feedback to your pupils? How do pupils respond to your feedback? How successful are your strategies? How could you improve them?
- How well do you understand the examination structure? How do you support your pupils' success in examinations? How could you improve it?

FURTHER READING

This is a teacher summary of the seminal paper (Black and Wiliam, 1998a – accessible to teachers) outlining the case for and use of formative assessment in the classroom: Black, P. and Wiliam, D. (1998b). *Inside the black box: Raising standards through classroom assessment*. London: King's College.

These articles contain a series of exercises to improve each component of your assessment literacy informed by the self-audits and exercises from Chandler-Grevatt (2019). Chandler-Grevatt, A. (2020). Six elements of assessment literacy. *Education in Chemistry*. Available at: https://edu.rsc.org/feature/6-ways-to-develop-your-assessment-skills/4013078.article

After two decades of Assessment for Learning, this book shows how the approach has been developed and spread globally, demonstrating our progress in understanding effective feedback and self-regulation, amongst other developments: Heritage, M. and Harrison, C. (2020). *The power of assessment for learning. Twenty years of research and practice in UK and US classrooms*. London: Sage.

BIBLIOGRAPHY

Andrade, H.L. and Heritage, M. (2017). *Using formative assessment to enhance learning, achievement, and academic self-regulation.* London: Routledge.

Best Evidence Science Teaching (2019). Best Evidence Science Teaching Homepage [online] York, UK: University of York Science Education Group. Available at: www.stem.org.uk/best-evidence-science-teaching

Black, P. and Wiliam, D. (1998a). Assessment and classroom learning. *Assessment in Education: Principles, Policy & Practice,* 5(1): 7–74.

Black, P. and Wiliam, D. (1998b). *Inside the black box: Raising standards through classroom assessment.* London: King's College.

Chandler-Grevatt, A. (2018). *How to assess your students: Making assessment work for you.* Oxford: Oxford University Press.

Chandler-Grevatt, A. (2019). *How to teach for progress: Classroom approaches for improving practice.* Oxford: Oxford University Press.

Department for Education (2013). National Curriculum in England: Science programmes of study. Available at: www.gov.uk/government/publications/national-curriculum-in-england-science-programmes-of-study/national-curriculum-in-england-science-programmes-of-study

Education Endowment Foundation (2018). Metacognition and Self-regulation Toolkit. Available at: https://educationendowmentfoundation.org.uk/tools/guidance-reports/metacognition-and-self-regulated-learning/

Harlen, W. (2007). *Assessment of learning.* London: Sage.

Harrison, C. (2014). Assessment of inquiry skills in the SAILS Project. *Science Education International,* 25(1): 112–122.

Hattie, J. and Timperley, H. (2007). The power of feedback. *Review of Educational Research,* 77(1): 81–112.

Hattie, J. and Yates, G.C.R. (2014). *Visible learning and the science of how we learn.* London: Routledge.

Mannion, J. and McAllister, K. (2021). *Fear is the mind killer. Why learning to learn deserves lesson time – and how to make it work for your pupils.* Woodbridge: John Catt Educational.

Ofsted (2021). Research review series: science [online]. Available at: www.gov.uk/government/publications/research-review-series-science/research-review-series-science

Stobart, G. (2008). *Testing times: The uses and abuses of assessment.* London: Routledge.

Xu, Y. and Brown, G.T. (2016). Teacher assessment literacy in practice: A reconceptualization. *Teaching and Teacher Education,* 58: 149–162.

7
HEALTH AND SAFETY IN SCIENCE

ALLISON CRANMER AND ANDY CHANDLER-GREVATT

CHAPTER OVERVIEW

School and college science laboratories are safe places for staff to work and for pupils to learn, and this is because teachers and technicians work within and apply the relevant legislation and guidelines. This chapter will focus on safe practice within the science laboratory. It will introduce you to working safely within your laboratory and supporting your pupils in doing so, with summaries of the key legislation that affects you as a student teacher, particularly your responsibilities of working in a school and a science laboratory. As a science teacher you use a wealth of potentially hazardous materials, so we highlight the main hazards and how to minimise these. Next, we consider the role of the technician and how to establish a good working relationship with them. Finally, we consider the health and safety considerations of extra-curricular activities and teaching outdoors, onsite or offsite. There will seem a lot to take in, but in your first years you will be developing your expertise in these areas, and working with other, more experienced colleagues will allow you to apply these to become an effective and safe science teacher.

INTRODUCTION

Science laboratories have features that are different from most other teaching spaces in schools. They have stools and higher tables, they have gas and electrical supplies, and they have sinks and taps; sometimes there are fume cupboards and demonstration benches. This chapter contains information about relevant legislation and guidance that underpins and informs school-based practice. It is not expected that you will be able to recall all of these, but they serve as a sound context and foundation for you working safely. The abundance of legislation and their references is not to be offputting but rather to reassure you that there is guidance and procedures in place to support and enable you to teach science safely. Chapter 8 will develop some of these ideas further as well as unpicking more about what makes practical work more successful in the classroom.

GETTING TO KNOW YOUR TEACHING SPACE: SAFETY FIRST

Before you start teaching in any laboratory there is much you should consider, and whenever you start teaching in a new laboratory check you know all the safety features. Box 7.1 can be used as a guide to ensure you are looking for the right things. If you are unsure of the location or use of any of the list, ask your technician or a teacher who already uses that room. Student teachers regularly teach in more than one classroom, so the list is helpful to annotate for each laboratory and then appended to your teaching file.

BOX 7.1 HEALTH AND SAFETY CHECK LIST FOR YOUR TEACHING LABORATORY

Make sure you know each of these in all the laboratories that you teach in:

- location of fire exit(s) for the laboratory
- the assembly point for evacuation
- procedure for safe evacuation of the laboratory
- location of the main gas tap
- location of mains circuit breaker
- location of the fire bucket
- location of the fire blanket
- location and types of fire extinguishers
- location of the broken glass bucket
- location of the eye wash station
- who and where the First Aider(s) is/are
- who to call in case of emergency
- how to report an accident
- how to report faults

ONGOING RESPONSIBILITIES AND WORKING SAFELY

It is your responsibility to report any faults or potential hazards when they occur or as you find them. Make sure you know who to report them to (usually the head technician and the head of science). Some of these may be ongoing maintenance issues such as a blocked gas tap or a slow draining sink, but others may require more urgent attention – for example, a potential gas leak. Less obvious are trip hazards caused by loose floor tiles and splinters from wooden desks, and the best approach is that if you have any question about a potential hazard then ask – better to be safe than sorry is a reasonable position to hold.

A good way to ensure pupils work safely is to lead by example. Follow the laboratory rules yourself and behave in the ways you expect the pupils to behave. Leading by example helps to reinforce safe working practices. The pupils are always very quick to point out that you do not have your eye protection on when they are being made to wear it. Model safe practice as well as safe behaviour.

IDENTIFYING HAZARDS AND PERFORMING RISK ASSESSMENTS

The terms 'hazard' and 'risk' are often misused or used synonymously. A hazard is something that has the potential to cause harm. A risk is the likelihood of potential harm from a hazard. In the science laboratory, there are three categories of hazard: biological, chemical and physical, and Table 7.1 lists common examples.

Table 7.1   Common examples of hazards in the laboratory

Biological	Chemical	Physical
Bacteria	Materials and substances	Electrical
Fungi		Musculoskeletal (ergonomic)
Viruses		Mechanical
Protozoa		Noise and vibration
Cell culture		Radiation (ionising/non-ionising)
Animal organs and tissues		
Plant specimens		

For every practical you do, you must risk assess it, practise it (see also Chapter 3 and Chapter 8) and decide how it is best used with a particular class. Remember the same practical may have different outcomes from a risk assessment depending on which time of day it is being carried out, the age of the pupils performing the task and the level of supervision required. As mentioned in Chapter 3, it may be a good idea for you as the student teacher to observe a more experienced colleague undertake this with the class to get an idea of the organisation of the room and how to mitigate the risks and hazards involved.

It is your employer's legal responsibility to make suitable and sufficient risk assessments, but you have a responsibility to risk assess all teaching and learning activities. This is usually recorded on lesson plans and/or schemes of work, but sometimes a dynamic risk assessment of changing situations during lessons may need to take place to maintain a safe environment (see also Chapter 8). The Health & Safety Executive (HSE) recommend five steps to risk assessment as shown in Figure 7.1 and CLEAPSS (2005, 2017) have clear guidance to support this process. It is important that you are aware of how to undertake a risk assessment and are able to adapt existing ones to the specifics of your practical work organisation and class. Although there will be generic ones which offer a good starting point, like any classroom resources, you will need to ensure they fit the need for your class.

Figure 7.2 outlines the general hierarchy of control of risk and can be further developed to include examples of typical precautions used in a school/college laboratory. When undertaking a class practical or observing a more experienced colleague undertake this, think about what control measures have been put in place to minimise any risk to the people that are in the room. Some suggestions for what can be done are also found in Figure 7.2.

TEACHING PUPILS TO WORK SAFELY

Encouraging learners to work responsibly and safely in the laboratory is an important aspect of managing a safe learning environment. We need to explicitly teach our pupils to work safely and we cannot rely on their common sense. However, pupils can behave unpredictably and do unsafe or even dangerous things. By having clear expectations and being consistent about the laboratory rules and expectations of specific risk assessments you can minimise risk. Science teachers generally do this well, as school laboratories are remarkably safe places to work in. As you gain experience these will become second nature, as it will appear to be with the teachers you are working with.

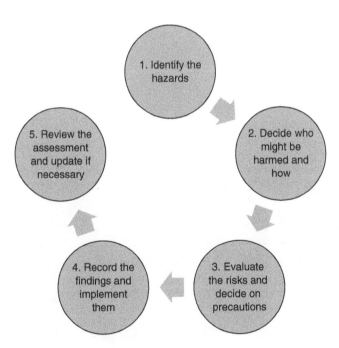

Figure 7.1 Five steps to risk assessment

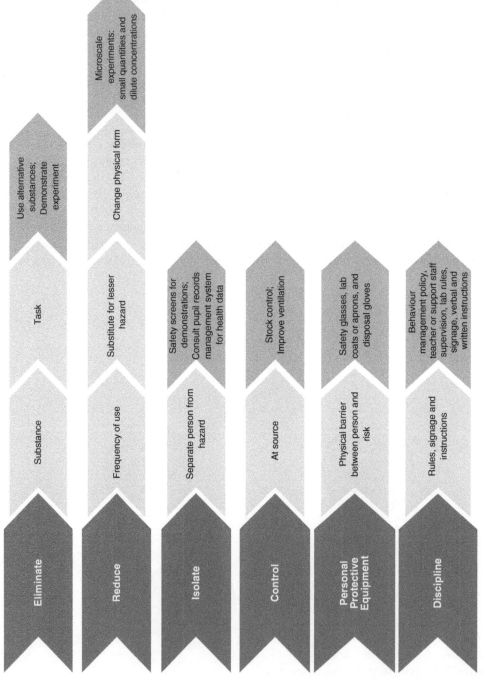

Figure 7.2 Hierarchy of control of risk for school/college laboratories

Most teachers set their expectations and safety rules at the beginning of the school year when they first meet their new classes. These safety expectations are reinforced throughout the school year at the start of each practical lesson. This early teaching involves breaking down barriers the pupils may have with practical work by explicitly teaching being safe in a lab, including things such as identifying different types of lab glassware, recognising the hazard symbols commonly found on the reagents and chemicals used, and the etiquette and behaviour expectations required of the pupils when they are in your lab.

HAZARD SYMBOLS

Any hazardous substance is classified by the United Nations Globally Harmonised System of Classification & Labelling of Chemicals (GHS). The European Union Regulation on Classification, Labelling & Packaging of Substances & Mixtures requires that manufacturers and suppliers must classify (based on properties and effects), label and package items safely. There must be hazard statements (of the principal hazards) and precautionary statements (of the principal control measures). There are a series of hazard warning symbols (pictograms) in the shape of a diamond with a distinctive red border and white background to easily and universally recognise these hazards. One or more pictograms might appear on the labelling of a single chemical. These are often displayed in the school science lab and are generally taught during the introductory lab safety lessons taught by science teachers every year. The up-to-date GB Classification, Labelling and Packaging (CLP) hazard pictograms can be found on the Health & Safety Executive website (Health & Safety Executive, nd).

LABORATORY RULES

Having clear expectations about learning and working in the laboratory is the first step to having pupils work safely. At the start of each year, it is good practice to familiarise your classes with the general 'Laboratory Rules' and the specific safety features of the laboratory they are working in (e.g. fire exits, fire extinguishers, eye wash station). Year 7 pupils usually have a detailed look at the laboratory rules and expectations over a few lessons, whereas year groups that have established knowledge and routines can be re-engaged with the rules through a quiz or question and answer session. Even though the pupils have been taught this before and should be accustomed to it, it is vital a refresher is carried out each year to minimise the risk of human error and the chances of an incident occurring.

Pupils need to be regularly reminded of the general expectations of safe behaviour in the laboratory. It is expected that the laboratory rules be displayed on a notice board in the laboratory along with first aid information and evacuation plans, although pupils will become 'blind' to these as they spend more time in the room. They often align being in the science lab with doing fun things; this can mean that reminders for pupils are often necessary, even when you think they should know better.

The Consortium of Local Education Authorities for the Provision of Science Services (CLEAPSS) have published ten lab rules for pupils (GL284) and it is essential you ensure you have access to them. In summary, they address access, behaviour management, environment, resources (use and disposal), personal protective equipment (PPE), emergency procedures and hygiene.

VIGNETTE 7.1   SETTING SAFETY EXPECTATIONS IN THE SCIENCE LAB

At the start of the new school year, Zoe taught her classes about the rules she expected them to follow whenever they were undertaking any sort of practical work in her lab environment. She gave the pupils time to do this independently by undertaking a 'spot the difference' activity between two different cartoon diagrams of a lab environment. Her pupils identified several different hazards the cartoon pupils are exposed to, before she asked them to come up with preventative measures. Not only was this asking the pupils to identify common lab risks and hazards, they were beginning to learn the notion of dynamic risk assessments in the lab environment which they could then implement, under guidance, when they performed practical tasks.

Zoe went on to refresh their memories on common glassware and equipment to help pupils build schema in their minds and familiarise themselves with how it all fits together to help them reduce cognitive load during practical tasks.

Activity: Consider how you will set the expectations for the pupils working in your lab or teaching space. How often will you remind them about the lab rules and how will you do this? What different strategies will you use with different year groups and why?

SAFETY ROUTINES

There are routines to establish so that pupils not only work safely but also know the reasons for the precautions they take. Ask any secondary school pupil what precautions they should take when doing a practical and most will reply, 'Wear goggles.' While not necessarily incorrect, they are not necessary for all practical work. However, it shows that although pupils know what working safely involves, they do not always know why they are doing it.

It is helpful to be explicit about the reasons for taking actions in order to minimise risk. Having said that, there are a number of routines you can establish to ensure that pupils work safely when doing practical work and these are elaborated upon in Chapter 8. For example, ensure that pupils:

- Stand at their desk, with the stool under the desk, and keep walkways clear during all practical work.
- Have a setting up routine which includes nominated pupils who collect equipment from particular places within the laboratory; specific pupils can take different roles – 'experimenter,' 'measurer' and 'recorder' – and these roles can be rotated.
- Have a clearing away routine which includes pupils taking responsibility for counting equipment returned to trays, putting equipment away in the right places and wiping down surfaces.

Ongoing checks through reminders, praise, and reprimand for repeat offenders helps remind and reinforce these expectations each time relevant activities take place.

In relation to this, it is worth bearing in mind that the collecting and returning of equipment almost always takes longer than you will anticipate, which may conflict with your lesson planning. Certainly, in the early stages of your teaching, be prepared within your planning to have elements that you can cut out until you are more experienced with judging how your classes function with these tasks.

WEARING SAFETY GLASSES

Safety glasses are one of the simplest, and most effective safety measures that can be implemented in the school science lab. Pupils don't often see the value of them,

Figure 7.3 Paper tissue in concentrated sulphuric acid (left), sheep's eyeball in concentrated sodium hydroxide (centre) and sheep's eyeball in concentrated sulphuric acid (right). Photograph used by kind permission of Dr Peter Borrows, ASE Health & Safety Group

preferring to use them as forehead protectors. It is therefore imperative that you, as the science teacher, enforce their correct use to minimise the risk when using any sort of hazardous material (biological, chemical or physical). Figure 7.3 illustrates the importance of pupils wearing safety glasses when using corrosive chemicals. (The sheep's eyeballs were left in either concentrated acid or alkali for 45 minutes, so results can be achieved within the timing of a typical lesson.) This is a demonstration with impact to illustrate the damage caused to the eye when in contact with such substances.

EMERGENCY ROUTINES

Schools hold fire drills to ensure that the school can be evacuated safely and efficiently. For whole class practicals, it is worth sharing clear expectations of what to do in the event of an emergency. For example, if a pupil's hair catches on fire, you need to be able to deal with it quickly and without having to worry that pupils elsewhere in the room are behaving dangerously.

With all classes, you can instil a 'Stop Safely' routine. If an emergency occurs (or, say, the fire alarm sounds), you need the whole class to stop doing their practical (safely) and stand still in their places. Your mentors may have such a drill in place. It must not be a 'stop and drop everything' routine, as this can be more problematic if pupils just stop and leave something heating or burning. The Stop Safely routine means that the class put down what they are using, turn off Bunsen burners or power packs and then stand still. They are responsible for making their space safe. You can practise this at the start of the year during a whole class practical for most classes, then just remind them of it whenever it is pertinent.

Share with pupils what they should do if a particular accident occurs, e.g. if you burn your finger, go straight to a tap and start running your burn under cold water and then get someone to tell the teacher. At this point we should add that these incidents are usually avoidable and therefore infrequent – but you need to know what to do to be able to act quickly, just in case. Finally, it is worth asking pupils what they would do if you, the teacher, were to have an accident; the most obvious instructions being they should know to go to the teacher next door or the technician.

One emergency scenario every science teacher needs to be aware of is fire during lesson time, as fire is an often-present risk in a typical laboratory. For a fire to start, there need to be three conditions: a heat/ignition source, oxygen and a fuel (a science lesson in itself) and this is known as the fire triangle. By removing any one of these through cooling, smothering or starvation, a fire will burn out. There are several sources of fuel present, such as paper, wood, dust and flammable chemicals, which may be used in class practicals. As the subject often uses an ignition source (most commonly the Bunsen burner), it is vital a science teacher knows the school fire safety procedure, where their nearest fire exit is and how to deal with minor incidents involving fire.

Under The Regulatory Reform (Fire Safety) Order 2005, employers have a legal duty to ensure that premises are safe by completing a fire risk assessment and taking general precautions. It is often the case that you will be asked to undertake mandatory fire safety training on commencement of employment or training at a different school; this will introduce you to the different types of fire extinguisher commonly found in schools and the type of fire they should be used to deal with.

Your primary responsibility is the safety of the pupils and yourself. Remember to always take a register at the start of the lesson and know where each pupil is at all times to allow management of an incident or emergency to be dealt with quickly and safely.

USING SPECIFIC HAZARDS IN THE SCHOOL LAB

As we described previously in this chapter, there are three types of hazard – biological, physical and chemical. When undertaking a practical, it is important to consider the risks that they pose and try to control the effects of these. In particular, you should consider the specific pupils in the class you are teaching – for example, the medical and allergy status of those in the class. It is important to consult the pupil records as well as pastoral and inclusion colleagues for health and wellbeing data at the start of the year, to inform planning and manage the risk appropriately in science lessons.

USING BIOLOGICAL SPECIMENS

Using biological materials, such as tissue specimens from animals or plants and microorganisms, is common in the biology classroom. These can pose their own risks, such as infection and illness. Mitigation measures such as personal protective equipment (eye protection and gloves), as well as robust sanitising regimes, should be implemented and explained to the pupils before and during the practical. Dissections are a common activity at GCSE and A-Level, using animal tissue samples in a class practical or demonstration. When selecting the specimen, you need to think about the individuals of the class to ensure that any religious or personal beliefs of the pupils are taken into consideration when choosing the source organism of the specimen.

Allergies of varying severity are increasingly common in the general population, particularly to common plant specimens. When planning practicals, ensure you are aware of any allergies in the class to avoid contamination and exposing the pupil to risk. Some allergies (by no means an exhaustive list) which are often in the forefront of a teacher's mind when planning practical work are peanuts and other nuts (now often not allowed in schools), kiwi fruit (sometimes used as a specimen for extracting DNA), celery and latex (can be found in some gloves used for PPE). It is essential that you look at the data for your class and tailor the specimens appropriately to avoid any exposure to potential allergens or medical triggers.

WORKING WITH PHYSICAL HAZARDS

Noise is very rarely a relevant hazard during science lessons, although sometimes there may be noise produced by practical demonstrations and experiments. For example, take care when demonstrating sound waves and the range of hearing using a signal generator and loudspeaker, particularly with high amplitudes and frequencies.

Radiation sources are used in the physics lab; they can be either ionising or non-ionising and can be emitted from natural or occupational sources. Radioactive sources held by schools and colleges are low activity, but there should be a Radiation Protection Supervisor to control the storage and use of ionising radiation. It is worth discussing this with the technicians or physics specialist in the department to make yourself aware of the regulations for storage and use of these substances in the class-room with pupils, as they do need extra care. Physics laboratories may also have lasers, but whilst these are not of sufficient intensity to damage skin, they can damage eyes, so precautions need to be taken on their use.

Electricity is an ever-present hazard in the school laboratory. There is a risk of electrocution if appliances and services are not regularly inspected and maintained. All electrical appliances should be inspected prior to class use by the user (teachers and support staff). They should also be periodically tested and inspected (Portable Appliance Testing – PAT) by a competent person. The science technician is often qualified to undertake this or works closely with those who are. Plug sockets should be covered when not in use and/or monitored to prevent foreign objects being pushed into them – many pupils have a particular tendency to store the last part of the splint used to light the Bunsen burner in plug sockets.

Tools and machinery pose mechanical hazards such as entanglement, friction and abrasion, cutting or severing, crushing and, stabbing and punctures. You will be unlikely to encounter many of these, but biology dissections, handling chemical glass-ware and heavy physics apparatus can introduce some of them.

Working at height may sometimes be necessary but can often be worked around. Rather than climbing onto chairs, tools or tables, use a kick step or stepladder and ask for assistance from a colleague to reduce the risk of falling.

WORKING WITH SCIENCE TECHNICIANS

All science departments should have at least one science technician; often they will have a Senior Technician and others with specialisms based on subject or phase. Your science technician(s) is a valuable, resourceful and professional person who makes your role as a science teacher easier. The Gatsby *Good Practical Science* guide (Holman, 2017: 13) states:

6 TECHNICAL SUPPORT

Science departments should have enough technical or technician support to enable teach-ers to carry out frequent and effective practical science.

From an outsider's perspective science technicians get equipment ready for science teachers and clear it away again. However, there is more to their role than this. They have expert knowledge about, amongst other things, health and safety, practicals, and maintenance and servicing of equipment that is used.

Getting to know your technicians, the systems and your responsibilities as a science teacher is essential to your integration into a science department. The number of science technicians in your department depends on the number of laboratories and number of pupils. However, also be aware that science departments may not have their full complement of technicians due to financial cuts, low pay, and reduced working hours (Chandler-Grevatt, 2017). Be mindful of how much time you demand of your technicians and ask your school mentor for a steer. You might be given some dedicated time to work with the technicians and actively contribute to the department. This is also covered in Chapter 8.

PREP ROOM ETIQUETTE

Prep rooms are your technician's workspace and they are busy places which require organisation, order and systems to ensure that the right equipment arrives at the right time, and is removed, sorted, cleaned and replaced quickly, ready for reuse. Here is a guide to prep room etiquette:

- Be respectful of technician time and thank them if they spend extra time explaining things to you.
- Understand their role; it is unlikely to be their role to do administrative tasks for you such as photocopying, so check before asking such things.
- Do not just take things from the prep room for your lessons – ask your technician first.
- Be specific about what you want in your weekly equipment requests – do not assume anything. If you are using Bunsen burners, you will need to order matches or lighters. If you need bottles of acid, state which type, concentration and volume (and in one or more bottles).
- If you are going to use unusual (balloons, specific confectionery, large volumes of food or chemical) or fresh (organs for dissection, pond weed) equipment, give plenty of notice.

Some ITT programmes have an hour a week given to student teacher–technician time. All science departments will give student teachers the opportunity to meet with and learn to work with the technicians, although this is often done informally, so that a working relationship develops between the technicians and the student teacher. Vignette 7.2 describes another way of approaching this, where a student teacher was given the opportunity to work more closely with technicians on a regular basis throughout her placement.

VIGNETTE 7.2   DEVELOPING A WORKING RELATIONSHIP WITH YOUR TECHNICIANS

In agreement between the ITT science leader, head of science, technicians and science mentors, one hour a week was set up for Anisa to work with a science technician throughout her placement. The activities that were carried out were to the discretion of the parties involved, and Anisa was able to engage with the following throughout her time in the school.

- Orientation of prep-room and equipment
- Preparation and practise of her own practical lessons
- Working with technicians / 'mucking in' / seeing behind the scenes
- Applying health and safety – general and specific
- Fixing equipment and making up practicals
- Improving her own subject knowledge development, particularly of practicals, e.g. colorimetry, radioactivity, distillation
- Developing (specialist) resources for whole department, e.g. videos, physics specific kits.

Anisa discussed a range of benefits from this student teacher–technician time including:

- Student teacher's understanding of technician's role within a science department
- Building positive relationships between student teachers and technicians, with mutual appreciation for each other's roles
- Raising the profile of technicians within the department
- Student teacher wider experience of practical work and health and safety lead to more confidence doing practical work
- Student teacher development: improved subject knowledge, integration into the department, increased confidence
- Impact on the department including extra help for technicians and the development of new resources.

Activity: When you are in school consider how you can use some of your non-teaching time to best work with the technician. In what ways can they support your wider subject knowledge development or skills as a science teacher?

WORKING OUTSIDE THE SCIENCE CLASSROOM

The educational benefits (both academic and pastoral) of extra-curricular enrichment activities to develop cultural (and science) capital, provide stretch and challenge, promote social skills and foster positive relationships are well known. Here we discuss three examples: STEM activities, educational visits and field studies.

Schools often offer these off-timetable sessions to enrich and broaden the curriculum, giving pupils the chance to explore STEM subjects like Science, Technology, Engineering and Mathematics (STEM) in less formal settings than timetabled lessons. Taking part in these activities is recognised in Standard 8 of the CCF and ECF. STEM Learning offers a programme of support and the Association for Science Education (ASE) and subject associations/learned societies (Institute of Physics, Royal Society of Biology and Royal Society of Chemistry) have devised a selection of suitable STEM activities. Just as you rehearse an experiment for the first time before you do it with a class, so you should review the risk assessment provided and trial these novel activities before use.

Educational visits are activities offsite which enhance and complement the core curriculum that cannot be done onsite, often due to a school/college not having the requisite resource or expertise. There are specific rules about financing such visits. If they are an essential part of the curriculum, then they should be free of charge for pupils, but if they are for enrichment, then they can be charged for. Many external organisations offer educational visits, produce learning resources and often have a dedicated Education Officer. The Department for Education (DfE) provides health and safety guidance for educational visits (DfE, 2018). The Outdoor Education Advisers' Panel (OEAP) also supports education establishments to develop good practice in offsite visits and CLEAPSS (2019) also produce a field-work student safety sheet.

Schools/colleges must have a visits policy. They should appoint an educational visits coordinator to oversee the administrative arrangements. Close liaison with the coordinator is essential to ensure all demands are met, but student teachers can only plan visits under the supervision of a qualified teacher. At times it can feel that the paperwork associated with offsite visits is cumbersome, but you should bear in mind that this has been generated as a source of support and protection for you as a teacher and for the pupils. In the event of unforeseen incidents this preparation is vital.

Field studies are key components of the biology and earth science curricula. Many schools have suitable grounds and playing fields, but others may need to travel further to visit suitable outdoor environments. Some local authorities and local companies have dedicated field studies centres that lead activities free of charge or for a modest cost. The natural environment has specific hazards, such as changeable weather, water bodies, uneven terrain, and wild animals and plants, so risk assess your activities with care and consult the pupil records management system for health and other data such as disabilities, allergies and phobias (and if visiting water, whether they can swim). The general advice for visits is applicable to field studies. The Field Studies Council (FSC) also supports outdoor education, with residential, day, outreach and virtual visits for all ages.

WORKING WITH HEALTH AND SAFETY LEGISLATION

Health and Safety legislation is a statutory framework that teachers must understand in addition to acting within the frameworks which set out their professional duties and responsibilities.

The Health & Safety at Work, etc. Act (HASAWA) 1974 is the key piece of health and safety legislation. It intends to secure the health, safety and welfare of employees at work and protect non-employees against risks to health or safety arising from or in connection with work activities. This act outlines the general duties of employers to their employees and to non-employees (pupils and visitors), plus the duties of employees to uphold the safety of everyone and themselves in the environment in which they work in the institution.

There are other regulations, approved codes of practice and guidance with which employers must demonstrate legal compliance. The Management of Health & Safety at Work Regulations (MHSWR) 1999 aims to improve health and safety management and it outlines the duties of employers to their employees.

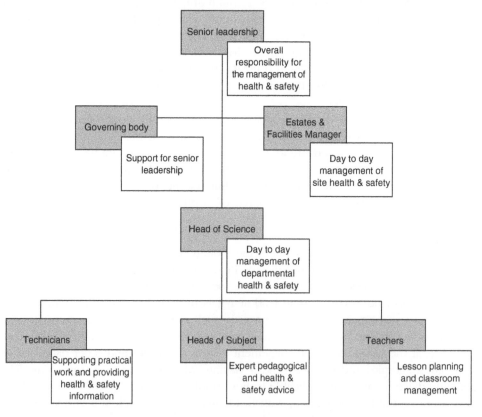

Figure 7.4 Typical organogram of health and safety management in a school/college

There is a chain of responsibility from senior leadership to employees, and a typical structure that might be found in a school setting is shown in Figure 7.4. It is important that you are clear about your role as a student teacher and then as a qualified teacher.

Your science department will have a policy, written by the head of science and/or those who understand the specific hazards. You must familiarise yourself with this and follow it when teaching. It is likely that your training provider will ask you to look at this as one of the first tasks when you start your placement as a student teacher.

It is the employer's legal responsibility under MHSWR 1999 to provide adequate training during working hours during your career:

1. Induction when you are first recruited.
2. When you are transferred to another department or your responsibilities change.
3. When new risks are introduced or there is a change in risk (such as new work equipment or existing work equipment is modified; new technology; or new system of work).
4. Periodic refresher training or Continuing Professional Development (CPD).

Pressures of time and workload often make accessing CPD challenging but health and safety is one aspect of your teaching that should never be compromised. As a student teacher you should be made aware of the safety expectations and ways of working within the department – and if you change schools for a second placement, ensure that you revisit these, as the schools may have different approaches to meet their needs.

A FINAL WORD

Ultimately, health and safety is everyone's responsibility. Whilst there may be changes in the policies and guidance over time, the sources of support will remain and it is essential you are up to date in the expectations of working safely. Ignorance is not an excuse.

WHAT TO LOOK FOR WHEN OBSERVING LESSONS

- How do experienced teachers ensure all pupils are using the expected PPE within a lesson?
- How is the collection and return of equipment organised in different lessons?
- What strategies do teachers use to remind pupils of safety and behavioural expectations within the science lab?

SUMMARY

Now you have read this chapter you should have:

- Details of your health and safety responsibilities within the classroom.
- An understanding of how to approach management of health and safety in the Science classroom.
- Greater awareness of the need for working closely with technicians.
- Understanding the need for maintaining professional knowledge and practice of health and safety.

REFLECTIVE QUESTIONS

- Do you consider health and safety when planning lessons and do you record the information in writing?
- Why is it important to instil safe behaviours in pupils?
- What is your personal philosophy on the benefits of extra-curricular enrichment activities?
- How will managing the Science classroom enable you to demonstrate that you are working towards and ultimately meeting the ITT, CCF and ECF?

FURTHER READING

This is particularly useful for Early Career Teachers in Science as it covers all the basics and some of the details that you need to get started with safe working in the school Science laboratory. It can be read from cover to cover, then dipped in and out of: ASE (2019). *Safeguards in the school laboratory*. Hatfield: ASE.

Chapter 24, written by Steve Jones, the Director of CLEAPSS, explores a range of health and safety issues also covered in this chapter: Banner, I. and Hiller, J. (Eds) (2018). *ASE Guide to secondary science education*. Hatfield: ASE.

The CLEAPSS website is accessible with a login which should be provided from member schools. It is an invaluable source of guidance and documentation to enable safe working in the science classroom: www.cleapss.org.uk/

BIBLIOGRAPHY

Chandler-Grevatt, A. (2017). Losing our technicians: The crisis facing schools. *Education in Chemistry*. Available at: https://eic.rsc.org/feature/losing-our-technicians-the-crisis-facing-schools/3008169.article

CLEAPSS (nd). GL284 Lab rules safety poster [online]. Available: science.cleapss.org.uk/Resource-Info/GL284-CLEAPSS-Lab-Rules-Poster.aspx

CLEAPSS (2005). *L196 Managing risk assessment in science.* Uxbridge: CLEAPSS.

CLEAPSS (2017). *PS090 Managing and recording risk assessments in school science.* Uxbridge: CLEAPSS.

CLEAPSS (2019). *SSS075 Fieldwork. Student safety sheet 75.* Uxbridge: CLEAPSS.

Department for Education (2018). Health and safety on educational visits. Available at: www.gov.uk/government/publications/health-and-safety-on-educational-visits/health-and-safety-on-educational-visits

Health & Safety at Work, etc. Act (HASAWA) 1974. Chapter 37. UK: The Stationery Office.

Health & Safety Executive (nd). Hazard pictograms [online] available: www.hse.gov.uk/chemical-classification/labelling-packaging/hazard-symbols-hazard-pictograms.htm

Holman, J. (2017). *Good practical science.* Gatsby Charitable Foundation. Available at: www.gatsby.org.uk/education/programmes/support-for-practical-science-in-schools

The Management of Health and Safety at Work Regulations (MHSWR) 1999. UK: The Stationery Office.

The Regulatory Reform (Fire Safety) Order 2005. UK: The Stationery Office.

8
PRACTICAL WORK IN SCIENCE

MARK LANGLEY AND JESSIE MYTUM-SMITHSON

CHAPTER OVERVIEW

This chapter builds on the content of the previous chapter, considering the reasons for doing practical work to promote and support learning. We will outline the importance of practical work having purpose and how it can be used to support conceptual development, rather than just engage pupils on a superficial level. The chapter content will also outline the organisation and planning of practical work so that it is well managed within your science lessons.

LINKS TO ITT CORE CONTENT FRAMEWORK AND EARLY CAREER FRAMEWORK

This chapter supports development of:

- Standard 3 - demonstrate good subject and curriculum knowledge
- Standard 4 - plan and teach well-structured lessons
- Standard 5 - adapt teaching
- Standard 7 - manage behaviour effectively

INTRODUCTION

Practical work is seen as an essential part of secondary science education, by pupils, teachers and the wider world. Within the UK, we carry out more practical work than most other countries and are lucky to be well provided for, in terms of dedicated laboratories, technicians and equipment. It provides opportunities for pupils to engage with learning in different ways to other subjects and can excite pupils about the world of science around them. It is also key to the National Curriculum and embedded as part of all 14–16 and post-16 science qualifications and is a requirement for pupils to experience high-quality practical science.

However, practical activities are frequently chosen by science teachers because they think they should be doing them, rather than it being the most useful learning tool. Pupils often delight in a practical lesson – and it can be the most common question as pupils enter the science classroom, 'are we doing a practical today?'. However, pupils can often enjoy practical work as they see it as an easy activity, to enable them to not write much and give them opportunity to waste time … rather than because they think it helps them learn the subject (Woolnough, 1995). Many practical activities are also quite unscientific and unstimulating, not meeting their intended outcomes, apart from developing student's ability to manipulate equipment (Abrahams and Millar, 2008: 1945). A key skill of a developing science teacher is to know when to deploy practical activities to maximise their effect and not falling into the trap of doing practical work for the sake of it.

High-quality practical work is not just the doing phase, but also the thinking and discussing phases (Millar, 2004). A common issue with practical work is that it is rushed, and the lesson concentrates on getting the activity done. Many pupils do not understand why they are carrying out a practical, and it is always interesting to ask pupils what they are doing and what they are learning. In many cases, if pupils are asked a few weeks later about the practical, they are likely to only remember superficial details around the practical, rather than what it shows.

Many 'wow' demonstrations fall into this trap – for example, the 'screaming jelly baby' practical (CLEAPSS, 2019) when a jelly baby sweet is dropped (usually head-first!) into a boiling tube of molten potassium chlorate (V), where it reacts violently with a purple flame, lots of steam and soot, and sometimes a howling noise. A teacher might try and use this to show how much energy is contained in the jelly baby as part of a respiration topic. Ask pupils a few weeks later, and they will remember the jelly baby reacting, but are unlikely to remember what it showed, apart from the noise and jelly baby plunging to its fate. As an aside, they will never have come across the oxidising agent before, so how are they to know that the energy is not coming from the chlorate (or even understand the meaning of oxidising)? This practical can then also sow some alternative conceptions for pupils which will have to be unpicked later.

All practicals should be planned and undertaken with effective learning objectives in mind that are specifically for the practical. Teachers usually set learning objectives (and where appropriate, success criteria) for the subject knowledge of a lesson, but rarely for the practical. This leads to pupils (and sometimes the teacher) not really knowing the purpose of the practical, or where it leads next.

If practical work is purposeful, varied and well planned, it can help students immensely. Just following a recipe time and time again will not. Students need to develop their understanding so they will be able to apply this in unfamiliar circumstances as well.

WHAT IS PRACTICAL WORK FOR?

Practical work can support learners in three core aspects of science education (Millar 2004):

- Knowledge and understanding of science – such as being able to state observable features, state or use a classification system, state a relationship between variables and show understanding of scientific theory.
- Practical skills – including being able to identify equipment, use equipment, describe a standard procedure, carry out a standard procedure.
- Scientific approach (scientific enquiry) – for example, propose a question, plan a strategy, evaluate risk, collect and present relevant data, interpret data, state a conclusion, evaluate a conclusion.

An additional two further broader purposes have been highlighted by the Gatsby Charitable Foundation's *Good Practical Science* (Holman, 2017):

- To develop higher level skills and attributes such as communication, teamwork and perseverance.
- To motivate and engage pupils.

Practical work helps pupils understand the links between two key domains – one of objects and observables (things they can manipulate and see) and the other domain of ideas. However, often too much time is spent on the former, with very little discussion or application of the ideas. Too many practical activities are done on the basis that if pupils see or experience something, then the explanatory ideas will emerge from the practical. This is the fallacy of induction; just because a student sees something, does not mean they will understand it.

For example, if pupils are carrying out a series of displacement reactions, of different metals and corresponding metal solutions, just because they see their results, does not infer they then understand the chemistry, or even which metal is more reactive than another (Royal Society of Chemistry, 2016).

It also can create confusion if there is the wrong answer produced during an experiment (such as a metal solution being acidic [to help the salt dissolve], so one metal reacts with the acid rather than displacing the other metal from solution, giving a particularly vigorous reaction). Then the teacher must correct the pupils' results, leaving them sometimes wondering why they did the practical when they are going to be told the right answer in the end. Or even worse, pupils are left confused about what has happened. Allowing time for the discussion and thinking parts of the activity are crucial for the practical to make sense - remember the mantra 'Hands-on, Minds-on' for any practical (Millar, 2004). Ensure there is space for pupil and teacher talk, and make relevant links to other areas of science, and their everyday lives (see Chapter 11 in relation to teaching science in context).

PLANNING AND PREPARING

Setting learning objectives for a lesson (or series of lessons) that include specific objectives for the practical activities is key (see also Chapter 5 for planning objectives); once this has been done, then the most appropriate activity can be chosen. This will help ensure a purposeful experience for pupils. For some activities, success criteria will be appropriate such as 'a full table of data will be collected by the end of the practical'. Millar et al. (2002) outlined the importance of this and described two levels of effectiveness in relation to judging the success of a lesson. The first level compares task specification and classroom events and in short asks you to reflect on the extent to which the pupils did what you wanted them to do. This however does not assess *learning* through the practical work and so they suggest that a second level of evaluation has to take place which is the extent to which the pupils learned what you wanted them to learn – and the only way you can achieve this is by having those clear objectives for learning through practical work from the start.

Some learning objectives may require splitting into smaller chunks, possibly over several lessons, in order that sufficient time is given for students to effectively complete the learning activity. An example of how this might be achieved is found in Box 8.1.

BOX 8.1   AN EXAMPLE OF HOW TO ORGANISE LEARNING OBJECTIVES FOR PRACTICAL WORK

A physics required practical at GCSE involves measuring how the resistance of a wire changes by its length and/or diameter, in order to demonstrate compliance with Ohm's Law. This will require a generation of a large set of data by pupils for them to analyse, as well as constructing and using electrical circuits (Institute of Physics, 2021).

This practical is unlikely to be completed in one lesson without becoming rushed. A better approach would be to split this up, though it requires advance planning for technicians:

- **Lesson one**
  - o Pupils are expected to set up the equipment to measure the current and voltage at various lengths of a single wire. This would involve them setting up the circuit, fault finding, and producing a simple table of data - which could then be used to exemplify calculations of resistance. A homework is set for pupils to draw (or add to a part-completed) table for their results next lesson.
  - o The key learning outcome here is 'set up and fault find a circuit, to be able to make voltage and current readings for a wire'.

- **Lesson two**
  - o Technicians set up eight or ten sets of circuits (two of each thickness/ diameter) around the room, ready-to-use, all working, and pupils, in small groups, move from one set of equipment to another, completing their table, with repeat measurements as appropriate, for multiple wires, so they gather lots of data. They do not have to set up the equipment, as they have demonstrated that skill in the previous lesson. The analysis (calculations and graphing) can be started in the lesson or completed in the next.
  - o The key learning outcome here is 'use the equipment provided to gain a set of results of current and voltage at different lengths of different wires, to analyse next lesson'.

Similar approaches can be made in many practicals. If in a chemistry practical, such as making copper sulfate crystals, the key techniques you want pupils to learn and master are around reacting hot solutions, filtering while hot and recrystallisation. Therefore, do you need them to spend time weighing out the solid copper oxide, or pouring sulfuric acid into boiling tubes if these are not part of the learning objectives (CLEAPSS, 2016)?

If you ask pupils to measure out specific masses of reagents, and you only have two balances in a class, it considerably slows down the practical, and gives opportunities for misbehaviour as pupils queue up. On your requisition, if you give enough notice, technicians will often be able to prepare measured quantities, such as the approximate correct dose of copper oxide in small beakers, and the acid poured into boiling tubes. Although more time-consuming for technicians, it has advantages of reducing waste and possibly contamination of bottles. However, some schools are short-staffed with technicians, so always ask first; most technicians will be very accommodating.

A key consideration of any practical is the existing skillset of the pupils. What have they done before, in what context and how might you need to remind them of this? Looking back through the scheme of work to identify practical skills they should have encountered is a useful starting point – but bear in mind that even though they have done these before, if it was some time ago, you may need to revisit the basics. If you have to introduce new skills, such as handling a new piece of apparatus, then you will have to factor this into your planning and this is where clear progression routes in practical work, within any scheme of learning, is an essential element, but often lacking.

TRIALLING ACTIVITIES

Confidence in leading practical work is core for science teachers. Often we are faced with practical activities we have never come across before, even from our own time in school as a pupil. This is even more prevalent when teaching outside our own specialisms. As mentioned in Chapter 3 and Chapter 7, trying out in advance is essential, as it will enable you to identify pinch points, expected results and where you, or pupils, may have difficulties. It will also enable you to tweak the outcomes of the (model) risk assessment if appropriate – do not forget to record any changes you make to the risk assessment. This might include things such as 'ensure window is open – makes a lot of smoke' or 'use pre-measured quantities with group 7D and technicians to put into separate trays on teacher's desk'. Any changes you make to the practical that have an impact on the risk assessment outcomes *must* be recorded by law (HASAW Act 1974). Figure 8.1 shows an example of an annotated risk assessment used for a class practical.

Trialling activities usually means discussing with technicians so they can fit in your request. Due to space constraints, the actual trial might have to wait until the end of the school day. It is also important that you involve an experienced colleague to help, if it is something you have not come across before.

Technicians are a fount of useful information – and they may also be able to come and support you during the lesson, particularly with demonstrations, where they could do the demonstration, while you interact with the class. This is a very good use of their talents, and helps pupils understand more about the role of science technicians more widely. It is important to foster a good working relationship with your technician team, as they are crucial to the success of your practical science lessons.

You might also consider filming a practical when you trial, or at least take pictures of the set-up, especially where there are several steps, or apparatus unfamiliar to the pupils. You can then use this as a back-up in case an experiment fails, or to incorporate into instructions where appropriate.

Ref	Equipment and reagents	Safety notes
1	**Screaming jelly baby** (3 sets to use)	Bench near window (to get rid of fumes!)- ensure windows open in lab and prep room to allow smoke dispersal
	NOTE QUANTITIES (reduced CLEAPSS amount) of potassium (V) chlorate- oxidising. 7g in borosilicate boiling tube	
	Proper jelly babies only (only put out two or three in packet)	
	All reagents on teachers bench	Smaller amount (7g) used to avoid spitting out
	More info in SRA001 Updated Nov 2019- see the new annotated copy in the prep room or HOD office.	
		Pre-weigh amounts in tubes- no stock bottle in lab. Loosely stopped with bung
	Extra PPE/equipment	
	Full HEAT RESISTANT GLOVE FACESHIELD LABCOAT Long TONGS SAFETY SCREENS (2)- use old marked ones not new	Spilled potassium (V) chlorate needs wiping up with wet cloth (wear gloves- nitrile) when cooled- cloth rinsed out (DO NOT USE PAPER TOWELS- can ignite late)

Figure 8.1 Annotated risk assessment

EMBEDDING POINT OF USE RISK ASSESSMENT INTO YOUR PLANNING AND LESSONS

Effective risk assessment is key, but so is communicating the outcomes (the things that people need to do/not do!) of your risk assessment to the people that need to know it. Most practical activities in schemes of learning have model risk assessments, but as mentioned in Chapter 7, these will need modifying/tweaking to suit your group, laboratory or how you will run the activity. The outcomes can be shared easily: on a presentation, embedded in a worksheet, in your planner, a reminder note to mention, on the technician's requisition, on (temporary) signs, equipment labels and so on. CLEAPSS (2017) guide PS090 (*Making and recording risk assessments*) and CLEAPSS (2020a) G030 (*Successful science practicals*) both have particularly useful information in and are key documents for every science teacher to read and understand.

What the risk assessment outcomes should NOT do, is sit on a form or electronic drive and not be used by anyone. Good risk assessment is helping you and others carry out the practical well. For most practicals, CLEAPSS and Scottish Schools Education Research Centre (SSERC) have produced excellent model risk assessments for their activities and these can be used as the basis for yours, but think how to best share the outcomes.

Many practicals do not work, or incidents happen, where teachers (and others) fail to fully read, and act, on the information provided. Never go against the advice from CLEAPSS or SSERC, as they are the experts in practical safety, and your employer should not allow you (or instruct you to) do anything that CLEAPSS and SSERC state should not be done.

A classic example is the methane bubbles demonstration (CLEAPSS, 2021) which must never be done on pupils' hands (although a responsible pupil can light it). Despite this instruction in the model risk assessment being in place for many years, teachers do it because of the wow factor – it's a fairly simple experiment, they have done it for years and see no need to read the basic information around it. However, pupils have been injured doing this, and if you go against the guidance given and an incident happens, it may place you in a very difficult position. So, for any activity in your scheme of learning, take a check on the CLEAPSS or SSERC websites for any updates or changes. New practicals are being added all the time, many of which are far better, quicker (and often lower risk) than more classic practicals that have found their way into schemes of learning.

As part of your planning for an activity, you must know what to do if something goes wrong. You should not be hunting round for the information or rely on someone else knowing. For most hazards, particularly chemical and biological, information from Hazcards, or similar, can be extracted into requisitions, your planner notes, into the notes of your presentation – anywhere you can easily get to them.

Remember you need to consider how you will manage and instruct people on:

- Spillages and breakages (who cleans them up – ok for students or needs a member of staff?).
- Splashes of chemicals on skin/eyes/clothing.
- Any gases/dusts that might be produced.
- Control of 'tempting' substances and equipment; counting in and out; where the technician will put it (such as giving you a roll of magnesium ribbon to keep safe, rather than leaving it in a tray for students to have unfettered access).
- If eye protection is required, what type? (Safety spectacles or splash-resistant goggles; be precise and check the safety information on Hazcards or similar).
- With reagents, consider what you are making, not just what you are ordering (and also what students *could* make, if they mix things they shouldn't).
- How to dispose waste from the lesson.

HOW LONG WILL IT TAKE?

There is a general view that it will take pupils three times as long to do a practical activity as it does a teacher. While this is not always true, it does highlight that pupils do take longer, and class practicals can easily overrun or become rushed (Ofsted, 2013). By choosing what parts of the practical need to be done (as determined by your learning objectives), you can reduce the time spent on aspects which do not contribute directly to the learning. How the equipment is presented to pupils, linked to the layout of the lab and how good the directions for carrying out the activity, are crucial in making it work.

You may be able to support how long the activity takes by using homework or the lesson before to go through key steps in the practical. If you expect pupils to be familiar with a technique (such as using a microscope, setting up a standard electrical test circuit or heating a beaker over a Bunsen burner to use as a water bath) then you can use the pre-activity time to assess their understanding. If it turns out they are lacking depth in some skills, then you can reassess how you do the practical.

It is also important to indicate to pupils that packing up and clearing away a practical does not mean the end of the lesson; set expectations that there will be other activities that follow a practical. Remember that you need to allow time for the thinking and discussing parts of the activity; it should not just be about the doing. This must be factored in when deciding where the hands-on activity takes place.

LAYOUT OF THE LAB (OR CLASSROOM…) AND ITS IMPACT

Secondary school laboratories vary enormously in their size and layout; however, there are three main types:

- Linear rows of benches facing the front
- Clusters of benches to form groups
- Freestanding tables with fixed benches around the outside of the room

There are pros and cons of all designs, but you will rarely have choice about the overall layout of your lab. However, bear in mind that there are standards from the Department for Education on labs (DfE, 2004), which includes distances between benches. If you have moveable benches, it may be that in one layout there is plenty of space for pupils to work, but in others the change to layout means there is dangerously little space for pupils to work and move safely. Although not perfect, a good starting point is at least 1 metre of space between any desks where you expect pupils to work or walk – more if pupils sit back-to-back. If it is less than this, then you may have issues.

The main teaching position is often dictated by a whiteboard (interactive or standard) and a projector/computer. However, this should not limit where a teacher is, particularly during practical work. A remote computer clicker/pointer is exceptionally useful, allowing you to move around the room, while still controlling a computer presentation. In some labs, a second plain whiteboard can be fitted on a side wall, so that you have an alternative position to write/teach from, which can be valuable as part of behaviour management.

During practical work, a teacher should move around the room, partly to help, but also to observe. You will pick up comments from pupils about the practical work, and can ask challenging questions as you go, so that you ascertain the level of understanding pupils are gaining – remember they are learning and not just doing.

When pupils set up equipment, they may require access to gas taps or electric sockets. This may be away from where they normally sit, such as in labs with only services around the edge of the room. This will require care with how pupils move, as it may mean they are more crowded and possibly have their backs to you. You will need to be visible, moving around the room and take great care in ensuring pupils are on-task. Do not be afraid to cut a practical short if the conditions in terms of behaviour, time available or other safety concerns become apparent. You can always continue another time, or in a different format (such as a demonstration).

Lab spaces need to be as tidy as possible and the greater the clear bench area for pupils to work, the safer and easier it will be to manage. Avoid piles of books, unused equipment, and random plants; find space elsewhere for these. In addition to the controls mentioned in the previous chapter, labs should be provided with basic equipment and you need to find out where they are, how to operate them and who to report things to if they are missing/broken. Remember that pupils need training in some things as well, such as immediate remedial measures and these can usefully be taught and revisited during practical lessons. CLEAPSS (2020b) guide GL120 (*About Hazcards*) covers these measures and can be adapted for pupils. Please note that these are updated frequently. Pupil Safety Sheets are ideal to use with pupils so they can develop a better understanding of control of hazard and risk.

Key lab requirements are:

- Adequate ventilation (at least five air changes an hour); opening windows is in addition to this. Poor ventilation is a challenge in many labs.
- Emergency shut-off controls for gas and electric (and possibly water).
- Eye wash provision (ideally plumbed in, or rubber tube in a bag, marked with the eyewash symbol, to be attached to a tap. Eyewash bottles are not recommended).
- Firefighting equipment (extinguisher and blanket – see previous chapter).
- Appropriate eye protection (usually safety glasses, with class sets of goggles available on requisition when a risk assessment outcome requires them).
- Place to store coats and bags (to avoid trip hazards).
- Hand washing facilities (with liquid soap and paper towels).
- Basic spill kit (often cat litter or sand).
- Waste bin.
- Dustpan and brush for clearing up broken glass.
- Glass bin (for broken glass NOT sharps, such as needles).
- Viewing panels in doors kept clear (unless you need to temporarily darken a room).
- Being able to unlock a door from inside without a key being required (so you or a student cannot be locked inside).

HOW WILL PUPILS ACCESS THE EQUIPMENT REQUIRED?

How equipment is presented for pupils to use should be based on a combination of the ability and behaviour of the group, how complex the practical is, the layout of the teaching space and the amount of time technicians have to prepare. The most basic, and fraught with difficulty, are pupils helping themselves to equipment from trays or cupboards. Pupils may not be able to identify the equipment by name or translate a two-dimensional diagram into what they are looking for. You can help by including pictures of set-ups (of actual equipment from your trials), or by careful labelling of cupboards and trays.

Group or individual sets of equipment can be time-consuming for technicians to produce, but they can save a lot of time within the lesson. If each group has just one tray, with everything (or nearly everything) they required in it, then either one pupil per group can collect it, or you as the teacher can deliver one tray per group. The latter can help with behaviour management, as it avoids pupils being out of their seats; for some groups this can reduce the opportunity for unwanted interactions. Box 8.2 outlines how grouping can be used effectively within science lessons.

BOX 8.2   GROUPING FOR PRACTICAL LESSONS

Grouping pupils effectively is really important to have practical work go well - and not something that just happens (see Vignette 8.1 for Elliot's reflection on practical work during his school placement). There are many ways of organising groups, but simple random choices can be as simple as 'the person collecting the glassware is ...'

- The person whose birthday is next.
- The person who has the smallest hands.
- The person who takes the longest to get to school.
- The oldest/youngest student.

A halfway house may be to have trays of the reagents or basic equipment per table/ group, but still expect pupils to get more recognisable equipment, such as Bunsen burners and tripods out for themselves. Again, only having one person per group as the nominated 'equipment collector' (and you may do the nominating) can help with maintaining a sensible flow around the lab. If you are tight on space due to the size of your lab, then keeping movement to a minimum is important.

For some practicals, as mentioned earlier, it might be worth asking technicians to pre set-up the equipment. For example, the first time pupils use a microscope, it may be more appropriate to have them around the edge of a room, with slides set on, so pupils have limited manipulation to do and can concentrate say on drawing/describing what they see. For some younger pupils their manipulation skills and strength may be a limit to them carrying and safely handling equipment. Having complex equipment, like distillation, set up for a demonstration can save time, if appropriate to your learning objectives.

VIGNETTE 8.1   WHAT WENT WRONG IN PLACEMENT 1 FOR ELLIOT

Elliot had come onto his PGCE after working as an analytic chemist in industry for 10 years. He felt confident in relation to his approach to practical work having the work experience he did. He soon found out, however, that there was a significant difference between his own work in the lab and managing a class in one.

He was teaching a lesson which aimed to allow the pupils to differentiate between acids and alkalis. Although it appeared that the pupils had made progress and met the aims of the practical – as all had ended up with a completed table correctly identifying unknown solutions based on their use of universal indicator – when he talked through the lesson with his mentor, he reflected on the organisation of the practical and how the pupils tackled the task.

He found that the groups he had were too big at each station within the classroom and he hadn't given set times for them to move on, so the movement around the room was quite chaotic. After some thought during his mentor meeting, Elliot decided that he could have reduced the movement around the classroom by using the technician's expertise to set the practical up differently or by providing equipment collection stations around the room to minimise pupil movement.

Due to the time it took for the groups to get the equipment they required and gather a completed set of results, he dismissed the pupils from the lesson without any consolidation of what they have done or learned. Elliot then had to ensure that the learning from the practical was achieved during his next lesson with the group, and that he was not doing practical for the sake of it.

Activity: Consider the different ways in which Elliot could have organised this practical activity and what he could have done to ensure there was some consolidation or assessment of learning before the pupils left.

If items are tempting targets for theft (e.g. magnesium ribbon, alkali metals), or have higher associated risks (e.g. scalpels, dissecting scissors), then you might want to count these out and in. On your requisition, you may want to indicate where they will be left by the technician, such as on your teaching bench or in a cupboard. It is also worth double counting the number you have as technicians are very busy, and they may have miscounted. If you do not recount, then you might be chasing for a missing bit of equipment that does not exist and this can make pupil–teacher relations deteriorate if classes are held back for no reason, for example. However, if things do go missing, then it must be investigated and escalated to other staff, to the head of department or higher, and be seen as a serious offence by pupils.

You are likely to work during your career with pupils who may have limited mobility, such as being a wheelchair user, having broken an arm or having other SEND requirements (either temporary or permanent), which means that they cannot interact with a practical activity in a classic way. Here, you need to ensure that they can still engage with the lesson and meet the outcomes in a similar way to other students; any disability they have should not mean they are discriminated by not doing practical (see also Chapter 10). You might find that individual sets of equipment are useful in trays, so they can work sitting down; or you may use hot water from a kettle rather than using a Bunsen burner. It is worth considering them taking the same approach for the entire class, so everyone is doing the same activity. Experience shows that if you adapt a practical for a specific user's needs, it often works out far better for the entire class. CLEAPSS (2018) guide G077 has a lot of useful, specific information for science in both mainstream and special schools. Figure 8.2 shows a set-up for a microscale chemistry

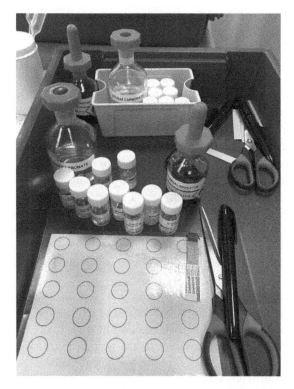

Figure 8.2 Microscale equipment which may support all pupils more effectively

experiment. The technician has set up all the equipment required in one tray and therefore may make it easier and more accessible for all pupils in the class.

Equipment will fail during a lesson, whether it's a power pack, bulbs, a blocked Bunsen or broken microscope. As technicians are very busy, they often do not have time to check equipment between lessons and your set of low-voltage supplies may be taken straight from your lesson into another. So if things don't work, then label them. A set of tie-on luggage tags with 'I am broken', or similar, can be very useful. For smaller items, have a 'poorly tray' in your lab, where things that have failed can go so the technicians can sort them out when they have time. If you suspect that a pupil has managed to contaminate a reagent even accidentally, put this to one side with a note on. This will help others in your department immensely and will be appreciated by technicians.

INSTRUCTIONS FOR PRACTICAL WORK

Instructions for practicals can be challenging for pupils to understand as following a worksheet, as a recipe, is not nearly as easy for many pupils as we might expect. Some pupils will find challenges with vocabulary, complex detail or insufficient key information. As a result, worksheet are often likely to need supplementing with direct instruction and this might include pictures or videos (possibly of your trial) to help them set up or use the equipment. However, avoid showing them what they expect to see happen. Integrated instruction worksheets are an excellent way to guide pupils through more complex steps of a practical and many schools have adopted these across lots of practicals, although often they do need tweaking to suit your activity or environment (see Chapter 5 and Chapter 10 for additional information about the use of integrated instructions).

You might want to focus on some questions before the practical, so it guides pupils to their observations. For example, with classic pondweed practicals, you might ask questions about photosynthesis so that pupils appreciate that oxygen is produced, then discussion around what would that look like on this plant in water... this moves the pupils towards looking for and then counting bubbles of gas (or measuring the volume). You might follow this up with a picture or video of a plant pearling bubbles of oxygen which they can then apply this to their practical. This is usually better than just asking pupils to take a measurement and helps them understand what that measurement is about.

Maths skills should be embedded within the practical where appropriate and can often be used to help pupils make sense of the practical. For example, if pupils will be expected to make a graph of data at the end of their experiment, then use sketch graphs (simple labelled axis with no numbers involved) to use for their hypothesis and have them talk through their graph so they demonstrate their understanding of what they have drawn. They can then compare and contrast their sketch graph to the one from their results (see Chapter 3 for further context around the use of maths in science).

Equations and conversions are frequently required in practical work and pupils should be challenged as they go through which might involve having a bank of questions available for you to use with pupils. It might be converting time from minutes to seconds, or cm^3 to dm^3; it may be having to rearrange a formula so they can process data. Choosing appropriate units, plotting tables and graphing can be supported by practical instructions, with differing levels of support being given if required. For example, blank tables may be appropriate for some pupils, for others, more information given. This adaptive approach allows pupils to be challenged and supported as you meet their individual needs.

VIGNETTE 8.2   HAVING THE CONFIDENCE TO STOP WHEN INSTRUCTIONS GO WRONG

When Lewis was on his final teaching placement of his training, his university tutor was coming in to observe his lesson – which, if all went to plan, would be the final sign off from that side of things. He was teaching a Year 9 class and looking at the effect of temperature on the reaction between amylase and starch, set up as a model gut using visking tubing and water baths. Lewis explained to the class what he wanted them to do, showed them all the pieces of equipment they needed and how to approach the task. He was nervous with having his university tutor there and as he walked around the room soon realised that the pupils were very confused, not clear as to what they were doing and how to do it. Panic set in; however, Lewis went to the front of the classroom and asked the whole class to stop – there were too many who were unclear on the process for individual interventions. He acknowledged to the class that his explanation and instructions were not as clear as they should have been and explained the method once again, this time using a diagram on the whiteboard to support, alongside a demonstration. The class then continued with the task and were able to get results successfully and without further intervention. Lewis finished the lesson with a summary of the work they had done that day, how it linked with their previous lessons and a short exam-style question for them to answer.

After the class left, his university tutor gave him feedback which Lewis anticipated being very negative. Both the tutor and Lewis acknowledged that there were problems with the first explanation. However, Lewis demonstrated that he was responsive to the needs of the pupils in his class, as he wasn't afraid to stop the lesson to provide a clearer explanation of what the pupils needed to do. They both felt that by doing this, he saved the lesson.

Activity: Consider how you will know if the lesson is not going as you planned and what you can do about this. What strategies could Lewis have used in the initial explanation to help prevent this taking place? How can you prepare a script for your explanations and instructions to make them as robust as possible?

CLEARING UP AND DISPOSAL

Disposal is the responsibility of the class teacher to work out, though in reality this is done with the technician team and should be planned in advance. Working out how things are returned to the technicians is very important – do they want things emptied out, or returned as is? It is essential that you establish what is to be done with contaminated equipment, such as after a dissection – is this to be fully dealt with by the technicians, or do pupils need to place all items in a suitable disinfectant, for example. Knowing what can be disposed of down the sink, put in the bin, neutralised or mixed is important. Waste pots can be very useful, labelled with what goes in them. Pupils will need clear instructions about how to dispose of materials from their activity which means that you also need to be clear on this. Technicians must not be faced with beakers of unknown materials as it is not their role to decipher what has been produced and how to get rid of it. Remember that many pupils will default to just putting everything down the sink or in the bin and so sharing information around disposal is key.

Other equipment, such as heat-resistant mats and Bunsen burners may be found permanently in a cupboard within the lab, so pupils will need to put these away. Ensuring this is done neatly is helpful and you can appoint pupils to take responsibility for a particular cupboard during that lesson, for example. Electrical equipment can be particularly challenging to put back neatly; this is where smaller group sets are useful, as each set can be quickly checked as they are brought back, rather than everything piled back onto a trolley. Figure 8.3 shows a neat and tidy way to help pupils identify how to pack equipment away. The instructions on the lid can easily be followed by anyone to ensure the correct equipment is stowed away safely.

Figure 8.3   Sets of electrical equipment to help manage resources

DEMONSTRATIONS

Demonstrations are an essential skill for science teachers to develop (Millar, 2004). Often a demonstration is exciting, engaging and can highlight phenomena, techniques or scientific principles that are challenging, unsafe, or too expensive to do as whole class activities.

Practise is key to ensuring that a demonstration works well, as well as planning when and how the demonstration will take place. Box 8.3 outlines some of the vital considerations for a demonstration to be successful.

BOX 8.3   CONSIDERATIONS FOR UNDERTAKING A DEMONSTRATION WITH A CLASS

- What is the learning objective for the demonstration?
- Where will the demonstration be set up: teacher bench, pupil bench, fume cupboard?
- How will pupils be grouped to view the demonstration? Do they need to move or is the demo easily seen from where they are (moving pupils usually involves disruption).
- Can the demonstration be recorded (so you can play it back and go through things) or projected via a webcam so everyone can see?
- If there is a lag while something happens, or you are setting up equipment, what will the pupils be doing? Are they working through questions or similar?
- Ensure you have enough 'teacher talk' and anecdotes to engage the pupils as the demonstration is working: a series of bullet point reminders can be useful. Talking through explanations and demonstrating simultaneously is something that requires practise.
- Don't forget to protect yourself as well as the pupils – so if safety screens are required, for example, they should protect everyone and not just on one side of an activity.
- Appropriate PPE (usually eye protection) will be required by all, but note that for some chemistry activities, for the demonstrator, full face protection (a face shield) may be required.
- Have an alternative or back-up ready in case it does not work. Don't lie to pupils if it doesn't go to plan, but be prepared to try again next lesson and be honest. A pre-recorded version of it (from your trial) might be useful to show instead.

ENQUIRY ACTIVITIES

Enquiry-based practical activities can be challenging to set up, but can work well to help pupils apply their scientific knowledge and understanding in a different context. True enquiry-based learning (in the sense of letting the pupils go and find out with little or no direct instruction) is not practised often in science, as it can have poor outcomes and is difficult to manage (Millar and Driver, 1987; Ofsted, 2021). Most scientific enquiry activities are more guided, but allow pupils more freedom to explore a topic, and can be particularly useful as an assessment activity as outlined in Box 8.4.

To enable pupils to carry out a more meaningful enquiry-based practical, pupils need both the substantive subject knowledge, and the practical apparatus and technique skills for them to be able to effectively tackle the question or problem set. If they try to learn the subject knowledge or have to develop new practical techniques, then they are unlikely to make progress (Ofsted, 2021).

It may be possible to set basic practical activities for homework; but bear in mind both access to even simple equipment (as not to disadvantage pupils) and the health and safety implications. However, some activities are fairly broad, such as sending pupils home with different coloured filters to look through different lamps (LED, incandescent, fluorescent, sodium) and report back their findings can be a useful starter to a discussion. Alternatively, some practicals can be done at home as an extension, or even if remote teaching is required, such as simple chromatography or environmental surveys.

BOX 8.4   EXAMPLE OF ENQUIRY AS AN ASSESSMENT

An example would be in physics, where pupils have carried out specific heat capacity practicals and calculations, then setting pupils a challenge of 'What is the power of a candle?' Pupils would be given access to a range of equipment and asked to work out the power of a small tea light candle. It would enable them to demonstrate they could apply a previous practical technique, but then they would have to use their scientific understanding, and mathematical equations, to be able to calculate an answer. They would generate an answer to which also the teacher is unlikely to know the 'correct' value (so pupils can't go 'is this right?') but can challenge pupils to justify if it seems sensible – and how effective the practical is.

In reality, this activity allows the teacher to spot pupils who are struggling with application, or are making fundamental mistakes, such as using decimal minutes in power calculations, rather than converting their stopwatch values to second. Help cards might be used on demand, such as with the equations on, to support pupils – this can provide scaffolding for those who require it.

Practical work, although an integral part of science teaching, is not an easy option. It is worthy of time invested in the planning and preparation stages to get it right from an organisational and learning perspective. In doing so the pupils will get more from it, your teaching will be more effective and it will enable greater progress in terms of learning. As already mentioned, the mantra to maintain is 'hands-on and minds-on' and this should enable you to develop further as a science teacher.

WHAT TO LOOK FOR WHEN OBSERVING LESSONS

- Ask the pupils questions about why they are doing the practical, and its purpose. Their responses may help you shape how you present future practical work.
- How do the teachers organise equipment for different classes and different rooms?
- Can you identify the learning objectives for the practical activity and how are these assessed?

SUMMARY

Now you have read this chapter you should have:

- An understanding of the need for practical work having a clear purpose and learning objective(s).
- Realised the multiple elements to consider when organising practical equipment and resources for the pupils.
- Furthered your knowledge of how to work safely and manage groups undertaking practical work.

REFLECTIVE QUESTIONS

- Think about practical work you remember from school – do you remember the practical or the learning from it? Think about why this is.
- As you plan your practical work can you identify where the pupils are developing their substantive *and* disciplinary knowledge?
- What considerations do you need to make before a practical lesson rather than a non-practical one? How will you manage the pupils effectively in both situations?

FURTHER READING

This is an excellent guide to the wide variety of physics equipment in schools, which differs much more considerably than typical chemistry or biology apparatus. It provides support for both physicists and those teaching physics who come from another background and includes typical practical uses and fault-finding. Many references are to the Scottish curriculum, but the majority of practicals are common across the UK: SSERC (nd). *Guide to practical physics.* Available at: www.sserc.org.uk/wpcontent/uploads/2017/07/Practical_physics_guide.pdf

This is essential reading for all science teachers, as it lays out the key stages for planning practical work and how to control hazards appropriately. It includes a very useful list of practicals that require extra care. Following this guide and the guidance in this chapter, will help ensure your practicals are high quality and effective: CLEAPSS (2020). *G030: Successful Science Practicals.* Available at: http://science.cleapss.org.uk/resource/g030-successful-science-practicals.pdf

This resource page collates the research and guides that exemplify the 10 practical science benchmarks, with useful resources to support your areas of development, particularly Good Practical Science Benchmarks 1, 2 and 7. Available at: www.stem.org.uk/good-practical-science

BIBLIOGRAPHY

Abrahams, I. and Millar, R. (2008). Does practical work really work? A study of the effectiveness of practical work as a teaching and learning method in school science. *International Journal of Science Education*, 30(14): 1945–1969.
CLEAPSS (nd). [online] Available: www.cleapss.org.uk/
CLEAPSS (2016). *PP027 Making copper sulfate crystals from copper(II) oxide.* Uxbridge: CLEAPSS.
CLEAPSS (2017). *PS090 Managing and recording risk assessments in school science.* Uxbridge: CLEAPSS.
CLEAPSS (2018). *G077 Science for secondary-aged pupils with Special Educational Needs and Disability (SEND).* Uxbridge: CLEAPSS.
CLEAPSS (2019). *SRA001 The howling/screaming jelly baby: Reacting a 'jelly baby' with molten potassium chlorate.* Uxbridge: CLEAPSS.
CLEAPSS (2020a). *G030 Successful science practicals.* Uxbridge: CLEAPSS.
CLEAPSS (2020b). *GL120 About Hazcards (2020 Edition).* Uxbridge: CLEAPSS.
CLEAPSS (2021). *SRA003 Igniting floating bubbles filled with methane (methane bubbles demo).* Uxbridge: CLEAPSS.
DfE (2004) Science accommodation in secondary schools: A design guide [online]. Available at: http://science.cleapss.org.uk/Resource/Building-Bulletin-80.pdf
Health and Safety at Work, etc. Act (HASAWA) 1974. Chapter 37. UK: The Stationery Office.
Holman, J. (2017). *Good practical science.* Gatsby Charitable Foundation. Available at: www.gatsby.org.uk/education/programmes/support-for-practical-science-in-schools

Institute of Physics (2021). Investigating the resistance of wires [online]. Available at: https://spark.iop.org/investigating-resistance-wires#gref

Millar, R. (2004). *The role of practical work in the teaching and learning of science*. High school science laboratories: Role and vision, Washington DC: National Academy of Sciences

Millar, R. and Driver, R. (1987). Beyond processes. *Studies in Science Education*, 14(1): 33–62.

Millar, R., Tiberghien, A. and Maréchal, J.-F. Le (2002). Varieties of labwork: A way of profiling labwork tasks. In D. Psillos and H. Niedderer (Eds), *Teaching and learning in the science laboratory* (pp. 9–20). Dordrecht: Kluwer Academic Publishers.

Ofsted (2013). Science education in schools: Maintaining curiosity [online]. Available at: www.gov.uk/government/publications/maintaining-curiosity-a-survey-into-science-education-in-schools.

Ofsted (2021). Research review series: science [online]. Available at: www.gov.uk/government/publications/research-review-series-science

Royal Society of Chemistry (2016). Displacement reactions between metals and their salts [online]. Available at: edu.rsc.org/experiments/displacement-reactions-between-metals-and-their-salts/720.article

SSERC (nd). [online]. Available at: www.sserc.org.uk/

Woolnough, B. (1995). School effectiveness for different types of potential scientists and engineers. *Research in Science & Technological Education*, 13(1): 53–66.

9
TEACHING TRICKY TOPICS AND ABSTRACT CONCEPTS

RANIA MAKLAD AND MICK DUNNE

CHAPTER OVERVIEW

This chapter will develop student teachers' knowledge and understanding of the importance of simplifying tricky topics and abstract concepts in Key Stage 3/4 science by using analogy, visualisation, metaphors, similes, and models to help them teach effectively. We will identify and examine the value of innovative pedagogic methods such as the use of games as means of accessing challenging aspects of science content. You will be encouraged to understand the limitations of these strategies in teaching science and addressing challenging concepts. The chapter will also identify, examine, and analyse relevant theoretical frameworks such as cognitive load theory and pedagogical content knowledge in terms of understanding the nature of an effective pedagogy.

LINKS TO ITT CORE CONTENT FRAMEWORK AND EARLY CAREER FRAMEWORK

This chapter supports development of:

- Standard 2 – promote good progress
- Standard 4 – plan and teach well-structured lessons
- Standard 5 – adapt teaching
- Standard 6 – make accurate and productive use of assessment

INTRODUCTION

What is 'tricky science'? Responses to this question might be: 'It's all tricky' to 'Isn't most of science tricky?' to 'I've always found a specific topic, idea, concept or theory tricky'. There is no consensus about what defines tricky science and you will have your own ideas; however, we believe some of the trickiest aspects of science relates to content that is fundamentally abstract in nature. Abstract concepts such as particle theory, charge, potential difference, protein synthesis and meiosis are complicated elements of science teaching and learning and demand an appropriate subject-specific pedagogy if they are to be taught well.

Learners of any science topic commonly demonstrate misconceptions of scientific ideas, often exiting science lessons having misunderstandings and misinterpreting some of what they were expected to learn (Driver, 1983; Taber, 2014); carrying misconceptions applies to teachers as well as learners (Taber and Tan, 2011). Identifying and tackling misconceptions, often tightly held by learners, adds to the trickiness of science teaching (see Chapter 3).

Another significant aspect of tricky science relates to scale, both at the macro and micro level. Science content of this nature has inherent difficulty and can be described, as seen in Chapters 3 and 5, based on cognitive load theory (Sweller, 1998, 2011), as having intrinsic cognitive load (this will be discussed in more detail later in this chapter).

Teaching science can be a multifaceted adventure and often unexpected things emerge regardless of all the careful planning that has been done. This chapter will provide you with both scientific and science-specific pedagogical information, resources and strategies as presented in the Early Career Framework (ECF) (DfE, 2019) that will support you in the teaching and learning of secondary science and help you manage some of the more challenging aspects of this fascinating subject. However, it is you that will choose the best approach for you and your pupils to simplify tricky topics and make them easier to understand while rectifying misconceptions.

WHAT MAKES TRICKY, TRICKY?

Science teaching is such a complex, dynamic profession that it is difficult for a teacher to stay up to date. For a teacher to grow professionally and become better as a teacher of science, a special, continuous effort is required (Showalter, 1984).

However we choose to teach any aspect of tricky science, language use and choice will be a critical consideration. Vocabulary must be accessible (age and ability appropriate) and contribute to developing scientific knowledge and understanding. Historically, scientists and teachers of science have, and continue to, use examples of commonly experienced everyday life to aid scientific understanding. To help pupils access and develop their knowledge and understanding of science concepts we often resort to using heuristic tools typically based on employing different types of comparisons. Such comparisons aid communication and are usually recognisable to the learner and often help them make better sense of the science we are teaching. These comparisons act as forms of cognitive scaffolding (we will return to this later), and even if we are not aware of their fundamental identity, typically involve employing similes, metaphors, verbal analogies and analogous models.

These comparators are not without their own limitations and although many teachers have a suite of favourites that they draw on there is no one perfect comparator. You may work with pupils from inner city schools that have never seen a field (a word often used when discussing gravity and magnetism). Can all pupils make sense of the solar system working like clockwork in this predominantly digital world? The rope model for teaching simple circuits or a zipped pencil case modelling a variable resistor, are most definitely imperfect, yet few would deny that they have value.

We now turn to a specific consideration of several comparators that help when teaching tricky science, beginning with examining the value of similes and their use in science teaching. Throughout the ECF (DfE, 2019), the need to make the learning accessible to all pupils is emphasised from different teaching and learning angles. For example, strong subject and pedagogical knowledge is highlighted (Standard 3) to motivate children and help them master foundation concepts and anticipate misconceptions. On the other hand, in Standard 4, the focus is shifted towards well-planned lessons, practical work, grouping of children and high-quality classroom talk. The following are examples of how to incorporate different teaching styles to make tricky topics accessible to young minds.

SIMILES

Similes are figures of speech. They make comparisons between two different things at the simplest of levels to make something more vivid and clearly understood. Whenever we say 'like a …' or 'as a …' we are probably using one type of simile. There are many examples of similes that are commonly used across the secondary age phase as identified in Box 9.1.

> ## BOX 9.1   EXAMPLES OF COMMONLY USED SIMILES IN SECONDARY SCIENCE
>
> - The heart is like a pump
> - The brain is like a computer
> - The eye is like a camera
> - The solar system works like clockwork
> - Electricity flows like water
> - A habitat is like a home
> - Particles are like the very smallest 'bits'
> - The sun is like a huge ball of burning gas

Think about how many times you have heard or used a simile in science – quite often we are not even aware of our use of them. Their effectiveness is in enabling pupils to visualise a scientific concept or idea through contrasting it with something else that is much more familiar to them. Similes can promote misconceptions and misunderstandings. For example, is the sun really a huge ball of burning gas? We now move to the value of metaphors – a more sophisticated comparator.

METAPHORS

It would be unusual if you were actually aware of how often you use metaphors in your teaching. Metaphors are words or phrases that are applied to objects or actions. They are not literally applicable but allow pupils to make concrete connections between abstract concepts and everyday knowledge and experience (Taylor and Dewsbury, 2018). Box 9.2 provides a range of examples, some of which you will be familiar with.

> ## BOX 9.2   COMMONLY USED METAPHORS TO SUPPORT SECONDARY SCIENCE TEACHING AND LEARNING
>
> - A circuit is a continuous path or track
> - The battery has died (or has gone flat)
> - Feeding relationships can be seen in food chains
> - The greenhouse effect is a big problem
> - A compass is sensitive to the Earth's magnetic field
> - The tree of evolution
> - The atom is like a tiny solar system

Like similes, they are making comparisons, but they may *not* be always helpful. For example, does a battery really die? Is the Earth really a greenhouse? Literal interpretation of both similes and metaphors can add to already established misconceptions and misunderstanding – is a cell (science concept) really a factory (metaphor)? What you may notice is the overlap between similes and metaphors – all similes are metaphors but not all metaphors are similes. While both can be helpful, they are not without problems. So long as you recognise this and act to ensure no lasting misunderstanding, they can help support science learning. Analogies can be very useful to aid learners in making sense of challenging aspects of science – this is what we consider next.

ANALOGIES AND ANALOGOUS MODELS

Think of an analogy like a word model that helps make an explanatory point through analogical thought. Metaphors and similes can be used to make an analogy. For example, electricity is like water and the heart is like a pump – yes, these link back to similes and metaphor, the key difference being how an analogy is used to make an instructive and illuminating point.

Analogous models are important in assisting you to help learners make sense of some aspects of science. Their value lies in how such physical models enlighten the learner by providing some insight into the associated idea (the world is flat) or concept (a kinetic energy model being used to illustrate that when molecules gain energy, they move faster and occupy more space). The following vignette exemplifies the use of one analogous model and how this model can be developed.

VIGNETTE 9.1   STUDENT TEACHERS AND MODELLING A BULB

PGCE secondary science students were asked to connect a simple filament (incandescent) bulb to a 1.5V cell using a single piece of aluminium foil - neither the cell nor bulb were in holders. Out of sixteen students only one was able to do this, the rest were genuinely flummoxed.

They were then shown an analogous model of a filament bulb (see Figures 9.1 and 9.2) that resulted in the success shown in Figure 9.3.

One student bravely traced the routes an electric current might take, orally describing to her peers what they were doing. She explained electricity may enter the bulb through the metal cap at the base, flow through the filament and then out through the shiny screw cap. She asked if it mattered whether the electricity travelled in the opposite direction and immediately answered her own

(Continued)

question by stating it made no difference whether it entered the bulb through the base or the side.

Figure 9.1   This shows the outside of a filament bulb

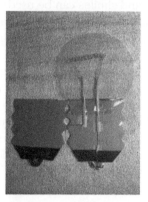

Figure 9.2   This shows the inside of the filament bulb. Importantly the student was able to trace with her finger the path electricity could take inside the bulb

Figure 9.3   The analogous model helped all students to complete the task successfully

This model was then used alongside a model cell and model wires to build other circuits of increasing complexity (Figures 9.4, 9.5 and 9.6 show some examples). It supported students' explanations of the differences between series and parallel circuits including an introduction to Kirchhoff's First and Second Laws. The use of these analogous models facilitated novel exploration of both Electron Flow Theory and Conventional Current Theory.

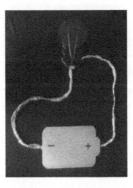

Figure 9.4

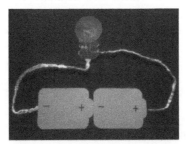

Figure 9.5

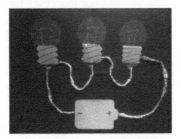

Figure 9.6

(Continued)

> **Activity:** Consider the following questions in relation to the model: Was this model analogous? Was it a reasonably accurate representation of the science being focused on? Did it, combined with analogical thought, provide a way to access information, primarily explanative in nature, that would have otherwise been difficult? Did it support personalised and wider learning? Does it have any weaknesses? Could you (would you?) use it?

DRAMA

The last specific method of visualisation we will discuss is drama – a pedagogic tool you will find particularly valuable in tackling tricky science concepts. Unfortunately, science can be perceived by some as the poor relative or even antithesis of creativity, clearly something we authors take exception to (see Robinson, 2017 for a thought-provoking discussion about this very subject). Direct, personalised, sensory engagement through the process of visualisation when learners mime, role play or hot seat, will support individualised and collective cognitive and procedural development of science (Taber, 2018). Additionally, we strongly believe this creative medium has the potential to promote affective development, greater learner-centred decision making and dialogic engagement as a social endeavour. Drama requires soft transferable skills (listening, communication …) and is fundamentally a collaborative venture. The cognitive benefits of participating in groupwork have been clearly identified (Love et al., 2014; Mercer et al., 2019). Effective use of drama has the capacity to support you in communicating abstract aspects of science through a variety of associated techniques (see Table 9.1). Most frequently in science, drama is used to model and recreate real-life situations.

Table 9.1   Different drama techniques and their use

Drama Technique/Teaching Strategy	Purpose
On the table	Pupils apply their senses to develop their observational skills and questioning skills to explore unusual objects located on a table or bench, perhaps in a display.
Spontaneous role play	In small groups, the pupils are placed in various situations and must take on varied roles to discuss contrasting views.
Hot seating	Someone is placed in an expert role and answers questions devised by the rest of the class.

(Continued)

Drama Technique/Teaching Strategy	Purpose
Miming Movies	Visual and auditory information is used to convey a different location or time in which the pupils must consider the consequences of happenings or events.
Miming Movement	Miming what it would be like to be something or to have something happening to them.
Freeze Frame	In acting out ideas they are asked to stop and explain their enactment and interpretations of it.
Modelling	Acting out what an object is or how something works.
Acting out mini-historical plays	Enacting aspects of scientists' lives e.g. Galileo Galilei - a 'college' drop out, a great observational scientist who was excommunicated from the church for his scientific beliefs, sentenced to life imprisonment and who spent the last years of his life under house arrest.

(Adapted from: McGregor and Precious, 2014: 35)

Think about the cognitive challenge of learning about state of matter, kinetic theory, some of the processes of physical change and chemical change, movement of thermal energy through a conductor, relative movements of earth, sun and moon and centripetal force… Role play can substantially contribute to aiding pupils' knowledge and understanding of these aspects of science so long as it is effectively planned and limitations are identified (Dorion, 2009). Acting out mini-historical events often focuses on the work of Curie, Darwin, Archimedes, Anning, Galileo, Newton, Goodall, Linnaeus, Ibn Sina (also known as Avicenna) or Crick. This can be very effective, and detailed paper-based and online research by pupils will be needed to 'bring them alive' through the media of drama; but mindfulness is needed about the potential of contributing to stereotyping scientists through cultural or gender bias.

Hot seating is a drama technique that we believe is not often used in secondary education, probably due to a combination of reasons based on a lack of pedagogical skill, a belief that it is time-consuming and the limited nature of pupil involvement. Green (2016: 45–46) provides examples of a form of hot seating referred to as 'Ask the Expert'. Pupils or teachers can be in the hot seat. Hot seating has resonance with a flipped learning as questions posed to the expert are not randomly thought of but based on systematic and informed background preparation. This drama technique can be used to develop thought experiment skills. Imagine the learning to be gained from interrogating any of the following in the hot seat – a seed, light, insulin, Covid-19 virus, a potassium atom, a parasite, or a water molecule. Similarly, the person in the hot seat could be pronuclear energy, genetic engineering or a developer wanting to build in a conservation area. This section began by stating hot seating was little used to support secondary science however, this is hard to reconcile given such a drama-based pedagogical approach (Villanueva Baselga et al., 2020) is novel, creative, active, personal, social, informed and has the potential to promote deeper levels of science learning. What we do with hot seating is a key to its success. Making sure that everyone knows why we are doing it and what is expected from the activity. This way everyone knows what they need to do, whether it is to ask specific, targeted questions or give well-developed and useful answers.

GAMES

It would be remiss not to recognise that other pedagogical tools can be used to support the teaching of tricky aspects of science.

Games have been designed to teach evolution, climate, cytosis, photosynthesis, intermolecular forces, bond breaker and Boyle's law, to identify just a few – it is easy to underestimate their value in supporting pupils' learning. *Angry Birds* and *Minecraft* are two well-known commercial games that are used to support scientific areas of learning such as aspects of environmental science, ecology, force, and movement. Games take a variety of forms: simulation; role play; case studies; quizzes; card games; and board games. Their value lies in them having an explicit goal, being interactive, the need to follow rules, their uncertainty (the roll of a dice, picking a card and so on), the necessity of having a plan/strategy, a fun experience and that they act as a 'hook' even for the more reluctant pupil (Turner, 2021a, 2021b). The CREST Awards (Taber and Cole, 2010) and the Institute of Engineering and Technology's (IET) Lego and Faraday Challenges are well-known examples of where gamification encourages active engagement with STEM-based activities.

Novel approaches such as gamification, which uses an aspect of a game to support educational gain, can be transformative for some learners and result in a positive shift in attitude towards science. As with any effort to utilise novel approaches to teaching and learning, much depends on the teacher and their 'expert' knowledge and understanding of science, science-specific pedagogy, and their pupils; this is what we now turn to consider.

PRACTICE–THEORY OR THEORY–PRACTICE

A central theme of this book is the relationship between theory and practice and so now we turn to some theoretical considerations. Despite the commitment and hard work of many teacher educators, many teachers perceive practice as being separate from theory. When first setting out on the journey to become a science teacher the significance of educational theory is often undervalued by many trainees as they prioritise developing pedagogic skills (planning, assessment, identifying useful resources and so on) and focus on developing specific aspects of subject knowledge. This is understandable but what any experienced teacher will tell you is that theory has a place and often helps to explain aspects of practice. Examples include why a dependable lesson that *always* works failed to work on a particular occasion, the pros and cons of group work, the value of dialogic engagement or why pupil X's home life is adversely affecting her schoolwork (Fung and Lui, 2016). However, acceptance of any theory remains the responsibility of the individual, i.e. you. We use this chapter to explicitly identify specific theoretical perspectives that we believe will be helpful to you. Knowledge of these theoretical frameworks can help explain the value and effectiveness of the approaches we are advocating.

PEDAGOGICAL CONTENT KNOWLEDGE

Pedagogical Content Knowledge (PCK) is a theoretical but useful way to conceptualise a teacher's professional knowledge and this section builds on what you have read in Chapter 3. Student teachers arrive on an ITT course with some relevant knowledge and understanding – this can be conceptualised as your existing PCK.

Further development of PCK will start at teacher education level and continue to develop through experience. Cycles of teaching, planning, classroom practice, assessment, evaluation and exploration of subject knowledge in the context of educational settings are important elements for PCK development. Continuous professional development (CPD) is also necessary for updating scientific knowledge and improving PCK, it provides resources and materials to support learning, and keeps teachers up to date with contemporary examples, applications and subtle shifts in scientific understanding.

When teaching any aspect of science, teachers draw on their knowledge and understanding of science, science-specific and general pedagogy as well as what they know about the target audience. Subject knowledge (ideas, facts, concepts, theories, laws and general principles) is referred to as CK (Content Knowledge – see Ball et al., (2008)) and how the teacher teaches is based on their PCK (Shulman, 1986, 1987). It is their PCK that determines the level of accessibility to the science being taught. PCK recognises misconceptions, represents their existing repertoire of lab/classroom-based praxis, likely to be underpinned by cognisance of relevant theory, and acknowledges the variability of pupils' needs; both competencies have a direct impact on ensuring pupils' progress. It is important to note that there are many different representations of teacher knowledge identified in research literature, but the authors believe limiting this to the concepts of CK and PCK is particularly helpful in terms of the focus of this chapter.

As mentioned above, CK and PCK exist in even the most naïve teacher, although it is quite likely that CK develops before PCK. Such a person will know science to a certain level, and have ideas (at this stage they are probably somewhat undeveloped and unsophisticated) about how it can or should be taught. Pre- and in-service courses, collaborative work with colleagues, personalised critical reflections of their own teaching, and self-determined learning, build on and refine both an individual's science knowledge base and their developing pedagogy, both general and subject specific. Aspects of a science teacher's PCK would include knowledge of specific misconceptions, how these can be elicited, how best to tackle them, and how to plan, organise, deliver effective practical work, best AfL (Assessment for Learning) practice and so on. Most teachers will agree that this continues unabated long after they gained QTS. So how does knowing about PCK and CK relate to teaching tricky aspects of science?

Teaching tricky science topics requires educators to have strong PCK, which requires the application of a teachers' developing cognitive ability to combine both subject and pedagogical knowledge (Kind, 2009). Lack of subject knowledge and subject-specific pedagogical knowledge, even in highly skilled teachers, can only lead to inability to form specialist PCK on a strong pedagogic foundation.

We recognise that not everyone will like the idea of utilising drama, games, poetry and analogies into their teaching, but those that do so, whether successfully or not, actively engage in the development of primarily their PCK. Green (2016) argues that dance, rap, silent debates, games and songs can be effective in supporting science teaching – we strongly believe such approaches can have a strength in supporting learners tackling some of the more challenging aspects of secondary science. However, in a world driven by outcomes this may require the teacher to move into aspects of pedagogy hitherto not experienced and perhaps perceived as not desirable – too much focus on process etc. It may require a degree of professional but creative subversion (see Kauper and Jacobs, 2019 for more information about this unexpected aspect of teacher professional competence) if deviation from existing custom and practice is frowned on! Having discussed PCK and CK, we need to analyse the use of some of the tools identified above, e.g. drama, analogies, in a little more detail.

Very early we identify scaffolding, a theory first introduced by Jerome Bruner in the 1950s, in the context of supporting pupils. The use of analogies, metaphors etc. provides an instructional scaffolding to enable the pupils improved access to scientific information. This has strong associations with Vygotsky's Zone of Proximal Development (ZPD) (Vygotsky, 1978). A scaffolding method such as the use of analogous models, e.g. a globe, or the use of role play, identified by a more knowledgeable other (the teacher), is used to enable the pupil to move from their existing knowledge and understanding or skill level to an improved learning position that must be within their ZPD. Sounds simple, but the reality is more complex than this.

The teacher must take cognisance of the pupils' social and cultural contexts in identifying what will be an appropriate metaphor, for example. The cognitive challenge must be recognised – progress needs to be in manageable steps. If the distance (i.e. challenge) to be travelled is too great, beyond the pupil's capacity (it extends beyond their ZPD), then it is very unlikely pupils will achieve the identified learning; from their point of view this bit of science would be perceived as being 'much too hard' to learn.

Equally important is not to judge the ZPD being so small that there is minimal intellectual test – it is perceived as being 'far too easy'; under such circumstances it may be that the 'more knowledgeable other' is not needed. ZPD can be conceptualised as that learning that is within the learner's supported capabilities – they cannot yet achieve this independently. So pitch is a critical consideration here, as is scaffolding, perhaps using the most appropriate metaphor, analogy, physical model etc.

Equally important is the teacher's knowledge of prior learning experienced by pupils; their prior science knowledge, understanding and past learning experiences are significant additional influencing factors. Combine these with the teacher's existing CK and PCK (see above) and only then can an informed judgement be made about the identity of the best instructional scaffolding to use. Furthermore, knowing that not all pupils learn in the same way requires the teacher to draw on additional contrasting relevant scaffolding methods. See Figure 9.7 which shows how a teacher's PCK, informed by such things as knowledge of the subject focus, of associated misconceptions, of the pupils themselves etc., is used to identify the most effective pedagogical approach to support their learning journey such as suitable methods of demonstration and practical activities to support mind-on learning. This diagrammatic representation accurately reflects an overview of process you experience when planning any learning event for your pupils.

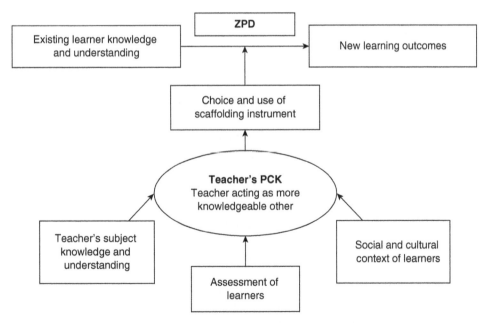

Figure 9.7   Showing how a teacher's PCK influences effective learning (M. Dunne)

The use of technology in science education has seen consistent, gradual growth for several decades. Technology is used in labs, field trips, hands-on activities, and data collection exercises. In Hennessy et al. (2007: 137), technology was praised in the way it moved children from using 'real experiments' to hypothetical 'what if' explorations and 'virtual tests' that offer immediate access to outcomes – still with strong teacher presence to rectify any cognitive conflicts and bridge the gap between scientific and informal knowledge.

With the significant changes made necessary by the Covid-19 pandemic, technology has supported the move from a face-to-face collaborative approach to a distant/online autonomous form. Online resources, to back a new form of science education, are on the increase with third parties starting to provide resources that support distant teaching and learning of the science subjects on multiple levels. BBC Bitesize has produced different resources to support children learning at home during Covid-19. The resources are aimed at parents as well as teachers and include interactive games, worksheets and curriculum-mapped video resources. The Association for Science Education (ASE) has also provided resources to support science teachers through this unprecedented time. It provided challenges to engage children and teachers alike as well as up-to-date reading materials, remote learning resources in addition to its regular journal publications. STEM Learning added a community app to its resources and a recovery programme to its normal resources. WOWSCIENCE, Pearson, the Wellcome Trust's Explorify are all providing similar services to science teachers, parents and learners.

WHAT TO LOOK FOR WHEN OBSERVING LESSONS

- How are teachers using models to support the pupils' learning?
- What similes, analogies and metaphors can you identify within a lesson?
- Can you identify opportunities where 'arts-based' approaches are or could be used within the science lessons you observe?

SUMMARY

Now you have read this chapter you should have:

- Identified some of the generic characteristics of what makes secondary science tricky including some examples.
- Focused strongly on concepts that are abstract in nature; but tricky science extends beyond this as with issues associated with scale.
- Realised that language is a critical tool in supporting the development of scientific knowledge and understanding.

- Recognised that engaging learners' affective qualities as through role-play, hot seating, modelling, etc. will not only aid cognitive development and support personalised meaning making but is likely to make the learning experience more memorable.

REFLECTIVE QUESTIONS

- The majority of our ITT students enthusiastically engage with centre-based drama activities and yet appear reluctant to use them during school-based training. Any thoughts about why this might be? Is it due to their lack of pedagogic skill and understanding? Is it too time costly? Is it linked to a lack of professional confidence? Could it be that many of our schools/science departments do not recognise the value of drama in teaching and learning science?
- Referring to Vygotsky's ZPD, how familiar are you with his ideas and theory? Can you identify connections to Piaget's levels of cognitive development when teaching any science topic?

FURTHER READING

Villanueva Baselga et al. (2020) highlight the value of arts-based approaches being used to support and enrich the teaching of secondary science and STEM education in general. The authors offer pragmatic ideas about how science content can be incorporated into drama-based activities that can be used to support even the trickiest aspects of science knowledge and understanding: Villanueva Baselga, S., Marimon Garrido, O. and González Burón, H. (2020). Drama-based activities for STEM education: Encouraging scientific aspirations and debunking stereotypes in secondary school students in Spain and the UK. *Research in Science Education*, doi: https://doi.org/10.1007/s11165-020-09939-5.

Keith Taber offers an important read for any teacher of secondary science. This publication identifies many of the issues faced by teacher and learner and those techniques that can be employed to overcome these challenges: Taber, K. S. (2019). *Masterclass in science education: Transforming teaching and learning*. London: Bloomsbury Academic.

Catrin Green's (2016) book is a very accessible tome offering wide-ranging guidance to the teaching of science. One of the things she highlights is the need to make this demanding subject memorable but for the right reasons: Green, C. (2016). *How to teach secondary science*. London: Independent Thinking Press.

BIBLIOGRAPHY

Ball, D.L., Thames, M.H. and Phelps, G. (2008). Content knowledge for teaching: What makes it special? *Journal of Teacher Education*, 59(5): 389–407.

Chandler. P. and Sweller, J. (1991). Cognitive load theory and the format of instruction. *Cognition and Instruction*, 8(4): 293–332.

Department for Education (2019). *Early Career Framework*. London.

Dorion, K.R. (2009). Science through drama: A multiple case exploration of the characteristics of drama activities used in secondary science lessons. *International Journal of Science Education*, 31(16): 2247–2270.

Driver, R. (1983) *The pupil as scientist?* Milton Keynes, UK: Open University Press.

Fung, D. and Lui, W.-M. (2016). Individual to collaborative: Guided group work and the role of teachers in junior secondary science classrooms. *International Journal of Science Education*, 38(7): 1057–1076.

Green, C. (2016). *How to teach secondary science*. Carmarthenshire: Independent Thinking Press.

Hennessy, S., Wishart, J., Whitelock, D., Deaney, R., Brawn, R., la Velle, L., McFarlane, A., Ruthven, K. and Winterbottom, M. (2007). Pedagogical approaches for technology-integrated science teaching. *Computers & Education*, 48(1): 137–152.

Kauper, K. and Jacobs, M.M. (2019). The case for slow curriculum: Creative subversion and the curriculum mind. In C. A Mullen (Ed.), *Creativity under duress in education?: Resistive theories, practices, and actions* (pp. 339–360). New York: Springer.

Kind, V. (2009). Pedagogical content knowledge in science education: Perspectives and potential for progress. *Studies in Science Education*, 45(2): 169–204.

Love, A.G., Dietrich, A., Fitzgerald, J. and Gordon, D. (2014). Integrating collaborative learning inside and outside the classroom. *Journal on Excellence in College Teaching*, 25(3&4): 177–196.

McGregor, D. and Precious, W. (2014). *Dramatic science: Inspired ideas for teaching science using drama ages 5–11*. London: Routledge.

Mercer, N., Hennessy, S. and Warwick, P. (2019). Dialogue, thinking together and digital technology in the classroom: Some educational implications of a continuing line of inquiry. *International Journal of Educational Research*, 97: 187–199.

Renkl, A. and Atkinson, R. (2003). Structuring the transition from example study to problem solving in cognitive skill acquisition: A cognitive load perspective. *Educational Psychologist*, 38(1): 15–22.

Robinson, K. (2017). *Out of our minds: The power of being creative*. Chichester: John Wiley and Sons.

Showalter, V.M., 1984. *Conditions for good science teaching*. National Science Teachers Association, 1742 Connecticut Ave., NW, Washington, DC 20009.

Shulman, L.S. (1986) Those who understand: Knowledge growth in teaching. *Educational Researcher* 15(2): 4–14

Shulman, L.S. (1987). Knowledge and teaching: Foundations of the new reform. *Harvard Educational Review* 57(1): 1–22

Sweller, J. (1998). Cognitive load during problem solving: Effects on learning. *Cognitive Science*, 12(2): 257–285.

Sweller, J. (2011). Cognitive load theory. *Psychology of Learning and Motivation*, 55: 37–76.

Taber, K.S. (2014). *Student thinking and learning in science: Perspectives on the nature and development of learners' ideas*. Routledge: London.

Taber, K.S. (2018). Representations and visualisation in teaching and learning chemistry. *Chemistry Education Research and Practice*, 19(2): 405–409.

Taber, K.S. and Cole, J. (2010). The CREST Awards Scheme: Challenging gifted and talented students through creative STEM project work. *School Science Review*, 92(339): 117–126.

Taber, K.S. and Tan, K.C.D. (2011). The insidious nature of 'hard-core' alternative conceptions: Implications for the constructivist research programme of patterns in high school students' and pre-service teachers' thinking about ionisation energy. *International Journal of Science Education*, 33(2): 259–297.

Taylor, C. and Dewsbury, B.M. (2018). On the problem and promise of metaphor use in science and science communication. *Journal of Microbiology & Biology Education*, 19(1), doi: 10.1128/jmbe.v19i1.1538..

Turner, I. (2021a). Games in FE: Part One – Why Games? [online]. Available at: www.youtube.com/watch?app=desktop&v=_nJWPxueRhI

Turner, I. (2021b). Games in FE: Part Two – Making Games [online]. Available at: www.youtube.com/watch?v=QtpdcfeWDgk

Villanueva Baselga, S., Marimon Garrido, O. and González Burón, H. (2020). Drama-based activities for STEM education: Encouraging scientific aspirations and debunking stereotypes in secondary school students in Spain and the UK. *Research in Science Education*, doi: https://doi.org/10.1007/s11165-020-09939-5.

Vygotsky, L.S. (1978) *Mind in society: The development of psychological processes*. Cambridge, MA: Harvard University Press.

10

TEACHING PUPILS WITH SPECIAL EDUCATIONAL NEEDS AND DISABILITIES (SEND)

ROB BUTLER AND ADAM HIGGINS

CHAPTER OVERVIEW

This chapter will show you how to adapt your lessons to meet the needs of your pupils. We will introduce you to a range of strategies to support your planning and teaching, and as you use these strategies more and more, they will become second nature and you'll use them without thinking about them. We will outline some key policy documents before describing the SEND conditions you are most likely to meet early in your career. You will see examples of materials used within the classroom to support pupils with SEND and what their work can look like with such scaffolding in place. We offer practical tips that help you to plan and teach all of your pupils as well as possible.

LINKS TO ITT CORE CONTENT FRAMEWORK AND EARLY CAREER FRAMEWORK

This chapter supports development of:

- Standard 2 – promote good progress
- Standard 4 – plan and teach well-structured lessons
- Standard 5 – adapt teaching
- Standard 8 – fulfil wider professional responsibilities

INTRODUCTION

The right of pupils with special educational needs to an appropriate education is enshrined in law. Teachers often think that teaching pupils with special educational needs (sometimes referred to as additional support needs) is something of a dark art or a skillset that they don't have. Quite often, all that is needed are simple modifications and adjustments to the way that you teach, and these tweaks will help the other pupils to progress as well. Other groups of pupils who might benefit from these strategies include those who have English as an additional language (EAL) and those who have prior low attainment. This chapter will help you to adapt your teaching to meet the needs of all of these pupils.

Just like driving a car, don't try to do everything at once but instead prioritise an area of need for your own situation and try some of the strategies suggested, widening your scope as you become more confident.

THE IMPORTANCE OF SPECIAL EDUCATIONAL NEEDS AND DISABILITIES TO THE TEACHER

The DfE SEND code of practice defines a pupil as having special needs if they have significantly greater difficulty in learning than the majority of others of the same age, or if they have a disability which prevents or hinders them from making use of facilities of a kind generally provided for others of the same age in mainstream schools or mainstream post-16 institutions. There is a long and complex document of guidance that sets out the expectations of schools in law (Department for Education, 2014). The devolved nations have their own versions of this legislation which have similar expectations and use similar language (although Scotland uses the term 'additional support for learning' or ASL) and links to support these are in Box 10.1. For a classroom teacher, the expectations, and strategies you will use in the classroom would be the same.

BOX 10.1   DEVOLVED NATIONS SEND CODE OF PRACTICE

SEND Code of practice for England: www.gov.uk/government/publications/send-code-of-practice-0-to-25

SEN code of practice for Northern Ireland: www.education-ni.gov.uk/articles/review-special-educational-needs-and-inclusion

Additional support for learning guidance for Scotland: www.gov.scot/policies/schools/additional-support-for-learning/

Special educational needs: code of practice for Wales: https://gov.wales/special-educational-needs-code-practice

---

The pupils that schools have identified as having additional needs will have their names put on a register to help the schools direct additional support and make sure they are making appropriate progress. This register has two lists of pupils: those who have their needs met by the school (school support) and those who need additional support so have an education, health and care plan (EHCP). An EHCP is awarded at the end of a graduated response from the local authority and is a statutory document that needs to be reviewed annually.

The teacher needs to know these learning needs to adjust the planning and delivery of lessons. Many schools create a pupil profile (some still use individual education plans, or IEPs) which summarise this information for the teacher. In the 2020/21 academic year, the Office for National Statistics reported that in England, 12.2% of pupils were in need of SEN support and 3.7% of pupils have an EHCP, and that these numbers are increasing year on year (UK Government, 2021). It could also be helpful to have a wider appreciation of the catchment area and specific issues that individuals face within your placement school community – for example, low levels of parental engagement, low aspirations, high local unemployment.

It is important to note that not all pupils who have special needs will have been identified or have individual pupil profiles. Each teacher and student teacher needs to check data available on the school's information system to see which pupils have learning difficulties, as not all will come to lessons with a teaching assistant in tow. Pupils with English as an additional language (EAL) could have similar needs to some pupils (e.g. poorer vocabulary and communication skills) but they might not qualify for SEN support unless they have additional needs related to their learning.

Individual schools have vastly different numbers of pupils with SEND, but it is worth remembering that the strategies will benefit all pupils including those who have prior low attainment, as suggested with respect to practical work in Chapter 8. It is important to distinguish between ability and attainment when referring to these pupils. Teachers often refer to pupils as 'low ability' when they mean pupils with prior low attainment. A pupil with undiagnosed learning needs can be 'high ability' but what you see in lessons is low attainment, as their needs are not being met. This kind of language can shape the attitude of teachers and lead to stereotyping and a culture of low expectations.

Classroom culture is often overlooked as many teachers are often driven by the content of the lesson. By the time they start secondary school, most pupils with special needs have experienced failure time after time and have started to adopt strategies to avoid having to fail. Many of these pupils expect to keep failing, which makes them reluctant to put their full effort into their work, or they might be reluctant to read/write in class. Experiencing success, combined with praise and reward, has the power to change their attitudes to learning. You will find the strategies in this chapter will help these pupils succeed, which will in turn make them more confident about the next task as their self-esteem starts to grow.

SPECIFIC NEEDS IN SCIENCE

In this section, we will introduce you to some of the main categories of special needs and examples of the types of strategies and approaches that you can use for pupils with these needs. This section gives a very short overview of these needs, but you can find out more by visiting the website of the National Association for Special Educational Needs (https://nasen.org.uk/).

You will find that pupils who have identified special needs often have a diagnosis detailing the cause (if known) and the nature of their special needs. This information is useful to you as a science teacher because it helps you to plan to meet these needs and to reduce barriers to learning. Be mindful of the fact that each learner is an individual and what works for one pupil with an identified need might not work for another. Don't be disheartened if a strategy doesn't work first time (or if it doesn't work at all). As your experience grows, your range of teaching strategies will grow and you will become much better at teaching these pupils, so hang on in there!

Some schools in England may refer to the categories of special need from the English 0–25 SEND Code of Practice (2014). This lists four broad areas of [special educational] need and support:

- Communication and interaction
- Cognition and learning
- Social, emotional and mental health
- Sensory and/or physical needs.

The same code of practice (section 6.27) emphasises 'The purpose of identification is to work out what action the school needs to take, not to fit a pupil into a category. In practice, individual children or young people often have needs that cut across all these areas and their needs may change over time … A detailed assessment of need should ensure that the full range of an individual's needs is identified, not simply the primary need' (Department for Education, 2014: 97).

For this chapter, we have focused on the needs you are most likely to meet in your classroom. In addition, CLEAPSS (2018) has produced a supportive guide which supports you in making practical work accessible for all pupils and offers adaptations you may wish to consider making.

AUTISM

Autism, also referred to as autism spectrum disorder (ASD) or autistic spectrum condition (ASC) is a lifelong condition that is characterised by areas of difference in communication, social interaction, managing change (restrictive behaviours) and sensory differences. Because it is a spectrum, not all pupils will be the same, so some characteristics, such as repetitive or restrictive behaviour, will not be displayed by all autistic pupils (NHS, 2019; National Autistic Society, nd). Sometimes, autism can manifest in school as extreme anxiety, leading to withdrawal and a lack of engagement. From a science perspective, inference and application may be affected as well as organisational skills (we call these executive function skills) in practical lessons.

Establishing routines in your lab such as starting with structured instructions using words such as now, next, finally can be very beneficial. Seating plans provide reassurance for pupils with autism (ask your pupils where they want to sit, as they may be sensitive to white noise in the classroom like the whirring of an overhead projector). Routines around getting out equipment (from an identified location) and clearing away will benefit all pupils, not just those who are autistic. An uncluttered and tidy lab will help those pupils with sensory issues (this extends to wall displays, which can contribute to sensory overload of autistic pupils).

To help with their difficulty with managing changes you should warn your pupils of these in advance – for example, room changes or your intention to do practical work in the following lesson. An example could be a pupil with autism always asking the science teacher at the start of each practical lesson, 'will it bang?' The learner may well enjoy all types of practical but just had to be warned if something unexpected might happen with a comment like, 'this one might make a smell'.

Consider if you can support pupils with autism with visual instructions – for example, integrated instructions for practical work. Be sure to allow pupils with autism time to process a question before answering, do not expect an immediate response. One way to achieve this would be to ask a question before you take the register and then get answers afterwards.

MODERATE LEARNING DIFFICULTIES (MLD)

Finding a definitive meaning for pupils with moderate learning difficulties is challenging (see Norfolk Educational Psychology Service (2016) and Educational Psychologist (2016) as examples). What we do know is that generally they will demonstrate attainment below expected levels across all/most of the curriculum and this broad learning delay is also likely to mean that pupils have reduced literacy and numeracy skills as well as difficulties that could be science specific. Quite often pupils with MLD have a reduced working memory so that recall is severely impacted over both short and long term (Westerberg et al., 2004; Archibald and Gathercole, 2007). Their organisation skills (executive function skills) can also be poor.

Breaking activities down into smaller achievable tasks will benefit these pupils and help develop their self-confidence. Scaffolding literacy and discussion work will help remove the barriers imposed by weak literacy skills and allow pupils to demonstrate their science skills.

As with pupils with autism, allow pupils with MLD time to process questions; give them thinking time to answer and return to them if they haven't had time to come up with an answer.

SOCIAL, EMOTIONAL AND MENTAL HEALTH NEEDS (SEMH)

Children with SEMH needs often have difficulties managing their emotions and/or their behaviour (SEMH, 2021) and this leads to low self-esteem and self-worth and so there can be declining cycles of behaviour if unchecked.

It is important when working with this group of pupils that every lesson with you is a fresh start. Never refer back to previous incidents (even if in a previous lesson that day) but use this information to be prepared going forward. Establish seating plans and routines with clear expectations. Consistency is key, as many of these pupils will test the boundaries, so be firm and stand your ground. It may take time to establish a positive relationship (this isn't the same as being their friend, it could be showing an interest or treating them fairly) but don't take anything said to you personally. Make sure you refer to pupils by name and always say please with an instruction and thank you when they comply.

It might help to give livelier members of the class a job to do while the class settles (e.g. getting out trays of equipment) as this can reduce the likelihood of low-level behaviour occuring. Break tasks into smaller pieces (chunking) and use real-life situations (use the science capital approach described in Chapter 11). Use praise but remember that some pupils with SEMH needs don't respond well to praise in front of their peers, so write it in a planner, tell them individually or even phone home.

SPEECH, LANGUAGE AND COMMUNICATION NEEDS

According to the Department for Education (2021) census figures, these are the most common needs you are likely to encounter in the classroom and will encompass pupils with a huge range of difficulties. Teachers might observe difficulty with speech, with vocabulary, with communicating in general or a combination of these.

Try to make sure these pupils sit away from distractions and near to you so that they can see your face when you speak, as this will help them maintain focus on you. When you are talking to the class, provide opportunities for these pupils to ask questions and seek clarification, or alternatively ask them what they have been asked to do. Use bullet points, break tasks down to make them accessible, and try to use diagrams to support instructions. Try to reduce excessive teacher talk and break this talking into chunks interspersed with activity so they will not lose concentration. Model good language and try to develop vocabulary by introducing it, defining it and making sure pupils can read and pronounce new words. Encouraging work with a partner might also help develop language skills. Allow time for pupils to process any questions you ask before you expect an answer because it might take them longer to process your question and form an answer in their head. You might find having a bank of sentence starters useful for some types of activity.

EXECUTIVE FUNCTION SKILLS

Executive function skills are the skills you need to get things done and are important for:

- Paying attention
- Organising or managing time
- Staying on task
- Understanding different points of view
- Regulating your emotions.

These are divided into three areas:

- Working memory – this is the information you hold in your head while you are using it.
- Cognitive flexibility – being able to think about something in different ways (e.g. solving an equation in a different way, different ways of carrying out an investigation).
- Inhibitory control – being able to avoid distractions and control yourself – for example, to avoid shouting out answers/responses in class, asking unnecessary questions.

Possible strategies for the teacher include breaking tasks down into steps, using visual organisers and schedules (or visual instructions for practical activities). Use of timers or stopwatches can help pupils to monitor time use. Check lists and to-do lists are simple but effective – for example, putting tick lists of instructions that pupils can tick off as they work through them. One approach that can help ensure pupils will not be left struggling, is the grouping together of pupils who have weak executive function skills together with those who have stronger skills. If you remind pupils to discuss the steps of an activity as is it undertaken, they can reinforce the task set by the teacher. Text mark-up with a highlighter can help to focus on key parts of a text.

Inhibition control is a little harder (and requires more patience from the teacher) but a simple strategy is to encourage pupils to wait for a set amount of time before putting their hand up to answer a question. A challenging learner who would attempt to answer every question in class found question cards to be a good way of regulating his impulse; the pupil had a set number of question cards and for each question they asked or answered a card would be removed. This had the effect of encouraging the pupil to focus on questions before asking or answering and there was a marked improvement over a school year.

REDUCING COGNITIVE LOAD

Cognitive load theory (also see Chapters 3 and 9) is much better understood in schools now than in the past and describes the process of how information being taught is processed and remembered. Information taught in lessons is held in the working memory, and as teachers we need to make sure this information is transferred to the long-term memory where it can be recalled or linked to other pieces of information. Pupils with special needs often have a reduced working memory, which means it is even more important that we reduce cognitive load to enable a focus on the most important aspects of the lesson.

One of the simplest and most effective strategies is chunking or breaking tasks down into smaller achievable steps. When you give instructions, consider how you can structure the task so that pupils complete it in small, bite-sized pieces and Box 10.2 outlines some tips as you prepare resources. Working on smaller tasks with fewer steps reduces the cognitive demand (remember that pupils with special needs often have a reduced working memory).

Not only does this mean the pupils can complete the task but it will help develop their self-confidence and self-esteem (meaning they are more likely to engage in following lessons).

BOX 10.2   TIPS WHEN DESIGNING RESOURCES FOR PUPILS

When designing resources for pupils it is important to consider the cognitive load by following these steps (see also Figure 10.1 which gives a worksheet example):

- Is there plenty of white space? Dense text can be offputting to pupils with low literacy levels, as they find it overwhelming.
- Stop pupils having to flick between sources of information. This could be by using integrated instructions or making sure that you do not break text/ questions when printing resources back-to-back (this is why the exam boards leave blank pages in the GCSE exams).

- Using side-by-side examples provides a familiar structure and gives pupils the confidence to answer questions or calculations independently.
- Give your instructions in small blocks or chunks – remember pupils with SEND cannot hold multiple instructions in their working memory.

C/W   Lesson 2 - Kinetic Energy   _/_/_

Key Words	Translation
Energy	Energia
Speed	Velocidad
Velocity	Velocidad
Mass	Masa
Joules	julios

Find and fix the errors below:

Energy is measured in Joules	The energy stored in a battery is electric
Energy can be created and destroyed	The greater the height, the more electrostatic energy you have

Kinetic energy is the energy of _____. It is affected by:

1. How _____ something is moving
2. The ____ of the object

Kinetic energy = 0.5 × mass × speed²

Which **two** of the following factors will affect kinetic energy?

▫ Height   ▫ Speed   ▫ Mass

Which of the following will have a higher kinetic energy?

▫ A car at 50 m/s   ▫ A car at 20 m/s   ▫ A car at 10 m/s

Which of the following will have a higher kinetic energy when travelling at the same speed?

▫ A motorbike   ▫ A lorry   ▫ A car

Mass (kg)	Speed (m/s)	Working Type: 0.5 x mass x speed x speed	Kinetic energy (J)
20	40		
300	2		
0.5	35		
17	26		
65	5		
2.9	10		
66	4		
13	1		
1200	11		

4

Figure 10.1   An example of a worksheet created by Adam Higgins to support his teaching of pupils with SEND

An example of resource design to reduce cognitive overload would be the use of side-by-side instructions. This means that each part of a process or a task has been chunked into explicit chunks, with instructions for each section written next to where the pupil is writing. It also will have a worked example so that the pupil is clear on what is expected of them, and what a successful outcome will look like. This does not only help the pupil to know how to complete the process, but also promotes independence, as although the teacher and teaching/learning assistant (TA) will be available to support, it would mean that they can constantly refer back to these instructions whilst working at their own pace. This works particularly well in numeracy-based activities – such as the teaching of calculations, and it also works well for extended answer questions, but instead of having instructions for the process, hints for what to include in each section could be included as shown in Figure 10.2.

	1. A light bulb transfers 20 J of energy in 60 seconds, what is the power of the lightbulb?	2. A laptop transfers 50 J of energy in 50 seconds, what is the power of the laptop?	3. A mobile phone transfers 100 J of energy in 120 seconds, what is the power of the mobile phone?
State the values that you know	Power = ? Energy = 20 J Time = 60 s		
State the rearrangement of the equation	Power = Energy ÷ time		
Substitute in the values	Power = 20 ÷ 60		
State the final answer	Power = 0.3 W		

4. A lamp transfers 1000 J of energy in 500 seconds, what is the power rating of the lamp?

5. An electric car has a power rating of 15 000 W, how much energy will it transfer in 10 seconds?

6. An oven has a power rating of 2150 W, how long will it take to transfer 10 000 J of energy?

....

....

....

....

....

....

Figure 10.2 An example of how to best structure a numeracy-based activity, created by Adam Higgins

Cognitive science tells us that the more often a piece of information is retrieved from memory, the stronger that retrieved memory becomes. Teachers need to plan for this 'retrieval practice' in their lessons. One approach to this is to keep a set of retrieval practice books as a place where pupils could do a variety of retrieval activities without getting these mixed up in their normal exercise books. The content for retrieval activities can be planned into schemes of work and covered in 'spare moments' in class. Examples of suitable opportunities include when pupils complete a practical lesson early or you have had to abandon a lesson due to the fire alarm going off. The type of activity is less important than the information being retrieved, which gives you the flexibility to construct activities that suit your class.

Examples of possible activities include:

- Labelling simple diagrams – recall
- Answering short questions
- Retrieval roulette (banks of preprepared questions that select one at random)
- Flash cards
- Games like snap, 'beetle' or snakes and ladders (with questions on the board)
- Making models – like DNA/cells using sweets/Lego.

These activities will encourage learners to retrieve information and key vocabulary – for example, when labelling diagrams or answering simple low-stakes questions. The retrieval of information will make the recall stronger so learners will remember more. A useful summary of how the memory works can be found in the EEF *Improving Secondary Science* report (Education Endowment Foundation, 2018a).

Dual coding is when you combine words and visuals to provide two different representations of information (Cavliglioli, 2019). We often do this in science with the procedure for a practical lesson or for summarising processes (e.g. homeostasis, digestion). The visual element needs to be meaningful to the learner and helps to provide two different ways of understanding the idea. This also benefits learners who have weaker literacy skills as they can often follow a more visual approach. Take care not to include too much information leading to cognitive overload. An example would be including diagrams alongside a practical method or representing data with an accompanying infographic. Sometimes dual coding can be confused with the debunked VAK (visual–auditory–kinesthetic) learning styles theory which can still be floating around in some schools, but these are not the same.

DIFFERENTIATION

In this section we will introduce a model for meeting the needs of all pupils in your class. The SEND code of practice states that 'high-quality teaching that is differentiated and personalised will meet the individual needs of the majority of children and young people' (Department for Education, 2014: 25).

VIGNETTE 10.1   PATRICK'S EARLY TEACHING EXPERIENCES REFLECTING ON DIFFERENTIATION

When Patrick went to school, he remembered other pupils being taken out of the class for what were then referred to as 'remedial' classes. As he started to teach many years later, it was at a time when 'differentiation' was emerging on the teaching agenda. The way it manifested in the classroom was through a very mechanistic approach – there was a 'core' set of work for the majority of the pupils in the classroom, extension tasks for those who finished first and an easier version for those who were less able. The senior leaders who would do what are now called learning walks would look to ensure that this was taking place in the lessons they visited. Differentiation by outcome became a default for many.

As Patrick reflected on how he had been teaching prior to this 'three-stage' approach he realised that this new approach was actually doing less to support the pupils in front of him. Those who were most able in the class were being given additional work to do, so it became clear that some just took longer with their work to avoid being given the extra work. Handing out the less complex worksheets highlighted the lower achieving pupils in the class. Fast forward to today and what we see in classrooms is far more beneficial to all. Trainees are expected to have high expectations for all their pupils. They should be setting appropriate challenges and stretching pupils to the best of their abilities – whatever that ability is. As teachers we have the benefit of knowing more about how pupils learn and how we can adopt strategies such as dual coding to support teaching and learning. Differentiation has moved on from three different worksheets for a class to being able to better support pupils of all abilities within the classroom through considering better questioning, grouping and how we work with individuals and small groups as teachers.

Activity: Make a list of different ways in which you can differentiate teaching and support within your lessons. Consider when you will use these and evaluate them in discussion with your mentor and host teachers after the lessons.

Differentiation in the classroom can focus on removing barriers too. Teachers often pitch their content to the top of the classroom and put support in place to help pupils who are struggling to get there. This support could be as simple as a printed title, a results table or set of axes for a graph (one experienced colleague would let pupils select their own support, such as choosing from a selection of blank tables).

Some schools use pre-printed booklets, which takes away some of the literacy pressure. It means that not only do pupils worry less about the quantity of notes they will take, but it also means in the future when they refer to these, they are easier to read.

Some pupils struggle to make sense of their own notes when they come to revise (either because of illegible handwriting or because they have not written the important facts down). There are two approaches which experience tells us works for booklets:

- For younger pupils these are more flexible and the content covered can be adapted slightly with the focus on solidifying the core scientific concepts in their mind. These booklets are printed page by page and put into a file.
- For older pupils where making sure all content is covered – for example, as part of the GCSE course, a more rigid booklet is used. This means that if a pupil misses a lesson, it is clear what needs to be addressed. However, these structures are not set in stone, and the flexibility with lower attaining pupils is a key attribute to acquire.

A great number of pupils with autism and Asperger's syndrome like routine. The use of booklets with a similar lesson structure means that some of this potential anxiety is taken away and they are more content with being in the lesson and focusing on the learning. It is important to remember that not all SEND pupils are lower attaining, a lot of them are very able, but just need routines and strategies to help them to reach their full potential.

Another way of scaffolding activities like calculations and chemical problems (writing word equations, organic chemistry problems like cracking alkanes) is by using side-by-side instructions, as we have demonstrated earlier in this chapter.

TEACHING STRATEGIES

In this section we will look at some of the specific teaching strategies that you can use with pupils with SEND. For each of the strategies we will also give you an idea of the rationale so you can prioritise which strategies to adopt for each group.

Pupils with special needs can struggle when faced with tasks that other pupils find simple. The key to success is to work out what the barriers to learning are and consider how these can be removed (or how you can help the pupil overcome them). These barriers could be weak literacy skills, poor communication skills, issues around processing and retaining information (see earlier in the chapter for details of some specific needs).

SCAFFOLDING

Scaffolding can also help those who need a little extra help. Scaffolding is about breaking down a task and providing a structure or process to help pupils complete the task and develop their understanding. Scaffolding helps overcome the resistance that SEND pupils often have when starting a daunting task and can help build confidence.

Application of science knowledge to new or unfamiliar contexts is a key part of science and forms a large proportion of the marks at GCSE. Pupils often see a question with an unfamiliar context and think that they cannot answer it, throwing away valuable marks. This simple scaffold is a way to support pupils when this happens:

1. What is the scientific idea behind the question?
2. What do I remember about this scientific idea?
3. What could the question be asking about this science?

This process provides support and reassurance for our pupils with SEND, how you implement the scaffold and the wording you use is down to the individual teacher (you could use a mnemonic to help make it easier to remember).

Many teachers will have come across writing scaffolds (or writing frames). These help the pupils to focus on the content and remove barriers created by having to get their thoughts in the right order. As the pupils become more proficient you can tweak the scaffolds to reduce the support they give.

It has been suggested that science writing uses a non-familiar style of writing (Wellington and Osborne, 2001). As science teachers, we have to help pupils master this style of writing, and structure strips are an excellent strategy to support this. They provide a sequence or structure down the side of a page – an example of this can be seen in Figures 10.3, 10.4 and 10.5. They also develop self-confidence and self-esteem as pupils see a page of text that they have created. Contrast that with the apathy felt when completing a worksheet which might fall out of their books and become lost. There is also an environmental benefit from using less paper and glue (in fact you don't even have to glue in the structure strips). As with all unfamiliar techniques, we would recommend that the teacher model using a structure strip for the first time until pupils become proficient in their use.

VOCABULARY

Pupils with special needs can also struggle with the vocabulary and format needed to explain a scientific idea. This can make it difficult for them to write practical conclusions and answer extended response questions in their exams. A successful way to model how to answer questions and write in a particular way (e.g. writing conclusions), is to use a technique called 'Steal the Style', an example of which can be seen in Figure 10.6.

By lowering the literacy demand of the task, pupils can focus on the content and the understanding. The steal the style technique involves giving a related example, but

Compare inhalation and exhalation	
Describe what happens in inhalation How do the ribs move? ☐ What happens to the diaphragm? ☐ What happens to the volume of the chest? ☐ In which direction does the air move? ☐	....
Describe what happens in exhalation How do the ribs move? ☐ What happens to the diaphragm? ☐ What happens to the volume of the chest? ☐ In which direction does the air move? ☐	....

Figure 10.3   An example of a way to structure the pupils' writing (created by Adam Higgins)

one that is not specific for the question that the pupil is completing. The pupil uses this as a model for their own writing. These can be very effectively used in the forming of evidence-based conclusions that can be drawn after an investigation. We know that ideally, we want the pupils to form a link between two variables and use a set of evidence to support this, but this is harder said than done. With the example the pupil can highlight (steal – it makes the pupil feel like they are cheating a little bit, which they love), they then can change the specifics to fit their situation. By highlighting both the parts that they steal and recycle, they get used to this structure, and can recall this by heart when the support has been taken away.

PUTTING IT INTO CONTEXT

The ASPIRES research from UCL refers to 'science capital' and the positive impact on engagement and attainment. As scientists we have the advantage that everything we teach has real-life applications because science teaching is simply about understanding the universe around us. Make sure that you include real-life examples in your teaching so that science lessons are not just a string of abstract ideas and facts. In a

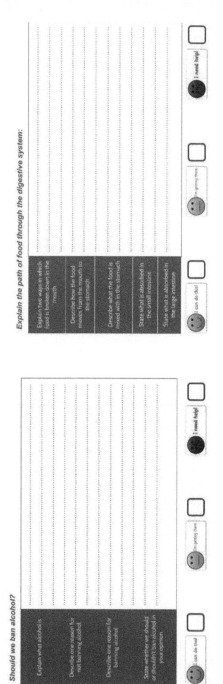

Figure 10.4 and 10.5 Example of structure strips (Adam Higgins)

	Steal the style, highlight the parts of the model conclusion that you will steal for yours	From my results I can tell that temperature does affect solubility. I know this because at 20°C 50 g of sodium chloride dissolved, whereas at 60°C 98 g of sodium chloride dissolved. This shows that the higher the temperature the higher the solubility.
Conclusion		....
	Write your own conclusion using the parts that you have stolen from above	....

Figure 10.6 An example of 'Steal the Style' (Adam Higgins)

Year 8 topic on nutrition and digestion, for example, pupils might look at a famine story from the news and unpick what was happening. Then pupils can be asked why the aid charities were handing out peanut butter sachets. Pupils are able to see the application of the work they had done on nutrition and the link to real life helped with engagement and retention. Refer to Chapter 11 for more information on utilising and boosting the science capital of your pupils.

ACCESSING THE CURRICULUM

The science curriculum is important for your SEND pupils and it must be appropriate. It should have high but realistic expectations and teachers of all career stages can lack the confidence to change this to suit their pupils. Ask yourself which pupil will make the most progress and have the best experience in science, the pupil with 100% superficial coverage of the science curriculum or the pupil that covered 80% of the curriculum with depth and embedding of concepts. Each cohort of pupils is unique, so the decision of what to focus on and what (if anything) to skim has to be taken by the teacher that knows them. This could be a good topic of discussion with your line manager in school.

TEACHING ASSISTANTS

Many, but far from all, pupils with SEND will be supported by a teaching/learning assistant (TA). It is important that as the teacher, you have considered the role the TA will play in your lesson. Getting a TA to support a small group of pupils instead of an individual is a good way to maximise their effectiveness and helps to develop valuable social skills as well. You can find out more about maximising the effectiveness of teaching assistants by reading the report from the Education Endowment Foundation (2018b).

In some cases, the teaching assistant will come to every lesson, while in others, they are targeted at the lessons that the pupil needs the most support in. The best practice for working with teaching assistants is to plan lessons together; however, few teachers can fit this into their schedules. If you keep your lesson plans in your online calendar you can share individual lesson plans with the teaching assistants who will be supporting your lessons so they have a little bit of a head start when they arrive at your lessons. It is not unusual for the teacher to have little say in the choice of teaching assistant that will be deployed by the school to work with an individual; however, consistency of support would be preferred as would having support who is familiar with the content of the science curriculum.

USING TECHNOLOGY

Spreadsheet software is a powerful tool to help pupils visualise results from their practical work. A template set up on the teacher laptop can average results and plot the results, allowing pupils with poor numeracy skills to see trends (e.g. limiting factors in photosynthesis). Be sure to set the template up with correct numbers of decimal places or axes on graphs and then lock the cells and protect the template. This means that pupils can only click on the parts of the spreadsheet that you have allowed them to, and they won't accidentally delete formulae or graphs.

Document editing software can check your documents for readability as part of the spelling and grammar check. This can be useful if you want to check resources you are going to be using in class, or you can paste in text from a website for checking.

WHAT TO LOOK FOR WHEN OBSERVING LESSONS

- Can all the pupils access (understand and complete) the work?
- Has the teacher given everyone the same work? What support have they provided to the learners who have struggled because of their needs? Have they provided scaffolding or modified resources?
- How did the teacher assess the learning that had taken place in the lesson for their learners with SEND?

SUMMARY

Now you have read this chapter you should have:

- Greater awareness of strategies that you can use with these learners in your teaching, which range from simple tweaks to whole activities.
- Recognised the need for planning and differentiating your lessons, and the resources you use with your learners, so you will be able to meet the needs of learners without a massive increase in your workload.
- A better understanding of the term special educational needs and disabilities (SEND) and associated terms and how complex defining these can be.

REFLECTIVE QUESTIONS

- Do you know who your pupils are who have special educational needs or those who might need modifications to the way you teach them?
- Have you identified general strategies that might help your pupils to make progress? You can use these strategies with any of your classes to try them out.
- Does your classroom/laboratory need any modifications to help establish routines and a productive learning environment for your classes.

FURTHER READING

The EEF Improving Secondary Science report offers a useful overview of how memory works and how teachers can support pupils with remembering information: EEF (2018). *Improving secondary science – guidance report*. Available at: https://educationendowmentfoundation.org.uk/tools/guidance-reports/improving-secondary-science/

This book clearly explains what Specific Learning Difficulties (SpLDs) are, and describes the symptoms of conditions most commonly encountered in the mainstream classroom. There are also dedicated chapters on helping students with SpLDs to develop effective revision skills and exam techniques: Hudson, D. (2015). *Specific Learning Difficulties: What teachers need to know*. London: Jessica Kingsley Publishers.

This offers a comprehensive and practical guide for teachers and SENCos to understand Autistic Spectrum Condition and help them put in place the right support and expectations: McCann, L. (2017). *How to support pupils with Autism Spectrum Condition in secondary school*. Cheshire, UK: LDA.

BIBLIOGRAPHY

Archibald, L. and Gathercole, S. (2007). The complexities of complex memory span: Storage and processing deficits in specific language impairment. *Journal of Memory and Language*, 57(2): 177–194.

Caviglioli, O. (2019). *Dual coding with teachers*. Woodbridge: John Catt Educational.

CLEAPSS (2018). *G077 Science for secondary-aged pupils with Special Educational Needs and Disability (SEND)*. Uxbridge: CLEAPSS.

Department for Education (2014). *SEND code of practice: 0 to 25 years*. 11 June [online]. Available at: www.gov.uk/government/publications/send-code-of-practice-0-to-25

Department for Education (2021). Statistics: special educational needs [online]. Available at: www.gov.uk/government/collections/statistics-special-educational-needs-sen

Education Endowment Foundation (2018a). *Improving secondary science: Guidance report.* 21 September [online]. Available at: https://educationendowmentfoundation.org.uk/tools/guidance-reports/improving-secondary-science/ (accessed 15 July 2021).

Education Endowment Foundation (2018b). *Making best use of teaching assistants.* 12 October [online]. Available at: https://educationendowmentfoundation.org.uk/tools/guidance-reports/making-best-use-of-teaching-assistants/ (accessed 15 July 2021).

Educational Psychologist (2016). Moderate Learning Difficulties, General Learning Difficulties, Intellectual Disability, what does this mean and are they the same? [online]. Available at: https://educational-psychologist.co.uk/sen-resources-blog/2016/2/9/moderate-learning-difficulties-general-learning-difficulties-intellectual-disability-what-does-this-mean-and-are-they-the-same

National Autistic Society (nd). What is autism? [online]. Available at: www.autism.org.uk/advice-and-guidance/what-is-autism (accessed July 2021).

NHS (2019). What is autism? [online]. Available at: www.nhs.uk/conditions/autism/what-is-autism/ (accessed July 2021).

Norfolk Educational Psychology & Specialist Support (2016). Moderate learning difficulties [online]. Available at: www.norfolkepss.org.uk/information/moderate-learning-difficulties/

SEMH (2021). SEMH meaning – What does SEMH mean? [online]. Available at: https://semh.co.uk/social-emotional-and-mental-health-semh/semh-meaning-what-is-semh/ (accessed July 2021).

UK Government (2021). Special Educational Needs in England. 24 June [online]. Available at: www.gov.uk/government/statistics/special-educational-needs-in-england-january-2021 (accessed 15 July 2021).

Wellington, J. and Osborne, J. (2001). *Language and literacy in science education*. Buckingham, UK and Philadelphia: Open University Press.

Westerberg, H., Hirvikoski, T., Forssberg, H. and Klingberg, T. (2004). Visuo-spatial working memory span: A sensitive measure of cognitive deficits in children with ADHD. *Child Neuropsychology*, 10(3): 155–161.

11
PUTTING SCIENCE INTO CONTEXT FOR PUPILS

JESSIE MYTUM-SMITHSON AND MATTHEW LIVESEY

CHAPTER OVERVIEW

The purpose of this chapter is to consider ways in which science can be made to be seen as more relevant by pupils to their own lives. We will suggest some of the simple changes you can make to engage your pupils with science and give them confidence that it is a subject they *will* be able to master and succeed in. It will also cover the theory of science capital as a teaching approach and how you can link science in your lessons to the everyday, lived experiences of your pupils. The chapter will offer practical long-term strategies to increase engagement, progress and also reflect on the potential impact on behaviour management.

LINKS TO ITT CORE CONTENT FRAMEWORK AND EARLY CAREER FRAMEWORK

This chapter supports development of:

- Standard 3 – demonstrate good subject and curriculum knowledge
- Standard 4 – plan and teach well-structured lessons
- Standard 7 – manage behaviour effectively
- Standard 8 – fulfil wider professional responsibilities

INTRODUCTION

Over the years, there has been much research into how best to engage and inspire pupils to take up careers in science; however, the number of pupils taking up science careers has remained the same (Archer et al., 2020). One of the most substantial long-term studies has been carried out by Professor Louise Archer and her team at University College London and Kings' College, London. From their extensive research and studies, the term 'science capital' was coined. The term science capital describes a 'bag you carry throughout life' (Godec et al., 2017: 7) that contains everything you know, think and experience about science as well as your science-related contacts (Archer et al., 2015; Godec et al., 2017). In short this refers to how 'sciencey' a pupil feels.

At the start of your teaching career, it is reasonable that in lessons you concentrate on the context and explanations of science concepts, perhaps overlooking how this relates to everyday life. It may not be a priority to think about how placing the science content into an everyday context or setting might make the difference between a pupil being interested in the lesson or another switching off and not engaging at all.

It is important that you take time to think about the context you are setting the science concepts you are teaching in. This can help the pupils to see where science fits into their life. As a student teacher or early career teacher, you may think it is difficult to link the areas of science you are teaching with a suitable context, and you may not always be confident about the associated subject knowledge to explore this context in detail – especially if unexpected questions are asked by the pupils. This chapter will help to support you with this.

One of the concerns around teaching in this way is that introducing such a context-based approach will be time-consuming and take up so much of a lesson that there will not then be enough time to teach the main science content. By using a science capital approach, which can involve tweaking rather than substantially rewriting lessons when planning, the time invested in preparation and therefore teaching time used to contextualise learning can be minimised, whilst still providing a link to 'real world' science (Godec et al., 2017).

It is worth noting that this science capital approach can also be considered a tool for social justice, as this approach focuses on improving science engagement and participation for both the personal and public good. The ASPIRES 2 project, a longitudinal research study looking at the career aspirations of 10–19 year olds, identified several key factors that influence the way in which young people see their scientific identities and aspirations. These include class, gender, ethnicity and whether the person has had opportunities in life to experience and succeed in areas related to STEM (although we recognise that some of these terms are argued about in themselves and can mean different things to different people, which is also acknowledged by the ASPIRES 2 project). Adopting a social justice approach is complex and it is not simply a case however of having a 'science capital lesson' every so often but more of a long-term overarching pedagogical approach to informing and teaching lessons and consistently over time, building a pupil's science capital (Archer et al., 2020).

VIGNETTE 11.1   RELATING SCIENCE TO EVERYDAY LIFE

Agnieszka first realised the power of using familiar contexts as a student teacher when she had to teach a lesson about quarrying to Year 10 pupils who lived in a city. The pupils had little or no experiences of quarries, where building materials came from, and consequently were not invested in writing about the pros and cons of a new quarry being developed.

When she reflected to her mentor that the lesson had not gone well, she kindly pointed out that the pupils could not relate to the lesson as they really did not care about a hypothetical quarry. Agnieszka was dreading teaching the same lesson to a different group later that day. Her mentor had a quick suggestion to shape the lesson from focusing on discussing a hypothetical quarry to saying that the quarry was going to be made just down the road from the school and would impact on the sports fields and play areas. The lesson went significantly better than earlier in the day and the pupils were able to state reasons why they would want it to be made and why they would not want a quarry. After this, she was convinced that providing a context that links to pupils' lives was one of the keys to engaging them and she has subsequently used this approach throughout her teaching career.

Activity: How can you find out about the local area to ensure that you are able to draw upon experiences the pupils can make sense of? Try to identify businesses and industries that are dominant in the locality.

SCIENCE CAPITAL AS A TEACHING APPROACH

When teaching science, you will often find pupils ask questions about how science relates to them and their lives – 'when will I ever need to know this?' and 'how will this help me in everyday life?' are quite common examples. To address some of their concerns, a science capital teaching approach can be adopted when planning lessons, to try and increase pupil engagement and progress, alongside building positive relationships with your pupils.

Science capital draws upon the work of sociologist Pierre Bourdieu, who in the simplest of terms described 'capital' as being a notion of accumulated economic, social and cultural experiences and how having a high capital allows individuals to progress through life (Bourdieu, 1986). The science capital concept considers all the science-related knowledge, attitudes, experiences, and social contacts that a pupil may have and (generally) how pupils with a higher science capital go on to take science qualifications beyond 16 years old and will often work in science-related careers. Ways in which science capital can be developed for pupils are discussed later in the chapter. Pupils who have a low connection with or experience of science, and therefore often a low science capital, are seen to rule themselves out of science careers and study beyond compulsory education. They are reported to find the subjects difficult to engage with and study (Archer et al., 2020; Godec et al., 2017).

Science capital is not fixed and can change throughout your life. Therefore, most importantly as a teacher, it is possible to increase pupils' science capital by adapting and tweaking the content of your lessons. The foundations of a science capital teaching approach aim to broaden what pupils count as science, building the science capital in their 'holdall' that they carry with them throughout life. This is done by using the three pillars of the approach (Godec et al., 2017) which are described in the next section of this chapter and further on you will see how these can look in the classroom.

PILLAR ONE: LOCALISING AND PERSONALISING

Each school you work in is unique as an environment with its own set of pupils, and these factors should be taken into consideration when finding suitable links to the pupils' out-of-school 'real' lives. Localising and personalising are simple ways that pupils can relate to the science topic being taught. This is more than just putting the science into a context to help the pupils understand; a teacher needs to ensure that the context they are using is directly relevant and familiar to the pupils sat in the class in front of you. For example, you could use local landmarks to aid discussions and explanations in the classroom. In your area there may be a local statue or building you can use to create a discussion about the effects of acid rain or weathering. If it is unaffected by such factors as the pupils to predict what it would look like if it was in the future. If it already is affected, ask them to consider what could have been done to prevent this.

You can identify where there are local industries and how their products are used more widely. It is about enabling the pupils to see that science is *there* on their doorstep.

PILLAR TWO: ELICITING, VALUING AND LINKING

This pillar stems from the need to understand the preconceptions and prior understanding a pupil has about the science that surrounds the world in which they live (see also Chapters 3 and 5). It is based upon the use of questions posed to pupils to draw out the personal, cultural or family experiences they have encountered that could relate to the scientific content that is being taught (and this, in many ways, is the nub of what science capital is). To embed these experiences and increase engagement, it is then important to acknowledge and value the contribution and experience, before explicitly linking it to the content being taught in the lesson – you will see examples of this later in the chapter. It is hoped by doing this that a pupil is more likely to feel their contributions and experiences are valid and valued, ultimately moving them towards feeling that science is for them.

PILLAR THREE: BUILDING THE SCIENCE CAPITAL DIMENSIONS

There are eight dimensions of science capital (which are outlined in Box 11.1 and elaborated upon in a later section) and each one of these dimensions can enhance the extent to which pupils feel science is for them (or not). As a teacher of science, you can aim to build some of these dimensions into your teaching and the science culture of the school you work in. Some of the dimensions are easier than others and you should not feel like you must include all these dimensions within a single lesson. The more you practice adding these dimensions into your teaching the easier you will find it – and by sprinkling them throughout your lessons you can increase how 'sciencey' your pupils feel. As Box 11.1 outlines, this could result in greater engagement and progress in your classes.

BOX 11.1   THE EIGHT DIMENSIONS OF THE SCIENCE CAPITAL TEACHING APPROACH

The eight dimensions of the science capital teaching approach are outlined below, and found in the *Science Capital Teaching Approach* (Godec et al., 2017). Examples and practical tips on how to promote the development of dimensions in your classroom can be found later in the chapter.

(Continued)

1. Improving scientific literacy
2. Promoting science-related attitudes, values and dispositions
3. Highlighting knowledge about the transferability of science
4. Encouraging science media consumption
5. Encouraging participation in out-of-school science learning contexts
6. Identifying family science skills, knowledge and qualifications
7. Getting to know people in science-related roles
8. Encouraging pupils to talk about science in everyday life.

PRACTICAL WAYS TO MAKE SCIENCE RELEVANT

Now that we have considered what it broadly means to adopt a science capital approach to teaching, the following sections give examples of some of the main ways you can make science relevant to your pupils and encourage contextualised learning. As we have mentioned previously, this is by no means an exhaustive list or suggesting a one size fits all approach (in fact a science capital approach values the individual experience greatly), but some take away, practical tips that have worked in various settings previously. You may also find different ways of making the lessons more relevant and personalised to your pupils.

GETTING TO KNOW YOUR PUPILS

This may seem like an obvious thing to do, but getting to know your pupils can be difficult when you teach a class of 30 a few times a week. However, making the effort early after meeting the class for the first time can open the door to many opportunities to making links and improving contributions in the future lessons. Some ways you can find out about the pupils' experiences are:

- Using the start of the lesson when meeting and greeting the pupils to ask how their weekend was or what they are doing after school.
- Finding out what they do for a hobby or activities outside school. You can then refer to this when relevant in class. It is difficult to find a role or pastime that ultimately doesn't engage with science in some way.
- Finding out what their career aspirations are. Even at an early stage in their school career, it is often a good question to ask, as there may just be a spark in someone's imagination that you can tap into and help flourish.
- At the end of any assessment, if there is any unexpected time, you could ask a series of questions that relate to their interests or views on science. So rather than

them sitting there waiting for everyone to complete their tests, you could ask them to draw an image of a scientist (this often changes over the year); ask them to write down as many scientists they know; any job that you need science for; their favourite animal; an interesting science fact they know or two things that they like doing in their spare time. Then when you mark the tests, you can easily read it and try and link this information in your lessons.

DISCOVERING PUPILS' EXPERIENCES

This is a quite straightforward, low resource way of increasing the science capital of your pupils. The first step is to ask your pupils open-ended questions such as 'what do you know about …?' or 'have you ever seen a …?' and promote your pupils talking about their own experiences. It can be done through questioning techniques or as a 'think, pair, share' activity to allow quieter or less confident pupils to take part. Once your pupils have shared their knowledge it is important that this is visibly valued by you as the teacher. When you acknowledge their contribution, this needs to be more than a generic great/good/excellent comment at this point – you need to ask for further details to allow your pupils to elaborate further (which is part of good feedback – see also Chapter 6). You can then summarise this and repeat back to your class to demonstrably value the pupil's contribution to the lesson showing that *their* knowledge is important.

The main danger point at this stage in the lesson is that the context link becomes the priority and the science content slips off the agenda, so you should ensure the discussion is moved forward to align with the learning objectives. It is a real positive to encourage your class to have appropriate discussions taking place, but time limits should always be placed on such activities to stop conversation drifting and taking up too much time.

Sometimes elicitation may occur spontaneously as a natural part of the lesson and the contribution still needs to be valued and discussed – never reject a contribution without hearing it first, as outlined by Saif's experience in Vignette 11.2.

VIGNETTE 11.2   A SPONTANEOUS CONTRIBUTION OF EXPERIENCES

Saif was in a discussion with Year 8 pupils during a biology lesson on reproduction and pregnancy when a pupil asked if they could talk about the birth of their dog's puppies. Saif allowed the pupil to share their experiences as it was directly related to the lesson aims. He interjected at times with an enthusiastic 'wow' and a big smile as the story unfolded. The pupil described how each puppy was

(Continued)

contained in a separate amniotic sac and how their family members had removed each puppy from the sacs one by one.

By allowing the pupil to describe their observations and offering praise throughout and at the end, rather than just stating 'that was interesting' before moving on, ensured that the pupil felt their contribution to the lesson was valued. It was then important for Saif to make connections with this to the content of his lesson, so he then linked the pupils' description back to the function of the amniotic sac and fluid during human pregnancy. Saif then knew that this pupil had a new litter of puppies and could refer to this when talking about animal development in future lessons.

Activity: By the nature of these being spontaneous, such incidents cannot be planned for. Consider the ways you can quickly identify if an anecdote from a pupil is going to be relevant and useful to the lesson or how you can record this for later use. You will need to be certain that you do not get drawn into irrelevant conversation but maintain a lesson focus – again, think about phrases you can use that do not dismiss pupils but make it clear that some stories are not for now.

USING HOOKS TO ENGAGE LEARNING

'Hooks' are a short, low resource way to immediately engage pupils with a topic you are about to teach them and explore their curiosity and wonder. These may take the form of unusual images with a question, a video of something exciting, an interesting object or demonstration. Ensure that the hook is linked to the lesson's aims and objectives to ensure time in lessons is not wasted and the activity is purposeful (see also Chapter 5 for views on the use of hooks in lessons).

A good example of a hook for a biology lesson on Mendelian inheritance is an image of a cat with polydactyly, accompanied with the task to explain what is different about the cat and how it could have been caused. Once the pupils are hooked into the lesson, they will be more likely to listen to the theory about the genetics behind polydactyly, learning the required content along the way.

Such images can be turned into activities which encourage pupils to be the 'expert in the room'. This involves them talking about their experiences and knowledge rather than simply giving them facts about the material shown. They offer an opportunity for you to ensure their contributions are fully valued through referring to something about the discussion later in the lesson, which also supports positive relationship building between you and your pupils.

VIGNETTE 11.3 GETTING THE MOMENT OF WONDER

Cameron was teaching a lesson to Year 8 on air resistance. After teaching the pupils about drag during falling objects and as the final act of the lesson, he showed a short video clip of a bowling ball being dropped alongside a feather in a vacuum (this last piece of information, however, he did not divulge to the pupils). Before commencing the clip, he conducted a class vote on which one would fall to the ground quickest - naturally the bowling ball won the class opinion.

He could really see the sense of wonder and amazement in the faces of the pupils as they were watching this clip. Without explaining why the objects fell at the same rate, Cameron called the class to order and began dismissing them from the classroom. He could hear the conversations between the pupils as they were leaving the classroom, puzzled but trying to apply their knowledge and work it out. One pupil who is often disengaged from lessons, came up to Cameron on his way out and said: 'That was amazing! Why was that? I can't wait to find out next lesson!'

Activity: Think about the timing of when you use hooks or wonder moments - can they be at any point in the lesson? How can you make sure that they support the teaching and learning without distracting the pupils from what you need them to know?

DEVELOPING SCIENTIFIC LITERACY AND ENGAGING WITH MEDIA

It is always worth trying to encourage pupils to engage with a wide variety of media sources, which expands the scope of the curriculum. Arguably, this is particularly important with pupils in the higher key stages, when application of knowledge is emphasised more and requires a greater degree of scientific understanding. However, it is vital that pupils engage with science-related media, including books, magazines, television and internet content, from an early stage in their schooling. You might find that your pupils often spend time watching clips on social media or television documentaries without knowing explicitly that it is scientific content. Perhaps prepare a list of tried and tested resources you can give them at the start of the topic to watch independently.

It is also a good exercise to ask the pupils to spot the 'bad science' that they see in the media, before critiquing it and explaining to their families or fellow classmates. This might include errors on diagrams shown on the news or incorrectly presented data.

Getting the pupils to bring their understanding of scientific concepts and begin the task of challenging things they see around them is a good way to promote an increase in science capital.

The more that your pupils are talking or reading about science, both in and out of school, the greater the opportunities are to consider their use of specific vocabulary and their understanding of concepts. In class when introducing new terminology, it is always worth exploring where pupils have used or heard of key words before – this can also support your assessment of prior learning. Mary Myatt (2018: 93) suggests that building vocabulary is an important aspect of teaching for 'closing the gap between those who come from rich-language backgrounds and those who do not'. In the same vein, if we want to develop the science capital of pupils, then we need them to be using scientific language confidently. She goes on to say that 'if the purpose of curriculum design is to ensure that pupils have access to and master deep subject knowledge, then one of the most efficient ways of doing this is to expose them to the technical vocabulary and subject-specific terminology of a subject area' (Myatt, 2018: 96). Science offers many opportunities to engage pupils in the ancient roots of language which can support them as they progress in their school and future lives as a way of being able to unpick meaning and understanding of wider language.

PROMOTING STEM CAREERS

The Gatbsy Charitable Foundation with Professor Sir John Holman produced a report in 2014 which outlined careers benchmarks. Benchmark 7 specifically states that 'All teachers should link curriculum learning with careers. STEM subject teachers should highlight the relevance of STEM subjects for a wide range of future career paths' (Holman, 2014: 7). One strategy to promote STEM careers and roles with your pupils is to find out if any other parents or carers (or wider family) have occupations that are science based or related. Try to select a range of occupations to highlight the usefulness of science – for example, it is obvious that doctors, midwives and health-care workers use science skills but perhaps less obvious that artists, hairdressers and nail technicians also use some aspects of science in their job. Find out which of your pupils have people in their lives who hold these positions or roles. By doing this you can challenge the pupils' stereotypical perceptions of a scientist and again help them to see the relevance of science to their future lives.

Schools can act as a platform to introduce pupils to a wider range of STEM careers and people who are in roles which are less familiar. Promoting these scientific careers and disciplines gives pupils the opportunity to gain information about what it might be like to work in a science-related job. It is worth exploring where you can establish links to local people or school alumni who have careers in various science disciplines. This will give you scope to include these, in person or virtually, in your lessons or special talks that can showcase what is on offer. The ultimate aim would be to weave the knowledge of STEM careers into lessons where their input as a career might be relevant to the content that is being taught.

Displays can also be a useful tool for showcasing science jobs, including those jobs that might not be considered a 'traditional science' job but draws upon science skills. Social media is a fabulous resource for images and details about scientific jobs.

The UK has a free STEM Ambassador programme promoted by STEM Learning that links up people in industry who would like to work with pupils to schools. Many industries and businesses will willingly visit schools or bring pupils on their sites to find out more. More information on the STEM network can be found in Chapter 13.

EXTRA-CURRICULAR ACTIVITIES AND OUT-OF-SCHOOL EXPERIENCES

Science clubs are a good way of creating out of classroom learning experiences while still in school. These clubs can often give you the opportunity to carry out practical work or talk about science-related ideas that are not on your school's scheme of work. This has the potential to further pupils' involvement with science and help them to see it as less alien in their lives. Existing structures, such as British Science Week, offer a great opportunity to run trips and have science-related visitors into your school. The science subject associations (introduced in Chapter 13) also support out-of-class activities and opportunities for pupils which can be used to develop and promote interest in those science disciplines.

If pupils carry out activities outside of class, you might want to make a display that is placed in a communal area such as a corridor to ensure that the value of that experience is lengthened and shared more widely than the pupils who attended – it serves as a little reminder of memories for the pupils on what they have done. The use of your Virtual Learning Environment (VLE) or school media platform will give you another medium to value pupils' work.

ENCOURAGING DISCUSSION AT HOME

You can use homework to get pupils researching more about the impact science has on their everyday lives. In the past, many student teachers have had success by setting a 'What has science done for me?' homework, where the pupils are asked to produce a poster or presentation about something that is personal to (and hopefully interests) them. This could be anything from a pupil who wears glasses explaining about their lenses, to a pupil explaining that the plastic used to make their pens were developed by scientists (Livesey and Hoath, 2019). Encouraging pupils to discuss their findings and research with their parents can also help. Some other activities you may want to set your pupils to encourage discussion with family are:

• Watching science-focused documentaries or YouTube clips with family members, then in the next lesson, asking the pupil to talk about what another member of their household thought about a certain part of the programme.

- Asking family members to give their opinion on something related to the topic studied in lessons. The next lesson, pupils can then come with their opinion and the opinion of someone from their household.
- Asking the pupils to carry out 'extra credit' homework – for example, making a model of DNA or designing (and maybe build?) an aerodynamic car.

THE IMAGE OF A SCIENTIST

It is important that you remove as many references in your school and lessons as possible of a scientist as a male, in a white coat, with 'mad hair'. Try to draw upon examples that represent scientists being diverse and use these as the role models in your teaching. You need to portray scientists that look like the pupils in your class and not the stereotypical scientist. They need to be able to see themselves in the examples shown. Encouraging pupils to share these views at home is also important. Small changes such as this enable your pupils and families to be able to see themselves as a scientist in the future and develop a sense that science is, indeed, for them too.

VIGNETTE 11.4   THE UNLIKELY EXPERTS

Using familiar contexts in your lessons is not just about making it fun, but rather about giving everyone in the class a voice and allowing them to contribute. By relating the science content to the everyday lives of pupils, it allows the pupils to also become the expert in the classroom.

Joe recently had a pupil in one of his classes who was often not interested in the lessons and would attempt to cause disruption. During one lesson on generators and energy, this pupil was able to describe, in great detail, the workings of a diesel generator that his grandparents had on a farm. Joe valued his contribution, responding enthusiastically with praise and linking the narrative to the content of the lesson. This pupil then went on to do the best bit of written work they had done all year. In subsequent lessons, the pupil continued to increase his contributions, improve his written work and decrease his disruptive behaviour. Behaviour is too complex to suggest a simple cause and effect, but for Joe he felt there was an interest seen in science by some pupils that had not been there before.

When teaching about photosynthesis, another of Joe's pupils who felt she was often too shy to contribute to lessons voluntarily, described growing tomatoes in her grandparent's greenhouse. She explained that it was good to keep plants warm but not too hot and was able to link this to the enzyme activity topic that they had studied in the previous academic year. In subsequent lessons, other pupils were able to recall the description and set the context from this pupil's contribution. The pupil in question felt happy with herself that she gave something of significant value to the class to learn from.

Activity: When you know your pupils better, as the year progresses, think about how you can make sure that there are planned times for them to be able to contribute to the content of a lesson. Think about how you can find out more about the pupils who seem less enthused by science as a way of linking the content where possible with their own experiences and interests.

BRINGING THE REAL WORLD INTO THE CLASSROOM

As a student teacher or early career teacher, you should perhaps consider when this approach would fit rather than feeling pressure to consciously include an aspect every lesson. If you get into the habit of including more aspects of the science capital approach you will find that you increasingly use it in more lessons as you become more familiar with it as an approach. There are many facets to classroom life that you have to consider as a beginner teacher that lay down the fundamental aspects of successful science teaching and learning. Being realistic about your development in the early days of teaching, we would suggest having science capital on your radar is a good first step and as you gain in confidence try to add more of the approaches, more often, into your teaching.

WHEN OBSERVING LESSONS LOOK FOR

- How are teachers using the examples of science from outside the classroom in the 'real world' to support the interest and engagement of pupils within it? How localised are these?
- Do teachers use knowledge about pupils' personal interests to support the teaching of science?
- How are teachers using their own experiences and anecdotes to form a context around the lesson?

SUMMARY

Now you have read this chapter you should have:

- A better understand of the theory of science capital and how it can be developed within science.

- An understanding of some of the benefits of approaching science teaching using this approach.
- Strategies for using context to link science to pupils' everyday life.

REFLECTIVE QUESTIONS

- Think about your own science capital. Can you identify the influences in shaping your choices to further study science after school or to teach it?
- What media sources can you draw upon to enable you to show pupils that science is happening beyond the classroom?
- What approaches will you take to get to know your pupils so you can use this information to support your teaching of science?

FURTHER READING

This publication offers further details about the ASPIRES findings and examples of how teachers can practically incorporate a science capital approach to their teaching: Godec, S., King, H. and Archer, L. (2017). *The science capital teaching approach: Engaging students with science, promoting social justice.* London: University College London.

Although aimed at primary age pupils, this book offers diverse profiles of scientists from a wide range of disciplines: Allen, D. and Sinclair, A. (2021). *Superhero scientists.* Sandbach: Millgate House.

Published by the Association for Science Education, *SSR* has a full issue with the theme of Science Capital: *School Science Review: Everyday science*, edited by Geoff Auty and Keith Ross, 100(372) (March 2019).

This article outlines how Science Capital can be enhanced through the use of homework to develop links with science in school and outside of the classroom: Livesey, M. and Hoath, L. (2019). Using homework to develop science capital. *School Science Review*, 100(372): 41–43.

BIBLIOGRAPHY

Archer, L., Dawson, E., DeWitt, J., Seakins, A. and Wong, B. (2015). 'Science capital': A conceptual, methodological, and empirical argument for extending Bourdieusian notions of capital beyond the arts. *Journal of Research in Science Teaching*, 52(7): 922–948.

Archer, L., Moote, J., MacLeod, E., Francis, B. and DeWitt, J. (2020). *ASPIRES 2: Young people's science and career aspirations, age 10–19*. London: UCL Institute of Education. Available at: www.ucl.ac.uk/ioe/departments-and-centres/departments/education-practice-and-society/aspires-research/summary-reports-and-books

Bourdieu, P. (1986). The forms of capital. In J. Richardson (Ed.), *Handbook of Theory and Research for the Sociology of Education* (pp. 241–258). New York: Greenwood Press.

Godec, S., King, H. and Archer, L. (2017). *The science capital teaching approach pack for teachers*. London: University College London. Available at: www.ucl.ac.uk/ioe/departments-and-centres/departments/education-practice-and-society/stem-participation-social-justice-research/science-capital-teaching-approach

Holman, J. (2014). *Good career guidance*. London: Gatsby Charitable Foundation.

Livesey, M. and Hoath, L. (2019). Using homework to develop science capital. *School Science Review*, 100(372): 41–43.

Myatt, M. (2018). *The Curriculum: Gallimaufry to coherence*. Woodbridge: John Catt Educational.

12
CHALLENGING THE CURRICULUM
STUART BEVINS AND GARETH PRICE

CHAPTER OVERVIEW

This chapter explores the nature of curricula, their construction and to what extent they mandate the learning experiences in the classroom. In order to support you with what perhaps will be challenging content we will outline the development of the science curriculum in England and Wales since 1988 and the arguments about the curriculum content and context, before considering challenges to the current curriculum – including their justification and implementation. We will consider the role of teachers and pupils in the operation of a curriculum and give you two examples of relevant curriculum development: enquiry-led curricula and integrated approaches (STEAM). This nature of the content within this chapter means that vignettes are not used.

LINKS TO ITT CORE CONTENT FRAMEWORK AND EARLY CAREER FRAMEWORK

This chapter supports development of:

- Standard 1 – set high expectations
- Standard 2 – promote good progress
- Standard 8 – fulfil wider professional responsibilities

INTRODUCTION

As an early career or student teacher you may feel that the curriculum is something created by the government that is to be 'complied with' or 'delivered'. Matching the content and skills required by the science curriculum dominate many teachers' planning and feature regularly in the marketing from publishers of commercial schemes. This is now considered the norm – but what is this curriculum and why does it have such power over what happens in the classroom?

This chapter suggests that the curriculum is not holy writ to be followed slavishly but a dynamic construction that benefits from challenge and revision by its stakeholders. These stakeholders include the funders, government, teachers, pupils, future employers and society more generally. Government enjoys a dominant position given that it usually is the funder and develops the, potentially legally-enforced, framework the curriculum is developed within, but we contend that all stakeholders should have a voice. In particular, we explore two aspects of the science curriculum: the content it contains and the context in which it is developed and deployed.

The chapter ends with two examples of significant challenges to the existing science curriculum:

- STEAM, which draws together elements of science, technology, engineering, arts and mathematics into a coherent whole.
- Enquiry-led science, which looks at how enquiry seeks to reflect the practices of research scientists in the classroom environment by emphasising the procedures of science.

CURRICULUM AND CONTROL

This section describes curricula in general and provides a brief overview of the history of the science curriculum in England and Wales since 1988. As you read, we invite you to consider who should have a voice in curriculum design and what the cost and benefits are of a mandated science curriculum.

THE NATURE OF CURRICULA

A curriculum is an amalgam of content, skills and, occasionally, attitudes that the curriculum designer feels is appropriate. Material that is 'in' is privileged compared with material that is 'out'. However, the act of choosing what's in and what's out reflects a series of assumptions about many areas including:

- the purpose of the curriculum – this is often formalised in explicitly stated aims and can include training future experts for research and commerce, providing a general familiarity with the knowledge domain appropriate to all citizens or to promote personal development.
- the nature of the knowledge domain covered – in science this typically devolves to a discussion about whether it is a body of knowledge (a content focus) or a way of creating new knowledge (a process focus), although it can also draw in issues around single or integrated sciences.
- presumed pedagogical approaches – Singapore science is strongly enquiry-focused (Singapore Ministry of Education, 2021) while Next Generation Science Standards (NGSS) in the USA include the need to demonstrate engineering practices (NGSS, 2021). Even where curricula claim to leave pedagogical decisions to the teachers, the amount and nature of the curriculum content can drive particular approaches, e.g. a content-heavy science curriculum that emphasises factual recall is perceived by many science teachers in England to prevent a more practical or enquiry-rich pedagogy.
- the link between the curriculum and the society – does the curriculum reinforce existing power structures and privileges or is there a commitment to social justice (e.g. the relative absence of black or female scientists in the National Curriculum for England)?
- any political, ethical or spiritual dimension and intention – some science curricula promote a love of country and a commitment to developing a 'good citizen', while some schools avoid talk of evolution or contraception.

THE SCIENCE CURRICULUM IN ENGLAND AND WALES SINCE 1988

It is worth outlining the history of the evolution of the national curriculum as we know it today. The first nationally mandated curriculum for England and Wales was created in 1988 by the Baker Education Act. The Science Orders the Act formalised described the knowledge and skills that all pupils were to cover from ages 5 to 16 and drew on a considerable body of work by curriculum developers prior to the Act (e.g. *Science 5–16: A statement of policy in 1985*). A decision formalised in the National Curriculum was that all pupils would follow science courses for at least 10% of their timetable in primary schools and that these courses should be broad and balanced. In secondary schools most pupils would study science for 20% of their timetable, again in broad and balanced courses, with a minority following a 10% route to allow more time for a second modern language. The science teaching community broadly welcomed these changes though pointed out the complexity inherent in the Orders' 17 Attainment Targets (ATs) and some complained about the loss of separate science courses. By 1991, the 17 ATs had been merged to produce four, although the requirement for broad and balanced science at all levels remained (Department of Education for Science and Welsh Office, 1991). Since then, the curriculum has been changed in terms of topics included, how it is assessed, the requirements for balance and even the extent to which individual schools have to follow it.

The change of government in 1997 ushered in a flurry of reviews and modifications to the science curricula in 2002, 2005 (primary) and 2007 (secondary), alongside modifications to public assessment systems and a significant rise in funding. There was also an increase in the guidance offered by government-funded bodies that took varying amounts of direction from the Secretary of State. The National Numeracy and Literacy Strategies launched by the Labour government in 2003 had a significant impact on primary schools even though, officially, they were only guidance and not mandatory.

The general trend since 1988 has been a gradual retreat from detailed prescription about content with an open assessment system to a more general description of content, with some parts notably and notoriously cut. References to climate change were cut from the Geography curriculum for Key Stage 1 to 3 by the then Secretary of State for Education, Michael Gove. At the same time the rules on assessment have been tightened leading again, at times, to controversy when practical work was removed from GCSE science in 2016 (Ofqual, 2015).

So, the science National Curriculum is a document that has been evolving and changing ever since its first inception. At the same time, the structures and systems around the published curriculum document have also been in flux, including changes to content, funding (the austerity years from 2010 onwards), assessment (changes to GCSE and GCE, modifications to SATs and league tables) and even who owns and runs schools (the academisation initiatives). These have all had a significant effect on the experiences of pupils and teachers across the country.

Few aspects of the education system in the UK are not heavily constrained or, at least, strongly influenced by government. However, teachers do have some degrees of freedom and, driven largely by political ideologies, the grip of government on the curriculum strengthens and weakens over time. For this reason, teachers can usefully reflect on the curriculum offered in their schools and classes and, in some cases, challenge it and seek change.

CHALLENGING THE SCIENCE CURRICULUM

The next section invites you to consider curriculum content: what is 'in', what is 'out' and what criteria are used to make the decision? We will also consider curriculum context and the dominant assumptions and perceived needs of British society. We question if schools should just accept those assumptions or should they, and to what extent, seek to effect change?

THE NATURE OF SCIENCE AND SCIENCE EDUCATION

While the exact nature of science is open to discussion (Bevins and Price, 2016) most scientists agree that the discipline contains a body of knowledge and a set of skills. The exact details of what appears in the body of knowledge and how it is divided and subdivided is disputed, as is the exact codification of the skills required. To most practicing scientists these discussions are wonderfully irrelevant – they choose and use the knowledge and skills required to complete their work. However, to writers of science curricula, who have to catalogue the knowledge and skills that must be taught in schools, these discussions can assume considerable importance.

One view describes the body of scientific knowledge in terms of traditional disciplines like biology, chemistry and physics and, occasionally, new disciplines like biotechnology or geophysics. An alternative view suggests science should be taught in an integrated way, where the individual disciplines blur, and yet another in a problem-based or project-led manner, where real-world problems and issues become the organising principle and the parts of science (both knowledge and skills) required is mandated by the relevant problem.

Similarly, the exact description and organisation of the skills involved in science is disputed. Whilst some limit scientific skills to simple control of variables, strategy components and the hypothetico-deductive process, others suggest communicating or networking are now fundamental to science, while others would add creativity into the mix. In the same way, science education is generally agreed to be about helping pupils to become familiar with scientific knowledge and skills. A false dichotomy between 'knowledge-rich' and 'process-led' curricula has led to less than helpful discussions, and very unhelpful government instructions, on the relative emphasis that should be put on these two aspects of science given the limited time available in schools. The recent Ofsted research report (Ofsted, 2021) on science education points out that both the 'knowledge' (which it describes as 'substantive') and the understanding of the processes of science with the associated skills (which it describes as 'disciplinary') are essential in a high-quality science education. The exact balance of emphasis placed on each of these aspects is left unspecified and, in this vacuum, the demands of the assessment systems are likely to guide teachers. However, thoughtful science teachers will, and should, have their own opinions and these should be revised regularly based on their experience in the classroom and the ongoing data from reputable research.

THE PURPOSE OF SCIENCE EDUCATION

If the nature of science is open to some discussion, the purpose of science education is similarly a subject of debate. Is science education primarily about training the future scientists and technicians needed by industry and research, or is it to provide the scientific literacy needed by all citizens in a modern democratic society? Should the school science curriculum concentrate on the body of facts and theories associated with the separate sciences with the aim of contributing a strong foundation for further study and careers in scientific disciplines, or consider science relationship with human features such as social and ethical contexts (e.g. vaccination and global warming), essentially fulfilling the requirements of a scientific literacy agenda? Of course, a relatively simple response would be a balance between the two, but within an environment of high-stakes testing and high-stakes accountability this is far from simple.

THE CONTENTS OF THE SCIENCE CURRICULUM

The content of the science curriculum in the UK is controlled by government. The different nations in the UK have different rules and regulations but all maintained schools are expected to follow the requirements of the published Science Programmes of Study (PoS). Academies are explicitly permitted to diverge from the published PoS provided that they offer a 'broad and balanced curriculum including English, maths and science' (Department for Education, 2021). Free schools and private schools are not required to follow the Programme of Study.

The exact details of the science curriculum contents are not usually particularly controversial and few people can become very excited about the details of which Group 1 metals pupils must cover or the choice of mammal a primary school class will study. Indeed, looking at curricula from across the globe, the topics included tend to be remarkably similar – the packaging and emphasis may change but the same ideas about photosynthesis, the periodic table and electricity turn up everywhere.

Arguments about the science curriculum content tend to centre around:

- the balance of scientific domain knowledge (often codified in facts and theories to remember and sometimes called 'content') and skills (both in terms of the scientific method and practical work)
- the inclusion of socio-economic issues like climate change or population control
- the age at which a particular topic is introduced and the sophistication of its treatment.

Many teachers feel that the amount of material to be covered is too large but most are also unwilling to suggest which parts might be cut and generally tend to suggest cutting topics outside their own specialism. Biologists, for example, can often find parts of the physics course that can be removed – and *vice versa*.

Socio-economic topics like climate change, extinction and the safety of nuclear power have been shown to increase motivation amongst pupils but are inherently less easy to control, and simple 'right' answers are not always available. In 2013, the Department for Education had to publish a response to complaints that climate change had been removed from the Science curriculum because it was 'political' rather than 'science' (Department for Education, 2013). There is ongoing discussion and debate around how the latest government sustainability and climate change education strategy will be meaningfully integrated into teaching.

You will be familiar with arguments in the media about children not being able to do long division without a calculator or A-Levels not being as hard as they used to be, and although these are usually part of the annual exam-reporting copy, a number of educational developers are always arguing about the level of difficulty of a topic and when it should be introduced to learners. Topics have moved between key stages repeatedly (in both directions) and any decision is only a temporary compromise between competing views.

THE PLACE OF SCIENCE IN SOCIETY

In recognising that science is an important subject to be taught in schools, we need to offer some thinking about its place in, and offer to, society. We also reflect on pedagogy and the science curriculum, and the important roles teachers and pupils have in science education. The section encourages you to think about a range of issues, from the link between science and society to how you view your role as a science teacher.

SOCIAL BENEFIT OF SCIENCE EDUCATION

Science remains a core subject in England and Wales and so all pupils will have at least some exposure to its methods, key concepts and current controversies. For some pupils it will undoubtedly be the largest single influence on their understanding of 'how the world works' in physical terms. Pupils are unlikely to discuss gravity at home or consider the fate of Darwin's finches with their friends in the park or out shopping. Does this mean that science education has a particular responsibility to ensure that the issues that are facing us as a species (e.g. climate change, antibiotic resistance, pollution of the environment) should be central to courses at school? If pupils do not learn about these topics, will they then be prey to disinformation, or will the absence of the topics imply they are somehow unimportant?

Science's emphasis on evidence over opinion or finesse more generally also helps to protect against disinformation or 'fake news' from malign actors. Recent history shows that responses to pandemic control measures, (e.g. mask wearing, vaccination acceptance) can easily be affected by rumours and fake news, and a society which is unfamiliar with, or unskilled in handling, scientific evidence could be at risk, literally, of significant excess deaths.

Alternatively, an emphasis on socio-scientific topics could distort the science curriculum away from fundamentally important topics which do not have the glamour or appeal of a hot contemporary topic. Do socio-scientific issues 'dilute' the science curriculum?

SOCIAL EQUITY AND THE SCIENCE CURRICULUM

Science is a human construct and reflects the established assumptions of the society that gives rise to it. Social equity, whether that be, for example (but by no means limited to), race, religion, gender, identity or sexual orientation, is an issue which is extremely important and one which science teachers can begin to tackle in the classroom. The often reported differential participation rates for, say, genders and ethnicities amongst STEM disciplines or in the curriculum, suggest that science education is not immune from this issue. The solution to these wider issues is not as simple as including different images within lessons and books but requires more of a shift in society. As a science teacher you can support this by thinking about the examples you draw upon in your teaching; however, we acknowledge that this is a bigger issue than can be addressed within a chapter of a book.

By way of an example, the views of Francis Galton (see the Galton Institute website), an eminent Victorian scientist and cousin of Charles Darwin, on eugenics were considered perfectly acceptable at the time and he was awarded a knighthood in 1909. These views and work on eugenics have long been discredited and few would suggest that eugenics, as Galton formulated it, should be taught in science classes. However, are there assumptions behind our curriculum, some unrecognised by those making them, that will look equally troubling in the future?

THE RELATIONSHIP BETWEEN CURRICULUM AND PEDAGOGY

If the curriculum describes the knowledge and skills to be taught then pedagogy describes the assumptions (e.g. how children learn), strategies (e.g. how a course or topic is cut up into different lessons), and processes (e.g. using practical work or listening to a lecture) of teaching, effectively, 'how teachers teach'.

This section looks at the relationship between curriculum and pedagogy in terms of the roles and responsibilities of teachers and pupils and considers two examples of significant pedagogical challenges to the science curriculum: the STEAM initiative and enquiry-led science courses.

THE ROLE OF TEACHERS

Managing a science class of 25–30 pupils, who hold different knowledge and skills as well as competing interests and motivations, is a difficult task for the teacher. Focusing on individual learning or providing one-to-one guidance is near impossible for any sustained length of time. Instead, teachers are forced to concentrate, for much of the time, on whole class learning.

However, good teachers find ways to off-set these constraints and one of these ways is by bringing the curriculum to life by making the content relevant to pupils' interests and daily lives. Relevance constitutes different components born of individual, societal and vocational aspects linked to the intrinsic and extrinsic motivations of pupils (Stuckey et al., 2013). Teachers can include real-life problems (see Chapter 11) and issues linked to their pupils' environment and daily experiences such as problems encountered through flooding in certain UK regions due to climate change. Not only do real-life contexts bring science to life for pupils but they also aid examination of the interdisciplinary nature of science.

The findings from a study of pupils in England, aged 15 between 2006 and 2015 (Sheldrake et al., 2017), suggest that demonstrating the wider applications of science to pupils was the only teaching approach to positively associate with pupils' value of science. Teachers, then, have a crucial role in bringing the curriculum to life for their pupils and can help to develop positive attitudes towards science and society as well as knowledge and skills. Moreover, it is their professional responsibility to enact the curriculum in such a way as to inspire pupils through science to enhance the learning experience. While the curriculum is a fixed artefact, there is scope for the creative teacher to deploy content relevant to pupils that will avoid negatively impacting pupils' interest. Teachers do have some agency in opting for classroom approaches that alert pupils to how science is applied in society, its multidisciplinary nature, and its impacts on pupils' daily lives. This is a crucial and explicit component of science pedagogy where the teacher as key practitioner links expert subject content knowledge with pedagogical content knowledge to bring the theories and applications of science to life.

THE ROLE OF PUPILS

The vast majority of people in any classroom are pupils, yet they rarely have a voice in curriculum or pedagogy discussions. If teachers can – and they should – challenge the curriculum, to what extent should pupils do the same?

Involving pupils in discussions about ways of teaching, even potentially about topics to cover, is part of supporting their autonomy. By 'pupils' autonomy', we mean the opportunity for pupils to make meaningful decisions about their studies. Discussions about how to support pupil autonomy are beyond the scope of this chapter but Table 12.1 offers some suggestions.

Table 12.1   Autonomy-supporting teacher behaviour

Teachers reduce pupil autonomy when they...	Teachers promote pupil autonomy when they...
• Offer incentives, consequences, directives. • Deliver assignments. • Seek compliance.	• Promote interest, enjoyment, sense of challenge. • Create opportunities for initiative.
• Emphasise pressure, involve the ego. • Use 'should, must, have to, got to' statements. • Neglect value, meaning, use, benefit, importance of requests to pupils.	• Provide information in flexible ways. • Provide options and choices. • Identify value, meaning, use, benefit, importance of requests to pupils.
• Block/counter expressions of negative affect. • Stress that negative feelings are not OK, are unacceptable and something that needs to be changed/fixed.	• Listen carefully, openly, understandingly. • Accept negative feelings, complaints are OK.

CASE STUDIES OF CURRICULUM CHALLENGE

Curricula do change, but often over long periods of time and some of the changes keep coming round again and again. The two case studies that follow illustrate two ongoing challenges to the science curriculum.

• STEAM initiative – STEAM stands for science, technology, engineering, arts and mathematics and is a radical approach to build bridges between these different subjects.
• Enquiry-led science – enquiry-led science education (ELSE) emphasises pupils constructing their own understanding through investigations rather than being simply told the answer by their teachers.

THE STEAM INITIATIVE

Concerns have been expressed about the way STEM subjects are currently taught by focusing on a perceived lack of creativity, a need for more multidisciplinary work and STEM's marginalisation of fears for society and the environment (Colucci-Gray et al., 2017). To tackle this perceived problem some curriculum developers have suggested adding 'arts' to STEM to make it STEAM.

One of the strongest arguments for deploying an integrated STEAM approach in schools is driven by the view that creativity is a crucial ability in the 21st century (Trilling and Fadel, 2009). Consequently, the arts can offer an important way to cultivate creativity. Unfortunately, the current curriculum offers no guidance on how teachers might integrate creativity into STEM lessons and school departments rarely focus on interdisciplinary project work within lessons that might contribute to a STEAM approach.

Currently, few integrated STEAM curricula exist that can guide your thinking as a teacher, but those that do often attempt STEAM through cross-curricular project work (Liao, 2016). This approach tends to emphasise 'real world' problems and charges pupils with identifying potential solutions through small-scale research and development projects. This type of classroom approach is frequently referred to as Problem-Based Learning (PBL) and includes features such as hypothesising, research, data analysis and design. These features are common across a range of contexts, from architecture and construction to industrial design and agriculture (Kang, 2019). Additionally, as with an enquiry-led approach, exponents of PBL claim that learners can experience greater ownership of their learning and are more motivated through designing and engaging in their own projects (Minner et al., 2010).

While the above might be enticing to you as a teacher, be sure to weigh up potential risks. For example, a frequent criticism of PBL and enquiry-led approaches from teachers is that it can be very time-consuming and restrict curriculum coverage (Bevins et al., 2019). That said, there is growing interest in STEAM curricula amid claims by leaders in industry that schools are not engendering the types of skills required by employers, in particular, 'creativity'. So, schools and departments that encourage a collaborative STEAM effort may well be ahead of the curve, even if that effort is deployed through after-school clubs and other non-curricular activities.

ENQUIRY-LED SCIENCE EDUCATION

Enquiry-led science education (ELSE) challenges the notion that the science curriculum is simply a fixed diet of facts and theories that are passed on unchanged by the expert teacher to the novice pupils. ELSE courses assume that the pupil will construct their own understanding based on classroom experiences and their existing knowledge. An ELSE science course is perhaps best seen as a 'self-assembly curriculum – a conceptual flat pack bookcase'! This is not to say that there are no fixed, or common, components in enquiry-led science courses and Table 12.2 compares these with more teacher-led approaches.

ELSE courses tend to emphasise the 'scientific method' exemplified by the 'control of variables strategy' over the memorisation of facts and typically include practical work where the experimental procedures are designed by the pupils themselves. This is one of the key tensions in ELSE – the time taken for practical work, particularly if

Table 12.2 Enquiry-led and teacher-led courses

Enquiry-led Lesson Characteristics	Teacher-led Lesson Characteristics
Often pupil-orientated with pupils being active.	Mainly teacher-orientated with pupils as passive receivers of information.
Built around group or team work.	Tends to use individual work.
Often uses cooperative and collaborative learning.	Tends to focus on individual learning and assessment.
Uses open-ended problems with multiple possible solutions.	Uses closed problems with a single correct answer.
Uses investigations where pupils have to make decisions for themselves.	Uses 'recipe-style' work where pupils follow detailed instructions.
Emphasises 'hands-on' teaching with the teacher circulating in the classroom.	Emphasises teacher lecturing or demonstrating from the front.
Uses project work with the projects extending over weeks or months.	Uses lectures or classes which tend to be focused at single-lesson level.
Embeds conceptual material in real world issues and problems.	Tends to organise teaching around traditional knowledge structures.
Involves the teacher taking risks and trying new ways to teach and learn.	Teachers tend to 'play safe' and avoid change.
Often pupil-orientated with pupils being active.	Mainly teacher-orientated with pupils as passive receivers of information.
Built around group or team work.	Tends to use individual work.
Often uses cooperative and collaborative learning.	Tends to focus on individual learning and assessment.

experiments need to be trialled and modified, can be considerable. No one is suggesting that pupils are not learning anything during this time, and some would argue they are learning exactly what professional science is really like, but sometimes it is tempting to just tell them Ohm's Law (it takes five minutes) rather than devoting two hours to the practical!

A number of strategies have been developed to support the investigative work in ELSE and these are collectively known as scaffolding. They can involve the use of a model to copy, sheets to structure the investigation, part-completed investigation plans, pre-built tables to collect data and a clear steer towards a 'good' question or 'appropriate' body of knowledge to back up the investigation. Critically, the support must be temporary, with the aim that eventually it is removed and the pupils can design and carry out their own investigations without teacher support.

ELSE courses do not ignore theoretical knowledge but tend to emphasise conceptual understanding at depth, and application of knowledge rather than simply memorising facts. An ELSE course would typically not value memorising and reproducing long lists of foods and their main constituents but would reward pupils' ability to use their understanding of the nature of food and its use in the body to formulate an energy biscuit for use in an emergency situation. Part of the task would also be to justify all their decisions by reference to existing knowledge and any new data collected by their own practical work. This creative application of knowledge is a central feature of ELSE and sees its greatest sophistication in Problem Based Learning.

All ELSE courses offer more autonomy to pupils than teacher-led courses and this is the source of many of the benefits of the approach. ELSE tends to:

- improve motivation to learn – particularly when pupils are able to choose and develop their own investigations
- deepen understanding of theoretical material as pupils apply their knowledge in novel or exotic situations
- develop metacognitive and team-working skills
- reflect the reality of professional science and so prepare pupils better for careers in science
- develop investigative abilities (e.g. control of variables, data-handling) more widely so protecting against 'fake news' and misinformation.

SUMMARY

Now you have read this chapter you should have:

- An understanding of the relationship between curricula and presumptions of those who commission and develop as well as the discipline they describe. Different curricula have different degrees of compulsion, specificity and openness to challenge.
- An awareness that science has been a core component of the UK curriculum for many years although the balance of material included has changed over that time reflecting changes in political control and perception of what counts as 'science'.
- Recognised that the classroom experience depends on the curriculum, pedagogy and the assessment regimen, and increasing autonomy for pupils in a supportive environment shows significant benefits.
- Developed knowledge that STEAM courses integrate a number of disciplines to provide a more holistic experience for pupils.

REFLECTIVE QUESTIONS

- Which socio-scientific topics would you like to see added or removed from your current curriculum?
- What do you think should be 'in' and what should be 'out' for your perfect science curriculum and why? Are there any topics you might want to move up or down a year to better match the maturity of the learners?
- How willing are you to consider adopting a teaching approach that is more enquiry-led? What problems do you think you will encounter?
- A curriculum cannot remain fixed for ever but who should be involved in change? Who should have a voice in how a curriculum is modified?

FURTHER READING

This book considers theory, research and practice to consider ideas around curriculum design. It is constructed with short, accessible chapters for any experience of teacher: Myatt, M. (2018). *The Curriculum: Gallimaufry to coherence*. Woodbridge: John Catt Educational.

This article offers a review of a novel curriculum model for science that combines traditional 'content' and 'skills' with a discussion of motivation, showing how this theoretical model can be translated into classroom experiences: Price, G. and Bevins, S. (2021). 3D Science – theoretical model or potential classroom reality? *School Science Review*, 102(380): 75–81.

This report offers a review of current practice in science education with some guidance on both curricula and pedagogy: OFSTED (2021). Research review series: science [online]. Available at: www.gov.uk/government/publications/research-review-series-science.

BIBLIOGRAPHY

Bevins, S. & Price, G. (2016). Reconceptualising inquiry in science education. *International Journal of Science Education*, 38(1), 17–29.

Bevins, S., Price, G. and Booth, J. (2019). The I files, the truth is out there: Science teachers' constructs of enquiry. *International Journal of Science Education*, 41(4): 533–545.

Colucci-Gray, L., Burnard, P., Cooke, C., Davies, R., Gray, D. and Trowsdale, J. (2017). *Reviewing the potential and challenges of developing STEAM education through creative pedagogies for 21st learning: How can school curricula be broadened towards a more responsive, dynamic, and inclusive form of education?* London: British Educational Research Association (BERA).

Department of Education for Science and the Welsh Office (1991). *Science in the National Curriculum*, London: HMSO.

Department for Education (2013). Climate change in the draft National Curriculum [online]. Retrieved from: www.gov.uk/government/news/climate-change-in-the-draft-national-curriculum

Department for Education (2021). The National Curriculum [online]. Retrieved from: www.gov.uk/national-curriculum

Hofstein, A., Eilks, I. and Bybee, R. (2011). Societal issues and their importance for contemporary science education – a pedagogical justification and the state of the art in Israel, Germany, and the USA. *International Journal of Science and Mathematics Education*, 9(6): 1459–1483.

Jenkins, E.W. and Nelson, N.W. (2005). Important but not for me: Students' attitudes towards secondary school science in England. *Research in Science & Technological Education*, 23(1): 41–57.

Kang, N.-H. (2019). A review of the effect of integrated STEM or STEAM (science, technology, engineering, arts, and mathematics) education in South Korea. *Asia-Pacific Science Education*, 5(1): 1–22.

Liao, C. (2016). From interdisciplinary to transdisciplinary: An arts-integrated approach to STEAM education. *Art Education*, 69(6): 44–49.

Minner, D.D., Levy, A.J. and Century, J. (2010). Inquiry-based science instruction – what is it and does it matter? Results from a research synthesis years 1984 to 2002. *Journal of Research in Science Teaching: The Official Journal of the National Association for Research in Science Teaching*, 47(4): 474–496.

NGSS (2021). Appendix I: Engineering design in the NGSS [online]. Retrieved from: https://static.nsta.org/ngss/20130509/AppendixI-EngineeringDesignInNGSS-FINALII_0.pdf

Nuthall, G. (2005). The cultural myths and realities of classroom teaching and learning: A personal journey. *Teachers College Record*, 107(5): 895–934.

Office of Qualifications and Examinations Regulation (Ofqual) (2015). *Assessment of Practical Work in New Science GCSEs – Summary*. March. Ofqual/15/5627.

Ofsted (2021). Research review series: science [online]. Retrieved from: www.gov.uk/government/publications/research-review-series-science

Sheldrake, R., Mujtaba, T. and Reiss, M.J. (2017). Science teaching and students' attitudes and aspirations: The importance of conveying the applications and relevance of science. *International Journal of Educational Research*, 85: 167–183.

Singapore Ministry of Education (2021). Science syllabus [online]. Retrieved from: www.moe.gov.sg/-/media/files/secondary/syllabuses/science/2021-science-syllabus-lower-secondary.pdf?la=en&hash=5A2FDABB63C929FF42F96A0EC63BDCA8710B8AF1

Stuckey, M., Hofstein, A., Mamlok-Naaman, R. and Eilks, I. (2013). The meaning of 'relevance' in science education and its implications for the science curriculum. *Studies in Science Education*, 49(1): 1–34.

Trilling, B. and Fadel, C. (2009). *21st century skills: Learning for life in our times*. San Francisco, CA: Jossey-Bass.

13

FROM STUDENT TO EARLY CAREER TEACHER

LEIGH HOATH AND MATTHEW LIVESEY

CHAPTER OVERVIEW

This chapter will summarise various principles from the previous chapters and suggest ways in which you can continue to develop as science teachers through your careers. After your Initial Teacher Training, the learning will never stop as you embark on your Early Career Teacher years. This chapter will outline some of the main avenues you can explore to gain further support and highlight some of the subject associations and teaching bodies that are there to enable and support good-quality science teaching.

LINKS TO ITT CORE CONTENT FRAMEWORK AND EARLY CAREER FRAMEWORK

This chapter supports development of:

- Standard 1 – set high expectations
- Standard 2 – promote good progress
- Standard 3 – demonstrate good subject and curriculum knowledge
- Standard 8 – fulfil wider professional responsibilities

INTRODUCTION

This book set out to support you as a teacher through the training process and into the early stages of your career by giving you practical tips and ways to reflect on your own teaching practice. We are more than aware that the volume of information you have to deal with during your teacher training is huge – there are so many elements to what you are expected to do that it is nigh on impossible for you to learn and understand it all in a few short months, never mind the years that follow. With this in mind, it is integral to the profession that you never stop learning throughout your teaching career, as it is a role that is continually evolving and developing.

The jump from student teacher to Early Career Teacher can seem like a chasm. You will have built up your timetable gradually over several months, eventually being able to manage a classroom environment on your own, albeit with your mentor or host teacher close by. However, in September, the classroom is yours. It is your environment for you to set the tone for the pupils to learn and you will be fully responsible for the progress that they make in your lessons. This needs to be balanced with the need to develop your practice and understand further why things have or have not worked for you in the classroom. You will again have a mentor in your department who will work closely with you to support you through the ECT years, to share ideas and evaluate your practice. You will also have the support of fellow ECTs who are going through the same process as yourself, so tap into this community and share your experiences and ideas.

We hope this chapter will give you a starting point to establish your network of associations, bodies and people that you can engage with as you develop your career. Some of these you may have encountered as a student teacher, and it might be time to look at how you can become more involved. Others might be new to you and some we will caveat with an indication of the dangers of leaping in head-first.

THE SCIENCE TEACHER COMMUNITY

As with anything, there are bodies of people out there who can support you and many have their strengths and limitations. In teaching, we can often find ourselves talking with only the other science teachers in our school, or on occasion, on a course when we have the opportunity to participate in externally funded CPD. Many teachers value CPD sessions, particularly when they are given the time and opportunity to talk to people who are in similar and contrasting settings to their own. Talking things through can often give the confidence boost needed in those early years, reassuring that what you are doing isn't too far from the mark or generating discussion that leads you somewhere else with your teaching that you would not have achieved on your own. If we were to link this with any theory, teachers in this capacity can act as More Knowledgeable Others aligned with Vygotsky's work and support each other through a Zone of Proximal *Teacher* Development (Vygotsky, 1978). Coaching and mentoring happens in many other businesses and industries but seems to be sadly lacking for classroom teachers beyond the practicalities of where the photocopying goes, what the assessment capture deadlines are or where resources are stored. Opportunities are waiting out there for you to seek out and take.

By establishing a network through being involved with different associations and communities, you create a safety blanket where you can seek support and access opportunities that otherwise might not be available. By widening the range of people you talk to and share ideas with, you will develop your pedagogical repertoire by trying new things. Take the opportunities to try something new within your teaching and use your supportive network for the hints, tips and top picks.

VIGNETTE 13.1   TAPPING INTO THE NETWORK

If there was one thing Annie wished she had known the value of earlier in her career, it would have been that of how a network of people and associations can support teaching and learning. This is something that she has come to know more of in recent years and one thing she shares with people she is lucky enough to mentor in the early stages of their careers.

Early in his career, Tom was introduced to various science education communities and organisations through colleagues at his school, training university and science education Twitter. These introductions have opened many doors which he has further explored himself as a science teacher. The network of people he can now call upon for support and advice is growing, leading him to develop his career further with the support of expert colleagues outside his school environment.

Activity: Find out from teachers in school what additional networks they are involved in and where there are opportunities for support outside school.

SOCIAL MEDIA NETWORK

The world of social media is a very dynamic one and the favoured platform shifts with time. Facebook and Twitter have offered online communities that can support people with growing networks and making valuable connections, which are a source of instant feedback and answers. There are plenty of opportunities to share ideas and learn from others, with much social media content being supportive and positive. However, there are well-known issues with this type of media compared with a verbal conversation, and this is something to take heed of when embarking on exploring the digital world. It is generally difficult to capture nuances and complexities associated with pedagogy when working with limited character numbers and not hearing the tone of the author's voice that you would face to face. There is no silver bullet in education and no one-size-fits-all approach, so you need to approach social media with caution. It would be wise to understand that the answer to a question you post on social media will generally lie somewhere in the middle of, what can occasionally be, polarised views. Do also remember to uphold the professional standards expected of you on social media – many student teachers have fallen due to an offhand remark or comment that has been seen by those in school. Keep your personal life exactly that.

ATTENDING CONFERENCES AND SEMINARS

Many teachers will want to source their CPD away from schools to gain a different perspective on an aspect of teaching practice they want to improve upon. Subject associations will provide high-quality subject-specific CPD, which is often difficult to access in schools. These conferences will take various forms, from evening and weekend sessions hosted by regional branches, all the way to multi-day international conferences which attract thousands of like-minded educators from across the globe. These offer invaluable resources to gain ideas to trial in your classrooms and an opportunity to meet different people and expand your support network even further. Perhaps you may even consider sharing your own experiences and ideas by presenting a session at a conference yourself.

VIGNETTE 13.2   THE BENEFITS OF ATTENDING SCIENCE EDUCATION CONFERENCES

As a teacher, Annie didn't venture far from subject CPD centred around examination requirements or the latest trend in education. One year, she decided to branch out and attended a science education conference. Whilst in a session on assessment, a lady walked in and sat down next to her. She caught sight of her name badge and realised it was someone who was renowned in the world of science education (admittedly, she was now somewhat distracted from the assessment session!).

That conference was the start of something. She walked around and heard from many people who, up until that point, she only knew from seeing their names in print. She bumped into a good friend who was involved with the organising committee of the conference. They had coffee and Annie lost count of the number of times people stopped to say hello and have a chat to her friend. At that point, she realised everyone attending were just normal people, all with a common aim to develop themselves and their practice.

Fast forward 10 years and Annie was sitting having a coffee with someone from another university who was attending the conference for the first time. After noticing Annie saying hello to so many passing people, her question to Annie was 'do you know everyone here?'. She was asking who people were, and when Annie introduced her to the people who wrote the books she was reading or the speakers she had heard, she was also in that state of awe that Annie had found herself in at her first conference all those years ago.

Getting involved in that community and network has opened up doors and opportunities that otherwise would never have happened. Not only did Annie have the chance to travel to New Zealand to present at the subject association conference there, she has been involved in organising, attending and presenting at a range of events. It doesn't have to be onerous, and it gave 'something different' to the teaching role she much loved.

Activity: Think about the people you hold in high esteem in science education or your previous work experiences. What is it that makes them respected and admirable in this context? How can you access their expertise? Which conferences will you attend first as an ECT?

DEVELOPING YOUR CAREER BEYOND THE CLASSROOM

Progression within teaching can often feel linear. Most follow a curriculum path of promotion or a pastoral one. The levels and layers within a school are usually rigid and the scope to branch out is limited. We are not for one moment suggesting that being 'just' a teacher is not enough, but many people want to add a little more flavour to what they do, especially as they become more experienced, and this can often conflict with the desire to stay in the classroom or a school-based role.

By engaging with a wider network, it is possible to diversify opportunities without compromising where your heart is as a teacher. The next section will suggest other activities that you might consider as you progress that will add to your teaching.

WRITING FOR PUBLICATION

This may be something that you do not necessarily see yourself being able to do as a teacher. There are many classroom teachers who want to write academically but often just don't know where to start. Within ITT, there is a great opportunity to support individuals in starting on this journey. Student teachers can, and have been, supported through co-authoring articles in order to enable them to share their ideas or great assignments focused on an aspect of their teaching practice. Writing short book reviews for subject association publications (such as the ASE) is also a great entry into academic writing.

If this is something you are interested in, speak to the science associations, contact your university-based tutors if you have them or even contact us! We have all been at the point of beginning as a teacher, developing our careers and wondering where to start.

VIGNETTE 13.3   BUILDING CONFIDENCE TO WRITE FOR PUBLICATION

Early in her teaching career, Charlie was asked by a colleague who was on the editorial board of a science publication if she would write a book review - the best bit at the time was getting to keep the book. She is now convinced those 400 words were, without being dramatic, career changing. When that book review was published in the back of that science education journal it was disproportionately exciting to see her name in print! At a later date, two of her colleagues were writing an article for the journal and she looked at the draft before suggesting something that could be added - a paragraph at best, but she was named as the third author. After this, her decision was made - she wanted her own article. From that point, Charlie sought support with drafts and had her first independent article published in a journal later that year. After becoming a relatively frequent author for the journal, she was invited onto the Editorial Board, and five years after that, was appointed as Editor. Charlie fully maintains her drive to write was sparked by those first 400 words. It all has to begin somewhere.

Activity: Consider where you can write for publication through the science education associations and bodies - even your school newsletter could be a starting point. Identify something you have done in your teaching that worked really well that others would benefit from knowing.

CHARTERED TEACHER STATUS (CSCITEACH)

Becoming a Chartered Teacher is a widely recognised award, which tells people that you are committed to furthering your own development and advancing the field of teaching and learning.

The Association for Science Education (ASE – see later in the chapter), licensed by the Science Council, is empowered to award Chartered Science Teacher Status (CSciTeach) to active science teachers in the UK. There are many suggested benefits of this in relation to recognition of your expertise and skills, supporting your future professional development and developing a wider community of scientists working across sectors. There are criteria to be met which include a minimum of four years' teaching experience – but this is something to definitely hold in your mind as an aiming point as you further your career.

The Chartered College of Teaching (see later in the chapter) offer a Chartered Teacher (CTeach) programme. Although this is not subject specific, it is a good way of increasing knowledge of teaching and learning more widely, identifying techniques and tips you can include to develop your own, and your school's, teaching and learning practices. Again, certain criteria have to be met to enter the scheme, but it is well worth exploring after your ECT years.

FURTHER STUDY – MASTERS, PHD OR EDD

There are many debates amongst teaching communities on the benefits of undertaking further study in education. Depending upon your training path, you may well have accumulated credits at Masters level through completion of assignments, and these can be used to progress to a full Masters degree within a certain time period after qualifying. As your teaching experience develops, you may observe behaviours or patterns in your classroom that you are unsure of how to explain. You might want to know a little more about the impact of something you are doing, or you may just 'wonder' about an element of education. Ed Podesta, who co-authored Chapter 5, would describe this as being the 'stone in your shoe'. A Masters degree allows you to explore this wonder in a supported way. There are teachers who also just want to do further study – not with a particular 'stone' – but a sense of wanting to undertake that programme and this too is fine. There is a wide variety of courses on offer from different universities across the UK and finding one that is right for you can sometimes be tricky. Many offer part-time distance courses, with some full-time, in fields ranging from teaching and learning, educational leadership and research-informed practice. If in doubt, speak to the support network that you are building and find someone who has studied this course before committing to find out if it is truly right for you.

From Masters-level study, there are opportunities to undertake a PhD or professional doctorates in education – an EdD route. These are different to a traditional PhD in that they have a taught element to the programme, meaning there is a smooth transition to the demands of high-level academic writing. The reasons for doing this are no different from study at Masters – sometimes the stone in the shoe is just a little bigger or perhaps there are more of them.

VIGNETTE 13.4   STARTING A MASTERS IN EDUCATION WHILST TEACHING

Tom recently started a Masters in Education following sustained interest in his subject and to further develop his practice and career. He chose a specific course which gave him the independence to undertake a small-scale action research project in an element of teaching practice he wanted to develop in his classroom environment. The taught modules on his course are designed to support him through the whole research process – first to understand what action research is and then the common research methods used in education, and finally to undertake the research project under the watchful eye of a dedicated supervisor. He thoroughly enjoyed his first year on the course and gained a greater insight into academic writing and research. Tom recommends looking into further study, although a research focused degree might not be for everyone!

Activity: Explore the postgraduate study that is available to you in your area and how these different courses function. Can you identify the 'stone in your shoe'?

OPPORTUNITIES FROM SUBJECT ASSOCIATIONS AND ORGANISATIONS

In this section are brief descriptions about how the relevant organisations support Early Career Teachers and what is on offer from them. Do spend some time researching and engaging with the organisation before committing to joining. Of course, this is not an exhaustive list of organisations that are available, just a selection of those that are most commonly encountered by student teachers and the more experienced teaching community.

THE ASSOCIATION FOR SCIENCE EDUCATION

The Association for Science Education offers support for student teachers and ECTs through their conference programmes and publications. Their regional and national committees have a history of being composed of, and representing, current and former teachers. They have a wealth of resources available for teachers including Best Practice Guidance documents which will support you with areas such as maths in science, inclusion, and outdoor learning, to name but a few. Their secondary-specific journal (SSR – *School Science Review*) offers both practice-based and research-informed articles to support you in the classroom. The community that is available through the ASE is very strong. Through either the regional or international conferences, as well as local events, there is the opportunity to meet with many teachers and educators who are enthusiastic about science education, and the regional committees will welcome you to become involved – even as a student teacher or very recently qualified one.

The breadth of knowledge and experience held by the collective ASE membership is unparalleled, and the organisation is committed to doing all it can to make sure that it can be shared with those who need it most. As a cornerstone of that commitment, it works exceptionally hard with student teacher and early-career teacher members in order to help them through those critical years of training and early careers teaching.

THE CHARTERED COLLEGE OF TEACHING

The Chartered College of Teaching is the professional body for all teachers. They work to celebrate, support and connect teachers to take pride in their profession and provide the best possible education for children and young people. They are dedicated to bridging the gap between practice and research and equipping teachers from the second they enter the classroom with the knowledge and confidence to make the best decisions for their pupils. Membership of your professional body provides you with access to the latest research and classroom practice to support and inspire you and is half price for early career teachers. Your membership includes print copies of its termly, award-winning journal, *Impact*, which brings together the voices of teachers and researchers and considers the implications of research for classroom practice. Its member-only website, MyCollege, includes a range of different written and video resources showcasing what is happening in classrooms around the country and around the globe. An area of the website designed exclusively for early career teachers, the Early Career Hub, provides resources aligned to the Teachers' Standards and the Early Career Framework, including self-review activities, case studies, videos of classroom practice and subject-specific examples. The aim of the Chartered College of Teaching is to support you 'to thrive in your first few years as a teacher' (Chartered College of Teaching, 2021). This is not a subject-specific organisation but one that can offer support nonetheless.

STEM LEARNING

STEM Learning offers a range of CPD – from free online courses to intensive residentials. For many state-funded schools there are bursaries to cover the course fees and supply cover needed. Local Science Learning Partnerships (SLPs) throughout England support teachers, technicians and others with bespoke and short-episode professional development, while the National STEM Learning Centre at York provides intensive CPD. The specialist team often work with ITT programmes and continue to offer support through your early teaching careers through CPD, resources, activities and events. These are linked through the Early Career pathways that provide a guided route through the CPD offerings, as well as specific links to the free resource e-library. Collated collections within the e-library are chosen to support each stage of science, both by subject and phase, from primary to A-Level, while the STEM Community is a free professional online space for all teachers and technicians of STEM subjects to collaborate, with specific groups for early career teachers. STEM Learning also lead the STEM Ambassador programme on behalf of the UK government, linking schools with industry and research, as well as the STEM Clubs, Nuffield Research Placement and European Space Education Resource Office for the UK (ESERO-UK) programmes, all of which can be reached from the homepage of the STEM Learning website (stem. org.uk).

SUBJECT ASSOCIATIONS

The following organisations specialise in one of the scientific disciplines and offer support and resources for teachers of all levels, tailored to that discipline.

ROYAL SOCIETY OF BIOLOGY (RSB)

The RSB supports teachers through their freely available resources as well as individual or school membership and they are 'committed to supporting and encouraging the study of biology at primary, secondary and tertiary levels across the UK, working in coordination with our member organisations and with the broader scientific community' (Royal Society of Biology, 2021). Their *Journal of Biological Education* features research into teaching, learning and assessment and *The Biologist* offers classroom materials four times a year. Their website hosts plentiful resources which are aimed at all age phases of teaching and they have a Biology Week in October which is supported by the Society. They also run competitions for secondary-aged children, which is something you may want to consider as you move further into your teaching experience as another way of engaging your pupils' interests in science. The RSB also works in partnership with the Biochemical Society, which adds to the abundant resources already available.

ROYAL SOCIETY OF CHEMISTRY (RSC)

The Royal Society of Chemistry is committed to supporting chemistry education domestically and internationally and they exist to support future generations of scientists, believing everyone should have access to a high-quality chemistry education.

The RSC's education website helps teachers to find further support through a dedicated area on the website specifically for early career and trainee teachers with the overall aim to 'expand your skills, knowledge, expertise and confidence' (Royal Society of Chemistry, 2021). Teachers and trainees can gain unrestricted access to resources and view and attend events by signing up for a free teacher account.

Their resources are themed to support teachers and student teachers, including ideas for assessment, practicals, classroom activities, curriculum maps and anecdotes. *Education in Chemistry*, their print magazine for secondary teachers, offers a bridge between research and teaching and includes articles to support teaching practice and building a supportive department as well as cutting edge research and in-depth science features and news, views and perspectives on teaching.

Education Coordinators run workshops with student teachers and ECTs and can offer a bespoke package of support, sharing teaching resources, development opportunities, local events and competitions for pupils. These tailored workshops give teachers the tools to become more confident, better informed about new resources and ideas, and be professionally supported within their region.

INSTITUTE OF PHYSICS (IOP)

The Institute of Physics brings together a range of members from academia, industry, the classroom and technicians. Their aim to 'promote, develop and support excellent physics teaching through networks, CPD events and proven resources' (Institute of Physics, 2021) is enacted through their website, local meetings and courses as well as access to resources to develop subject knowledge and pedagogy. They do pivotal research into areas such as addressing gender imbalance in physics. Their 'Explore Physics' part of the website offers activities that pupils can do out of school which you can use as a means of continuing their engagement outside of the classroom. They provide support specifically for ECTs as well as those who do not have physics as their specialism.

Now that you have reached the end of this chapter, and this book, we hope you have, and continue to have, an inspiring journey through your teaching career. The benefits of really thinking about your practice and how to develop it have been made explicit throughout the book and we hope that you can see the sense of value in developing yourself professionally as you gain experience in the classroom.

SUMMARY

Now you have read this chapter you should have:

- Identified ways in which you can gain further support and CPD to develop your teaching practice further.
- Been introduced to various subject associations and bodies which offer support to Early Career Teachers.

- Enthusiasm for your future and be looking forward to the exciting teaching career ahead of you!

REFLECTIVE QUESTIONS

- What are the targets that I am going to take forward from my training year and into my ECT years? How will I go about developing these?
- Have I explored the support that is available to me from the subject associations? Could I explore the feasibility of attending one of their conferences or meetings?
- How can I build my network of support to develop my career outside school?

BIBLIOGRAPHY

Chartered College of Teaching (2021). [online] available: https://chartered.college/join/ect-membership/

Institute of Physics (2021). [online] available: www.iop.org/education

Royal Society of Biology (2021). [online] available: www.rsb.org.uk/education

Royal Society of Chemistry (2021). [online] available: https://edu.rsc.org/early-career-or-student-teacher

Vygotsky, L.S. (1978). *Mind in society: The development of higher psychological processes.* Cambridge, MA: Harvard University Press.

APPENDIX 1
PLANNING PROFORMA

LESSON PLANNING PROFORMA

Lesson Topic		Date of Lesson		Class / Group	
Learning context	*What have they already covered? What are they going on to learn in connection with this topic?*				
Which of my weekly science targets are being addressed?					
Planned progress and learning outcomes	**Objectives:** What **particular, specific** knowledge, concepts and skills do you want pupils to learn, develop or improve?		**Outcomes:** What will pupils have **done/made/completed**? Check these connect with your lesson objectives.		

(Continued)

	Misconceptions or preconceptions related to these objectives. Do I know enough? What should I learn more about?	
Enabling progress from a range of starting points	Details of specific educational needs or needs of groups of pupils, e.g. ethnic groups, EAL, gender.	How will you provide challenge and support for the specific needs in this group?
	Role of other staff members.	Significant H&S or other features of lesson or location.
Post-lesson evaluation of pupils' progress	How far were your lesson objectives achieved? What impact did your teaching have on pupils' learning? What progress did pupils make in this lesson? Evidence from individuals / groups (gender, minorities, PP, EAL, SEND) / whole class. **Focus on the specific things that pupils said, did, wrote, or completed in response to your teaching as evidence.**	

LESSON ACTION PLAN

Element (& Timing)	Teaching and Learning	Monitoring and Assessment
	Outline specific teaching and other actions, **and resources** with links to specific objectives. The lesson plan should be obvious from this column alone.	How will you know they have all grasped this? Especially if you're teaching online?
Start of Lesson Routine	Consider: • *Greeting, seating, establishing tone, bell activities, registration, dealing with latecomers, etc.*	If relevant
Introduction	Consider: • *Links to prior learning or overarching enquiries* • *Raising curiosity; levels of intellectual buy-in?* • *Sharing of lesson objectives, outcomes or other criteria if appropriate* • *Possible barriers or misconceptions which may appear* • *Timings!*	Consider: • *Learning or understanding students might show* • *How you will check on pupils' knowledge and understanding* • *What Key Questions / Concepts should they bring with them from previous lessons?* • *Whose knowledge and understanding you will be checking*
Development Sub-divide if needed	Consider: • *Key teaching points – new knowledge / ideas being developed and links to learning objectives* • *How activities will be introduced* • *Use of modelling* • *Strategies to tackle misconceptions*	Consider: • *How you will check on pupils' knowledge and understanding for each activity* • *Key Questions / Concepts* • *Whose knowledge and understanding you will be checking*

(Continued)

	• *Teacher actions during student working including work with specific groups* • *Opportunities for review* • *Possible barriers or misconceptions which may appear* • *Make each section of the development distinct and include timings!*	
Conclusion / Plenary / Review	*Consider:* • *How you will summarise key points* • *How you will celebrate achievement* • *How you might address any misconceptions* • *How you might make a link to the following lesson* • *Timings!*	*Consider:* • *Review of learning against lesson objectives* • *Whose knowledge and understanding you will be checking*
Homework / Out of class learning		
Homework to extend or build on pupils' learning in the lesson, or prepare for the next lesson - this section is essential to show that you can embed pupil progress over time.		

INDEX

Page numbers in *italic* indicate figures and in **bold** indicate tables.